T5-AGT-398

Disordered Lives

Disordered Lives

*Eighteenth-Century Families and
their Unruly Relatives*

Catharina Lis and Hugo Soly

Translated by Alexander Brown, M.I.L.

Polity Press

First published in 1996 by Polity Press in association with Blackwell Publishers Ltd.

2 4 6 8 10 9 7 5 3 1

Editorial office:
Polity Press
65 Bridge Street
Cambridge CB2 1UR, UK

Marketing and production:
Blackwell Publishers Ltd
108 Cowley Road
Oxford OX4 1JF, UK

Blackwell Publishers Inc.
238 Main Street
Cambridge, MA 02142, USA

ISBN 0 7456-1514-7

A CIP catalogue record for this book is available from the British Library and the Library of Congress.

Typeset in 10 on 12 pt Sabon
by CentraCet Limited, Cambridge
Printed in Great Britain by TJ Press Ltd, Padstow, Cornwall

This book is printed on acid-free paper.

Contents

Acknowledgements

The years of this book's gestation have left us with many debts. The first is to the Sub-Faculty of the History of Society (now the Faculty of History and Art Sciences) of the Erasmus University of Rotterdam, for the financial support they gave to Katelijne Bernard and Jan Van Ryckegem to explore certain sources; we are very grateful to both these graduate students for their research assistance.

In addition, we have been extremely fortunate to receive support from many friends and colleagues. Special thanks are due to Sabine Bocher and Anne-Marie Roets, who generously made data regarding private confinement in Bruges and Ghent available to us; without this information it would have been difficult to test certain hypotheses. We are also indebted to Christi Boerdam, Peter Burke, Leen Charles, Frank Daelemans, Francine de Nave, Karel Degryse, Marc De Laet, Marc Jacobs, Geoffrey Parker, Frank Scheelings, Stefaan Vandenberghe, Paul Vandenbroek, Carl Van De Velde, Herman Van Goethem, Adrienne Van Ham, Paul Van Heesvelde, Karin Van Honacker and Patricia Vansummeren, who provided useful information, offered valuable suggestions or were very helpful in other ways; we are very grateful to Marc Jacobs for preparing the manuscript for the press.

We would like to express our gratitude to the board members of the Nederlandse Organisatie voor Wetenschappelijk Onderzoek (Netherlands Organization for Scientific Research) for providing the means to cover the cost of translating our book into English. In this connection we would like to thank Alexander Brown, who took on the difficult task of turning our often awkward and obscure Dutch phrases into English prose.

Our final debt is to Patrick De Wilde, Chairman of the Research Council of the Vrije Universiteit Brussel (Free University of Brussels), who generously arranged for a subsidy as a contribution to the production costs.

List of Plates

Introduction

Even in present-day Western society it proves to be possible for people who have committed no penal offence or who have shown no sign of psychological disturbance to be locked away for long periods without ever being given a hearing. Since every case of unjust confinement goes against the fundamentals on which our society is based, revelations about sane persons languishing in mental hospitals rightly arouse indignation among the general public[1] and lead to controversies among lawyers and physicians over committal procedures.[2] The arguments between supporters of a legal approach and those of a medical one are not new. Throughout the nineteenth and twentieth centuries, both groups have defined the problems of improper confinement in very different ways. It could hardly be otherwise, since the former are concentrating on civil rights, while the latter are looking primarily at patients dangerous to themselves and others.

The controversies over committal procedures reflect the fundamental fact that legal guarantees and medical diagnoses alone cannot solve all the problems. In the case of enforced confinement in a psychiatric institution it is not only a question of human and citizens' rights and the psychological condition of the patient. Attention must also be paid to the factors leading up to a request for confinement, for there are two parties involved in this matter: the 'uncontrollable' person and his family. Anyone who ignores the petitioners is closing his eyes to the tensions and conflicts forming the background to compulsory admission and to the social context in which the whole affair is being played out.

From this perspective historical research is particularly illuminating. Up to the end of the *ancien régime*, petitioners were able to cite 'misconduct' as the only motive for 'private confinement' or 'confinement on request', and here their petitions offer us an opportunity to look into the nature of their problems, standards and values, their expectations and tolerance thresholds. From the early sixteenth century onwards there were people being confined in monasteries or public institutions because, according to their families, they had been leading 'unruly' lives and were not amenable to reason. Some of them were declared insane, but most had simply misbehaved – which was enough to deserve their incarceration. Such problems were dealt with in the houses of correction in the Northern and Southern Netherlands, the English Bridewells, the French *hôpitaux généraux* and the German *Zuchthäuser*: rebellious young people, adulterous women, drunkards, violent husbands and other persons with morally reprehensible behaviour – they had committed no legally indictable offence, but according to their families they were uncontrollable, and the authorities supported this view.

During the Age of Enlightenment, voices were heard in many Western European countries demanding that the possible abuses of the private confinement system be checked, in particular the risk of being locked away under false pretexts and/or for an indefinite period. In France the criticisms of forms of arbitrary confinement were closely bound up with changing concepts of political and personal liberty. The practice of confinement on request became increasingly associated with royal absolutism, symbolized by the *lettres de cachet*, arrest warrants that were private *ordres du roi* used as a means of summary incarceration without intervention by any tribunal or court. Yet historical research has shown that, far from being a formidable instrument of tyranny, the *lettres de cachet* in fact protected family interests: Claude Quétel has estimated that, from 1589 to 1789, between 100,000 and 200,000 such general warrants were issued for the whole of France, with nearly 98 per cent of these requested by family members themselves.[3] Many scholars have demonstrated, moreover, that towards the end of the *ancien régime* high officials did recognize certain abuses which had developed since mid-century, and diligently set out to correct them. Throughout his first term as minister of state (1775–6), and subsequently, Malesherbes continued to make procedural reforms in the private confinement system, calling for thorough investigations of each case by family courts and provincial commissions. In 1782 Minister Amelot declared that libertinism, squandering of goods and possessions and *mésalliance* would not be 'sufficient motives for depriving a man of thirty years of his liberty'. In 1784 Minister Breteuil sent all *intendants* a circular specifying that no detention could exceed three years, imposing further restrictions on the confinement of the insane, making it mandatory that marital disputes be settled in court and declaring that 'family honour' was not sufficient reason to deprive one member of his or her liberty.[4] It should be stressed, however, that these reform-minded administrators continued to defend the system in principle because they considered some form of discretionary authority essential for the 'salvation of families', and that their campaigns against the abuses of *lettres de cachet* were aimed chiefly at preventing middle- and upper-class families from using such *ordres* to hush up scandals or to settle private vendettas.[5]

For the French revolutionaries, *lettres de cachet* were synonymous with 'despotism' and the abusive authority of 'criminal ministers' . They considered any deprivation of liberty without the intervention of the courts as impermissible, for this opened the door to arbitrariness, which was irreconcilable with the Rights of Man and Citizen. The law of 16–20 March 1790, which subsequently came into force in the Belgian *départements*, expressly stipulated that insane adults could be confined only after the court had passed judgement of disability – but the recently achieved personal liberty could not be allowed to put public order into danger either. Hence the law of 16–24 August 1790 held municipalities responsible for any damage caused outside the home by 'dangerous lunatics and wild animals'. The decree of 19–22 July 1791 specified, moreover, that families who let 'dangerous lunatics' free to wander about would be punished by heavy fines. It is obvious that abuses could arise from this legislation; the more so, because court procedures were so expensive and time-consuming that most families simply turned to the executive power – the mayor – to commit an 'uncontrollable' member to an asylum.[6]

In eighteenth-century England the growth of a private, profit-oriented 'trade in lunacy', essentially unfettered by outside control, equally created concern about possible abuses, especially the confinement of sane persons in private madhouses as alleged lunatics. As early as 1728 Daniel Defoe charged that men often disposed of unwanted wives by committing them to such establishments; and by the 1760s the fear of wrongful confinement had become a major topic in fictional writings, pamphlets and newspaper articles, in which private madhouses were depicted as repositories for sane persons who had proved troublesome to their families. It would seem, however, that the problem of improper confinement was basically a middle- and upper-class concern. The 1763 Select Committee of the House of Commons recommended the interposition of the legislature only with regard to private asylums, and the 1774 Madhouse Act expressly excluded paupers from its purview, although such patients were most likely to suffer from neglect and ill-treatment. It should be noted, moreover, that the workhouses and houses of correction had come to contain many lunatics alongside the other inmates.[7] Neither the 1828 Madhouse Act, which stipulated that the admission of private patients required certificates signed by medical practitioners, nor further reforms in the nineteenth century relieved the

wealthier classes of their anxiety, as is apparent from periodic outbursts
raging against the 'mad-doctors' and the committal laws. 'These outbursts', as Peter McCandless has very properly observed, 'reflected the
anguish of a society convinced of the need for a system of involuntary
confinement, yet uncomfortable with the implications of its existence
and suspicious of the abilities and intentions of those charged with its
operation.'[8]

In short, whether committal procedures involved primarily a familial
judgement on unacceptable behaviour/madness or a legal/medical one,
the middle and upper classes remained very fearful of improper confinement, both in France and in England. Although the explosive growth in
the number of persons officially designated as insane in the nineteenth
century came overwhelmingly from the ranks of the labouring population,[9] little attention was being paid to the impact of social factors. Even
the most outspoken critics of the committal laws tended to concentrate
their attacks on the private asylums, and the major concern they had in
common was preventing the incarceration of sane individuals belonging
to the propertied classes.[10] In other words: the problem continued to be
defined in terms of arbitrary authority and abuse of power.

Some historians of psychiatry have recently emphasized 'the mix of
humanitarian and authoritarian goals in the asylum's foundation [and]
the profound tension between individual rights and social needs inherent
in the commitment process',[11] but the great central question remains:
how are we to explain the confinement of increasing numbers of the
poor? Was the nineteenth-century 'moral treatment' of the insane simply
a more effective means of coercion, as Michel Foucault has argued?
Although our book deals with an earlier period, these questions are
highly relevant to our purpose, because (1) the new realm of the asylum
had its roots in the eighteenth century, and (2) private committals to
public institutions by the end of the *ancien régime* had already originated
in the overwhelming majority from lower-class families, both in Paris
and in the Belgian cities we have studied.

Foucault's great achievement was in pointing out the ubiquity of
power: everything is enacted in a permanent continuum of power
relationships that manifest themselves as much within the family as in
the workplace and the public platform. His contention that from the
middle of the seventeenth century onwards the fabric of society became
permeated with ever more complex and drastic forms of coercion and
control is open to question, however. In his view, this is the context in
which the *lettre de cachet* system has to be placed. The state-led
movement to confine the idle and insane induced families to invoke the
paternal and tutelary authority of the father-king, whose interventions
enabled them to discipline their own members – the power-politics of

the state strengthening the authority of the *pater familias* and vice-versa. Since the *ordres du roi*, used by the central government to enforce security in the realm, and the *lettres de cachet de famille*, solicited by parents to incarcerate their children, had identical disciplinary aims, public order was synonymous with familial order: private tranquillity (re)produced a certain form of social tranquillity. One of the consequences of this process was that the *lettre de cachet* system came to reflect not so much royal absolutism as despotic familial power, since 'anyone can avail himself, for his own ends and against other human beings, of the enormity of absolute power . . . [and] anyone, if he knows how to play the game, can become a terrifying monarch over his fellows, subject to no law: *Homo Homini Rex*.' That does not, however, alter the fact that the machinery was started by the power-politics of the state, which offered it as a tool of family discipline and in this way could cast a wider net of social control, drawing ever greater numbers of people into its mesh. From Foucault's perspective, the abolition of the *lettres de cachet* only signalled the replacement of one form of coercion by another one, which was even more repressive because it corresponded to the imposition of 'a dense, differentiated and continuous network, where the various institutions of justice, police, medicine and psychiatry alternate, and a new discourse develops which employs a language pretending to be that of observation and neutrality.'[12]

Foucault's sweeping assertions make no answer to the question of why the *lettres de cachet* in eighteenth-century Paris 'originated in the overwhelming majority from persons of modest backgrounds'.[13] Why exactly was it that these families resorted to an external instrument for social control? Why did they not use informal ways of casting out those whom they called 'troublesome', and how did the latter come to be defined as uncontrollable or insane and as fit candidates for houses of correction or public asylums? Whatever merits Foucault's account may have as a portrayal of power-politics in France under the *ancien régime*, it corresponds in no way to developments elsewhere. In England there was no state-led move to sweep up the idle and insane from the streets during the seventeenth and eighteenth centuries;[14] and in the Austrian Netherlands, as we shall show, petitions for confinement had to be submitted to the local magistrates, who were prepared to place the unwanted person in a public institution at the expense of the city when the petitioners could not foot the bill. Why in fact did the aldermen in eighteenth-century Brabant and Flanders concur with requests for confinement which originated increasingly from lower-class families and in which there was no mention of psychological disturbances? Why was it that growing numbers of the latter took such radical decisions? Were they becoming more intolerant because they were having to suffer from

all sorts of misbehaviour more often than previously? Did social developments influence the frequency of misbehaviour and the attempts to
discipline the perpetrators?

Similar questions have been posed with regard to the gradual institutionalization of the pauper insane in the nineteenth century. As Michael
Ignatieff has remarked: 'A new "discourse" on the corrigibility of the
insane, on carceral utopias of reformative discipline comes into being in
the early 19th century and carries all before it. Yet the process by which
persons are first defined, stigmatized and marginalized as crazy must
always begin either at home or at work, and since the vast majority of
lunatics were paupers, it must begin within the working-class family.'[15]
Until now, few historians have looked beyond the walls of the nineteenth-century asylum to find out why this institution became acceptable
to lower-class families, and those who did tackle the problem have
stressed that the available evidence does not allow a direct test of widely
divergent (and often contradictory) hypotheses. In a penetrating study of
the social profile of admissions to the Lancaster Asylum between 1848
and 1850, John Walton has demonstrated that 'the roots of most asylum
committals clearly lay in domestic troubles, as families at the end of their
tether sought succour even though it meant the Poor Law and the
asylum', and that insanity in early Victorian England was a social rather
than a medical problem. Unfortunately, attempts to go beyond these
generalizations 'raise difficult issues, conceptually and in terms of the
interpretation of the abundant but ultimately frustrating evidence'.[16]

This is precisely the challenge we have undertaken. Thanks to exceptionally rich archival sources it has been possible to track and quantify
how and why it was that private confinement in the major cities of the
Austrian Netherlands – Antwerp and Brussels in the duchy of Brabant,
and Bruges and Ghent in the county of Flanders – took on ever greater
proportions, and why the petitioners and the unwanted persons increasingly belonged to the poorer segments of the urban population.

Our first aim was to shed light on all the aspects of the private
confinement drama:[17] the relationships between the 'uncontrollable'
individuals and those who were seeking their confinement; the host of
interpretations covered by the expression '*quaed gedragh*' (bad behaviour or disorderly conduct) and the term 'madness'; the nature of the
conflicts between, on the one hand, parents and children and, on the
other, married couples; the arguments put forward by the witnesses; the
motives of the authorities for helping those families who could not
themselves pay for the costs of confinement; the factors which determined the length of a prisoner's sentence; and the regime in private
institutions, prison workhouses and public asylums.

Our second task was to place the dynamics of private confinement in a social context. Relations between people living under the same roof or between relatives are after all influenced by the changes taking place in the society in which they act, think and feel. Different economic, demographic, political and cultural developments can bring about other kinds of social tensions and domestic troubles, which can lead to specific definitions being made as to what unacceptable behaviour is. Obviously only a comparative approach makes it possible to investigate and explain the variations in tolerance thresholds. This is why two cities – Antwerp and Bruges – have been put under the microscope, cities which in some respects had much in common and which in others differed to a remarkable degree. The thousands of case histories which were collected and examined enable light to be shed on the various material and emotional survival strategies lying at the heart of the requests for confinement and to relate those personal decisions to the changes taking place within the urban communities involved. The study of private confinement thus gives us a privileged vantage-point from which to gain insight into collective sensitivities and mental attitudes and, more importantly still, to understand interactions between social processes and personal experiences.

1

Confinement Requested

On 10 August 1796 a certain French *Représentant du Peuple* by the name of Lemane, who was on his way to Holland, learned by chance during a stopover in Brussels that the mother of Jean-Baptiste Verstraeten had requested the confinement of her son and that the *procureur* Verhulst supported her request, even though the young man had committed no legally punishable offence and demonstrated no psychological disturbance. Lemane was beside himself with rage. Had the republican armies not triumphed? Did the inhabitants of the Belgian *départements* still not understand that the Rights of Man and Citizen were inviolate? Were there still supporters of despotism at large? Lemane was so indignant and disturbed that he decided to stay a few days in Brussels in order to prevent someone becoming the victim of a *lettre de cachet*, the detestable symbol of royal capriciousness during the *ancien régime*. He informed the minister of justice, who praised his alacrity and gave him powers to prosecute the guilty parties. Lemane needed no second telling. He questioned all those involved in the case and scared the living daylights out of everyone – everyone except Commissioner d'Outrepont, who wrote to him laconically that there was no question of a *lettre de cachet*: private committals in this part of the world had never been signed by the monarch, let alone drawn up by him. Parents who sought forced confinement, because they feared their son or daughter would be ruined, had in the past been acting in accordance with the principles of the recently introduced law of 16–24 August 1790: they had turned to the aldermen, since without their permission no one could be put away for misbehaviour. His words counted for nothing. Lemane remained so implacably hostile that Mistress Verstraeten, opting for safety, withdrew her request to have her son locked up.[1]

Nonetheless, d'Outrepont was right. No one in the Austrian Netherlands could be put under lock and key without the express permission of the authorized judges. A number of unusual cases apart, there were three legal grounds for removing a person's freedom: legal prosecution (in which a written order for holding the suspect in custody was signed), imprisonment as the consequence of the judgement in a trial, and finally confinement at the request of members of a family, guardians or – if it was a question of people receiving charity – the directors of a public charitable institution. Contemporaries made a clear distinction between *collocatie* (private confinement) – the usual term – on the one hand, and preventive detention and imprisonment on the other: with confinement on request there was an objection to behaviour which from a formal point of view was not punishable by law, or only partly so, while in the two other cases there was suspicion or proof that the person involved had acted outside the law.

In order to be able to put away a family member it was necessary to go to the aldermen of the town or community in which he/she was born, or had been living for a number of years, as the case may be. In Antwerp, Brussels and Ghent only written petitions were accepted. Anyone who could not write thus had to engage the services of a notary or public scribe; the letter was then signed with a 'mark' or cross. In Bruges, on the other hand, it was possible to make a request for confinement verbally. Between 1740 and 1789 four out of ten petitioners made use of this method; they set nothing down on paper, but went personally to the aldermen. Did they choose this procedure out of fear that subordinate officials would give publicity to their case, thus threatening the family's reputation? This is not implausible since, in the towns where only written requests were accepted, some petitioners stated in their letters that they could not go into details on the matter without bringing the good name of the family into disrepute. It still seems unlikely that most of the verbal requests were made with such considerations in mind, however. Well-to-do families always made their requests to the aldermen in writing, taking care to phrase them in such vague terms that prying eyes would not be able to glean much from them. The desire for discretion is therefore not an adequate explanation. It is possible that some petitioners were of the opinion that a verbal exposé had greater persuasive power, especially where there were few 'hard' facts to back up a plea for confinement. Yet this could seldom have been the most important motive, since the aldermen acceded to as many written requests as verbal ones and they clearly employed the same criteria for granting them. For this reason we are more inclined to seek an explanation in the material need of the families involved: since they were too poor to pay for the costs of the confinement, it seems reasonable to suppose that they preferred a verbal procedure to save the expense of engaging a public scribe.

Cases speedily dealt with

Although private confinement brought a dramatic change to the social and emotional life of the unwanted person, the procedure in the duchy of Brabant and the county of Flanders was very simple and took little time to enact. Most families, it is true, did not lightly go to the *Edele ende Weerde Heren* ('Noble and Esteemed Gentlemen') with a request to put one of their number under lock and key, but once the first step was taken the case was quickly settled.

A request for confinement always led to an official investigation. In Antwerp, Brussels and Ghent the chairman of the aldermen, after receiving the request, immediately appointed two of his colleagues to question the petitioners and if necessary to seek information from persons who might be considered as privileged witnesses, such as relatives, neighbours, the parish priest, the employer, the landlord and, in the case of insanity, a doctor. If there were suspicions that the law had been infringed, then the representative of the central government – the *amman* – was also sent out; he had to advise the aldermen within three days. Once they had the reports of their two colleagues, the aldermen decided whether there were good grounds to grant the request and, if so, where the unwanted person was to be confined, for how long and at whose expense. In Bruges the same procedure was followed, it being understood that the petitioners often went to the town hall to make their request in person, after which the aldermen began their investigations.

Did this procedure provide sufficient guarantees against abuse – that is to say, against someone's being locked up on the basis of false arguments or untrue statements? Nothing could be less certain. The investigations were anything but thorough. In 96 per cent of the cases the aldermen took less than a week to come to a decision; if we exclude Sundays, then judgement was given in 80 per cent of cases in as little as three days after the petition was made.

As far as we can ascertain, the aldermen-commissioners restricted themselves in general to a hearing of the petitioners and the witnesses they called, so that the declarations were almost always one-sided. Of the 735 persons who provided testimony in Bruges in the period 1740–89 in connection with confinement petitions, only 28 did not fully subscribe to the viewpoint of the petitioners. Even in those few cases the latter succeeded in their petitions because the differences of opinion were not central to the matter in hand. If the request for confinement concerned an 'insane' person, then the commissioners contented themselves with the medical attestation provided by the petitioners. An independent 'expert' was seldom consulted, except in Bruges, where the head of St Julian's Hospital was obliged to 'examine' the patient on the orders of the magistrate.

Bruges was also the only one of the four cities under scrutiny where anyone whose behaviour was challenged by housemates or by relatives could make answer in person, and thus put his own view of the facts. In other places such a person's fate was decided without his being able to defend himself, or at least to give an explanation of his unusual or 'scandalous' way of life. Of course, most cases had a long history which was recounted with varying degrees of detail in the requests, so that it is quite understandable that the aldermen assumed that the person to be confined was not amenable to reason. The enforced silence of one of the protagonists in the committal drama, however, increased the possibilities of injustice.

In short, the available information suggests that the aldermen did not put themselves out to find out whether confinement was deserved – in other words, that they were generally inclined to accept the arguments of the petitioners without question. This can also be seen from the small number of requests that were rejected: in Antwerp only 12 out of a total of 864 in the period 1710–89 and in Bruges 90 out of a total of 766, or less than 12 per cent in the period 1740–1789. Most of the refusals were made to requests where insanity was given as the only, or most important, motive for private confinement. Thus the two brothers and the sister of the 24-year-old Maria Barbara van Dyck had their request rejected because they could not convince the aldermen of Antwerp that she had taken leave of her senses. The petitioners' intentions were indeed all too clear: they wanted at all costs to prevent Maria Barbara getting her inheritance so she could marry the man she loved, a hussar, who – according to the petitioners – was only out 'to rob her of her worldly goods on the pretext of marriage'.[2] The grandparents of the 22-year-old Maria Isabella Rottiers, on the other hand, did succeed in their efforts: the young woman was confined to a convent for a year, because she was 'sick in the brains', which must have been deduced from the fact that she wanted to enter into marriage with a barber's assistant who was barely able to maintain himself.[3] It is not easy to see why the aldermen of Antwerp took such different decisions in cases that – at least at first sight – were so very similar. There is nonetheless no doubt that more requests for confinement were refused in Bruges than in Antwerp because the real or alleged mental illnesses in the first-named city were always investigated by a neutral outsider.

The figures mentioned above clearly show that confinement on request in the eighteenth century was by no means an unusual phenomenon. However, it is not possible to deduce how many people were put under lock and key. Some petitioners asked the aldermen to extend a confinement or to lock up someone again after he had enjoyed a period of freedom. On the other hand, there were others who turned to the courts because they wanted some member of their family released from confinement. There were still others who asked for the detainee to be transferred to a less expensive institution. If we want to know how frequent confinement was, then we need access to information sources containing the various types of request. This is the case with Antwerp, at least from 1710 up to and including 1789.

Requests in Antwerp for confinement for the first time, as well as those for extensions, transfers and releases, were set down in special registers – the so-called *Requestboeken*, which have all been preserved. This source, as their title indicates, contains all sorts of requests reaching the magistrate, which means they cover an extraordinarily broad spectrum of subjects. For the period 1700–94 the series comprised no fewer than 108 volumes. Each volume was given an index by contemporaries, it is true, but this only mentions the names of the petitioners, so that it is not possible to find out which were the requests relating to confinement by this means. This can be done only by going through each register from beginning to end – a time-consuming process, which fortunately appears to be a fruitful one. After all the relevant texts had been tracked down and analysed, we noted that the series showed no gaps, except for the years 1700–09 and 1790–4, which were marked by political difficulties or military operations.

Apart from its completeness this source has another advantage: it is very reliable. True, it contains only copies of the original requests upon which the aldermen had given judgement, but the original confinement petitions were reliably copied. This can be seen not only from the scrupulousness with which it was noted which people had signed the document and whether they had done this with a signature or a mark, but also from a comparison of some ten originals that we came across in other archive lists with the copies thereof in the *Requestboeken*; there were only two occasions on which a word had been wrongly transcribed.

Let us now look at the figures. They are dry, but they speak volumes! From 1710 up to and including 1789 there were in Antwerp no fewer than 605 people put under lock and key for the first time upon request of other members of the family. Most of them were men: 391, or almost 65 per cent of the total. This percentage acquires even more significance if account is taken of the fact that the overwhelming majority of the Antwerp population consisted of women; in 1755 they constituted

Table 1.1 *Number of requests for confinement for the first time:
Antwerp, 1710–89*

Period	Men	Women	Total
1710–19	7	5	12
1720–9	22	10	32
1730–9	38	12	50
1740–9	32	17	49
1750–9	40	23	63
1760–9	59	27	86
1770–9	93	57	150
1780–9	100	62	162
Total	391	213	604

59.5 per cent of all the inhabitants above the age of 12 – in 1796 the figure was still 57.6 per cent. Men among those locked up were thus over-represented. That there was a greater need to discipline male housemates and relatives can also be seen from the fact that their confinement was extended much more often. Among the 391 men locked up there were 180 'recidivists' – almost 28 per cent of the total – while only 42 of the 213 unwanted women, or barely 20 per cent, ended up in an institution more than once.

Confinement on request came to the fore in the seventeenth century. Random samples from the *Requestboeken* show that very small numbers were involved, however, which otherwise explains why the Antwerp house of correction repeatedly – and often for long periods – could be used for other purposes. In this sense private confinement was a typically eighteenth-century phenomenon. Is it possible to be more precise about this? In other words: were the confinement requests more or less evenly spread over the period 1710–89 or were there any significant shifts in the numbers? Table 1.1 gives us the answer. Although the number of people placed for the first time in an institution by other members of a household or by relatives increased considerably, it is clear that the greatest concentration was during the 1770s and 1780s: during this time more requests were made and approved than between 1710 and 1769, which covers a period of 60 years. From 1770 up to and including 1789 the average number came to almost 16 per year, as compared with barely five per year between 1710 and 1769. The end of the *ancien régime* might thus be qualified as the period of family discipline.

In Brussels things were no different. Since we have not come across any sources in which all requests for confinement were registered, our analysis is based in this case on two random samples, involving the house of correction on the one hand and the *Simpelhuys* (mental home) on the other. We have found out how many of the capital's inhabitants ended up there for the first time through the actions of family members. For the house of correction we found 53 individuals in the first period and 130 in the second – i.e., about double – and for the *Simpelhuys* respectively 170 and 238 cases – i.e., an increase of 40 per cent. If we put both groups together, then the total number of men, women and children taken in for the first time during the 1740s against their will came to 223 and, in the 1770s, 368, or an increase of 65 per cent. These figures are only an indication. In contrast to Antwerp, it is not possible to ascertain in the case of Brussels how many unwanted people were confined in religious institutions at the instigation of fellow members of the household or relatives. However, both random samples show conclusively that towards the end of the *ancien régime* more and more families seemed to find the behaviour of their members intolerable as time went on.

We do have information on Bruges and Ghent. For both cities – the most important in the county of Flanders – it is possible to calculate by approximation the number of their inhabitants who were confined at the request of housemates or relatives during the eighteenth century. For Bruges, Sabine Bocher counted 368 initial requests in the period 1765–89, that is, almost twice as many as between 1740 and 1764, which then came to a total of 195. For Ghent, Anne-Marie Roets reached a figure of 83 in the period 1755–64 and 193 in the period 1775–84, thus more than double. In other words, in both these places we can see the same trend as in the large towns and cities of the duchy of Brabant – namely, a spectacular rise in the number of requests for confinement during the 1770s and 1780s. Just as in Antwerp, it was mainly the male inhabitants who were put under lock and key: in Bruges they represent 60 per cent of the total number confined and in Ghent about 55 per cent, although the greater part of the population consisted of women.

In order to compare the figures, we have related them to the total number of inhabitants, excluding the military and religious. In the period 1775–84 we counted an average of three requests for confinement for the first time in Antwerp per 10,000 inhabitants per year, in Ghent four and in Bruges nearly six. Since we do not know how many people in Brussels were confined in religious institutions at the instigation of their families, we can reach only a minimum figure for the capital, based on the total number of newcomers to the house of correction and the mental hospital: on average, this comes to five requests per 10,000 inhabitants per year during the decade 1770–9. At first sight the figures do not seem very impressive: but we should also take account of the fact that private confinement was a family matter. The requests do not allow us to reconstruct the whole network of family relationships, but we have been able to calculate how many households were directly involved in requests for confinement during the 1770s and 1780s: one in every 39 in Antwerp and one in every 23 in Bruges. The information on Brussels and Ghent covers only half of the period under consideration. If we extrapolate, then we get the following proportions: one in every 25 households in the first-named city and one in every 32 in the second. The ranking thus remains unchanged. In Bruges and Brussels private committals were proportionately the greatest in number and in Antwerp the least frequent, while Ghent occupied an intermediate position.

The differences cannot be ascribed to formal, legal factors, since the procedure was the same everywhere. Neither, given that the overwhelming majority of the requests were granted, could the criteria employed by the aldermen have played a part in this; as a matter of fact, we can see that the largest number of refusals occurred of all places in Bruges, where there were proportionately more inhabitants put in confinement by housemates or relatives than anywhere else. Were Antwerp families more tolerant perhaps, because they were confronted less often with all manner of unacceptable behaviour? This seems plausible, but such a hypothesis gives rise to further questions. Who in fact decided what behaviour was intolerable and why? Did the definitions vary according to social position and the nature of the family relationships? Did social developments influence the frequency of the 'refusals' and the attempts at discipline? Was confinement the only way of bringing 'difficult' family members into line or were there alternatives? In order to answer these questions we must first know who the people in confinement were.

From top to bottom

There is no doubt that people from the most varied social backgrounds ended up in institutions through the efforts of other family members. In 1730 the widow of the merchant Abraham Gansacker besought the aldermen of Antwerp to lock up her only son Joseph, because he was 'of such a bad and unruly disposition that not only had he squandered all his worldly goods, hereditary rental incomes and annuities but had also, within a period of nine to ten months, disposed of and fruitlessly squandered the sum of 7,000 guilders'; the 'wastrel', moreover, wanted to marry an innkeeper's daughter, and thus enter into a *mésalliance*.[4] Half a century later, the widower Franciscus Vervoort went to the magistrate in Antwerp, though he had very different reasons for seeking the confinement of his 19-year-old son Andreas. He was a poor man, whose income was insufficient to support his three children. Andreas nonetheless was refusing to contribute to the family income; he was not only a Jack-of-all-trades and master of none, but he squandered everything he earned drinking and gambling in public houses.[5]

Between these two extremes there was a wide spectrum of social backgrounds, as can be seen from the substantive information contained in some of the requests. In general, however, the descriptions of unacceptable behaviour do not give us a detailed profile of the social environment of the families involved. Nor does mention of professional situations enable us to judge their wealth and status. The problem is not so much that we might unknowingly be mistaken about the professional activities of some of the petitioners and the people in confinement as that an occupation of itself gives us little to go on. Of course, we could assume that persons on private incomes, merchants and notaries were well-off and that doctors, brewers and master mariners had some money behind them, just as we can scarcely doubt that dung-collectors (for manure), lace-makers and cotton-spinners had nothing save for their manual labour: but those in most other professions could equally well come from the 'middle stratum' of society as from its lower levels. A master silk-weaver, for example, was just as likely to be an independent producer (thus a small manufacturer) as a subcontractor working for a merchant-entrepreneur. We have tried to find indications as to the status of the petitioners from other sources, but this avenue of exploration yielded nothing. There are no consecutive lists of taxpayers which have survived. In Antwerp and Bruges there are registers, it is true, which throw light on the fiscal position of heads of families, but they cover only one year, namely 1747, so that it is not worth the trouble of going through them – particularly since in the middle of the century relatively few requests were made. Is it then impossible to divide the petitioners into social groups? Certainly not: the place of confinement gives us a solution, at least to a certain level. This point needs explaining.

In principle the petitioners themselves could choose the place of confinement. Obviously it had to be a place recognized by the authorities. During the first half of the eighteenth century the aldermen hardly if ever concerned themselves with choosing the place. At that time they even granted a large number of petitions in which there was mention only of 'a monastery'. In Antwerp this happened on no fewer than 36 occasions, which comes to a quarter of all the requests for confinement for the first time. The aldermen presumably did not bother to specify an institution under their jurisdiction, since it concerned respectable families, but it goes without saying that their negligence in this respect could have led to abuses. The risk was not imaginary that the unwanted person could be forgotten about altogether – that is, that he remained confined without the authorities' ever knowing about it. The central government recognized the danger and on 17 December 1743 issued an order which specified that thenceforth the place of confinement should always be stated and under no circumstances could an institution be chosen outside the territory of the Austrian Netherlands.[6] The law was observed relatively well: between 1750 and 1789 the Antwerp aldermen did note down where the unwanted person was to be placed in 96 per cent of cases.

Petitioners who indicated no particular preference and simply expressed the hope that the aldermen would 'collocate' or 'imprison' their relative 'in a secure place' were without means. This can be seen from the fact that the magistrate in such cases would decide to have the unwanted person placed in a public institution at the expense of the city. Now we come to a crucial aspect regarding the choice of place. The people responsible for running a correctional or mental institution took no one in unless the family or the authorities paid his maintenance costs. This is why a magistrate always conducted an investigation into the financial circumstances of families who declared that they were not in a position to pay the amount required. If in such cases permission for private confinement was given, then the city had to foot the bill. It is hardly surprising therefore that the aldermen paid close attention to the social position of the petitioners. Thus between 1745 and 1789 five people from Bruges ended up not in St Julian's Hospital, as their relatives had requested, but in a private institution, because an investigation showed that the families were not without means.

Expenses varied considerably from institution to institution. The Alexian Brothers, or *Cellebroeders*, who took in exclusively male mental patients, made unusually high demands. The cost to the city of providing board for the Bruges sculptor Hendrik Pulincx came to no less than 240 guilders a year from 1772 to 1781 – and that was a cheap rate, since the Alexian Brothers in Brussels, Diest and Ghent charged individuals at least 300 guilders a year. Nor did the female orders perform their charitable work for nothing, though they were satisfied with lower maintenance charges. During the second half of the eighteenth century they were asking individuals for 180 to 240 guilders for looking after a patient. Confinement in a public institution was less expensive. The managers of the *Simpelhuys* in Brussels charged individuals 150 guilders a year and those of St Julian's Hospital an average of 144 guilders. It was even more advantageous to confine a family member to a correctional institution. In the *Rasphuis* in Ghent maintenance costs came to about 100 guilders a year, and in the Brussels house of correction they came to between 50 and 150 guilders in 80 per cent of cases; the family of the *costcooper* (literally, the one 'buying' board and lodging) had also to be responsible for the cost of linen, hair-cutting and nursing. In the provincial penitentiaries in Ghent and Vilvoorde the same conditions applied, but the annual maintenance costs depended on the duration of confinement: 120 guilders for a stay of less than two years, 100 guilders for two to three years and 60 guilders if the confinement lasted longer.

The majority of the working population was certainly not able to foot such bills. The annual income of most male employees varied between 120 and 180 guilders. There were of course wage-earners who received more, such as printers and typesetters, whose income came to between 300 and 350 guilders, or the designers, plate-cutters and other technicians in the cotton-printing industry, who could earn up to 450 guilders a year, but they were a small minority. It is true that during the course of the eighteenth century more women and children contributed to the family income as time went on – but they too earned very little. At the end of the *ancien régime* most lace-workers and cotton-spinners in Antwerp were paid respectively two and three *stuiver* per day. If we assume that they worked 300 days a year, then the annual income of the former came to 30 guilders and that of the latter to 45 guilders. The average daily pay of boys between 11 and 15 years of age in the same city varied between 1.5 and 2.5 *stuiver*, which, reckoned over a whole year, comes to between 22.5 and 37.5 guilders.[7] Even if three of the four or five family members were wage-earners and in full employment, the average proletarian family would thus have had about 200 guilders a year, which means that after deducting general living expenses there was little or nothing left over.[8]

In short, the choice of place was essentially determined by the financial circumstances of the family involved, at least in the sense that anyone who could not pay automatically ended up in a public institution; the 'choice' was limited in such a case to a mental hospital or correctional institution, which implies that the description of the unacceptable behaviour was of the utmost importance. The fact that the expenses were borne by the city does not necessarily mean that the petitioners were desperately poor or that they were exclusively wage-earners; it indicates only that their financial means were insufficient. Given that even the lowest boarding charges always amounted to a considerable sum, we can assume that among the non-payers there were also people who ran small businesses. We know little about the families who did pay the maintenance costs themselves other than that they belonged to the property-owning classes. However, there is a shade more to it, since some of them gave preference to a monastery and others to a public institution: people had to pay more in the former case than in the latter, which suggests a difference in social circumstances. This is all the more

Table 1.2 *Distribution of Antwerp families in accordance with place of confinement, 1710–89*

Place of confinement	1710–69		1770–89	
	Number	%	Number	%
Monastery	203	69.8	108	34.7
Public institution, paid for by				
– the family	32	11.0	16	5.1
– the city	56	19.2	187	60.1
Total	291	100.0	311	99.9

probable because families who initially opted for a monastery were sometimes obliged after a time to have the person under confinement transferred to a public institution; the argument was always that they could no longer afford to pay the high boarding charges.

Although the information regarding the place of confinement does not afford us an insight into all the gradations of social position, it does shed some light on the most noticeable differences. For Antwerp we have worked out how many families paid for maintenance themselves, and here a distinction was made between confinement in a monastery and in a public institution. We have calculated the numbers of payers and non-payers for two periods, namely 1710–69 and 1770–89, so we could see if any shifts took place (see table 1.2). All figures cover requests for confinement for the first time. During the 1770s and 1780s more people were confined at the expense of fellow household members or relatives than in the period 1710–69: the average number rose from 39 to 62 per decade, and it should be noted that most of them ended up in a monastery – which means that they were from relatively well-off families. Nevertheless, the increase in their numbers was insignificant in comparison with the spectacular rise in the number of persons confined at the expense of the city: from nine to around 94 per decade – that is, 10 times as many, representing no less than 60 per cent of the total at the end of the *ancien régime*. In other words, private confinement was and remained a method of discipline used by families from the most diverse social backgrounds, but the greater concentration of its use had now shifted from the well-to-do to the lower classes.

In Bruges the less well-off population groups were represented in much greater numbers than in Antwerp, as can be seen from the figures regarding the place of confinement calculated by Sabine Bocher (see table 1.3). The period she studied was divided into two parts to show up any

Table 1.3   *Distribution of Bruges families according to place of confinement, 1740–89*

Place of confinement	1740–64		1765–89	
	Number	%	Number	%
Costs paid by family:				
– monastery	22	11.3	32	8.7
– public institution	24	12.3	31	8.4
– private institution	2	1.0	12	3.3
costs paid by city:				
– public institution	106	54.4	208	56.5
– private institution	41	21.0	85	23.1
Total	195	100.0	368	100.0

changes in the social profiles of the petitioners. The most remarkable finding is not that the percentage of persons confined at the expense of the city rose very slightly, from 75 per cent to nearly 80 per cent, but that it formed the majority in *both* periods. The extraordinarily large preponderance of this category in the middle of the century becomes even more significant if we bear in mind that at that time an average of three requests per 10,000 inhabitants was being made – i.e., twice as many as in Antwerp. The lower classes in Bruges were therefore much more readily inclined to discipline fellow household members or relatives, and they did this much more often than their counterparts in Antwerp. The difference between these cities was, it is true, less pronounced towards the end of the *ancien régime*, because the number of petitioners from modest backgrounds in Antwerp increased much more than in Bruges, though it still remained considerable.

The definition of 'misconduct' doubtless varied according to social position. It might also be considered that the nature of the family relationships played a role here: it was the immediate environment of the unwanted person which had most to do with his behaviour. This is why we have investigated how many relatives subscribed to the confinement requests in Antwerp and Bruges and what connection they had with the unwanted person. With regard to the first point we can be quite brief: in almost 90 per cent of cases the request was made by one or two people. At the other extreme we found on one occasion 11 signatories in Antwerp and on two occasions ten in Bruges. In the rest of the cases six was the maximum. For the study of the family relationships we took a

Table 1.4 *Relationship of the first petitioner to the person confined in Antwerp and Bruges (percentages)*

Relationship	Antwerp		Bruges	
	1710–69	1770–89	1740–64	1765–85
1	43.2	36.9	50.8	40.2
2	17.1	19.9	12.8	12.5
3	27.1	33.3	30.3	33.4
4	5.8	4.5	2.0	5.2
5	6.8	5.4	4.1	8.7
100% = N	292	312	195	368

close look at the first signatory, since he or she was obviously the chief petitioner(see table 1.4). To get an outline, we made distinctions between the following relationship patterns:

1 children or adolescents confined by parents or guardians
2 unmarried persons confined by relatives
3 married persons confined by their spouses
4 married persons confined by their relatives
5 widows, widowers or divorced persons confined by relatives.

It is clear that most committal dramas were played out either between parents and children or between spouses. Both in Antwerp and Bruges these categories always represented together more than 70 per cent of the total, and it is worth noting that it was parents who most often resorted to confinement. We cannot compare this information with that on Brussels without qualification, because it exclusively concerns unwanted people who were in the city mental hospital or house of correction. If we look into the relationship of these people with the petitioners, however, then it is quite clear that the latter were parents or spouses in the main: their proportion as a whole varied between 65 and 80 per cent. In consequence the conclusion could be drawn that the problems and conflicts arose mainly within the nuclear family. Other family members who took the initiative were only in the minority and then it was a question of relationships of second and third degree, in which brothers and sisters took the lead.

What reasons could so many parents have had for putting a son or daughter under lock and key? The phenomenon is all the more remarkable since, as time passed, more and more fathers and mothers from the lower classes were resorting to this practice. We must remember that they desperately needed every source of income, however small. For married workers and people with small businesses, the consequences of having their partners locked up were even more serious, at least on a material level. Why did growing numbers of them take such a radical decision? What patterns of behaviour were so intolerable that confinement seemed the best or indeed the only solution?

2

Unruly Living

Unruly living: this is what it was all about. The requests are full of descriptions which made it clear that the person to be locked up behaved in some abnormal way, was not amenable to reason and constituted a danger both to those closest to him and to society at large. 'Put my son Joannes under lock and key!' pleaded the widow Anna Theresa De Visser in 1773, 'because he blasphemes like a heretic, incessantly uses abusive language to me, gets drunk every day, frequents places of ill-repute – in short, he is not living as a Christian, but as an animal.'[1] Emmanuel Quaeyhagen had to be disciplined, according to his niece in 1778, because he was bringing the good name of the whole family into disrepute: even though his mother lay dying he still pestered her for money to go drinking, 'which turned him from a human being into a creature without reason'.[2] Most petitioners put things somewhat less drastically, but the tenor of their arguments was always the same: their relative was incapable of normal social contact, had no sense of responsibility, was bereft of all moral judgement and turned the lives of the other members of the household into a living hell. The theme was not without variations – quite the contrary. The expression 'inappropriate social behaviour' covered a host of interpretations, and confinement was considered as a remedy for 'maladies' of all manner and description.

Insane or debauched?

A relatively large number of petitioners stated that the person to be confined conducted himself scandalously, it is true, but that he could not be held responsible for his deeds because in the first place they were self-destructive, which according to the family was an indication of insanity. In both Antwerp and Bruges, 25 to 30 per cent of the requests for confinement for the first time involved people who were deemed by their relatives or others in the household to be insane. From the requests and medical attestations it seems that a very wide socio-cultural category was involved which had many manifestations and meanings. Nonetheless, however widely these differed, they did have one thing in common – that insanity was not interpreted in terms of sin or possession by supernatural powers, as was still often the case in the seventeenth century. During the period under consideration, even priests – who sometimes acted as witnesses – no longer considered insanity as a punishment from God or as the work of the devil. Just as did the petitioners and doctors, they associated deviant mental conditions implicitly or explicitly with 'disturbance'. While the syndrome was seldom if ever specified exactly, everyone defined insanity in secular terms: the person concerned was suffering from 'a deviant mental condition', had a 'muddled' or 'deranged mind', was 'touched in his powers of reason or his senses', 'troubled in his senses', 'suffered a sickness of the senses', or, in short, was 'sick in the head', 'sense-less', 'insane'.

Given that it was no crime to be insane, the authorities had not the slightest problem with the fact that mad people were walking about freely in society. These people were in any case an everyday phenomenon, in towns, cities and villages. They were familiar figures in the physical and mental landscape of the time. They – that is, the harmlessly insane – were considered as simpletons or innocents. The limits of the acceptable could not however be exceeded. If the insane person caused scandal or, worse still, constituted a threat to public order, then action was taken. The information available suggests, moreover, that the initiative was seldom taken by the aldermen. The majority of the insane who were locked up were clearly in an institution at the request of relatives or other members of the household, whose declarations were confirmed by third parties.

The view of society, in particular that of the people directly involved, was thus of decisive importance – especially since the contention of insanity was not exclusive to the domain of a specific professional group. The advice of doctors and surgeons doubtless tipped the balance, but their attestations show that the 'academic' interpretations of insanity did not differ greatly from the petitioners' ideas about it. It is possible that in the Austrian Netherlands, just as in eighteenth-century England,[3] a specialist expertise was gradually crystallizing, giving rise perhaps to new definitions of insanity. However, this had little influence on the daily conduct of affairs. In the medical reports made in conjunction with confinement requests up to the end of the *ancien régime*, it is difficult to find even the beginnings of an embryonic 'psychiatric' diagnosis.

The requests and witnesses' testimonies show that contemporaries were looking at external appearances. According to them, insanity could be recognized in certain patterns of behaviour which were perceptible to everyone. It showed itself in a number of symptoms: an abnormal manner, a bizarre appearance, an odd way of speaking, eccentric habits. The person concerned looked mad, talked gibberish and behaved idiosyncratically. An attestation from a Brussels doctor in 1770 put it in a nutshell: Laurent Speltincx was insane because

> . . . after I had examined his manner, the movement of his eyes, his mouth, his pulse, and had studied him in all his moods and made various interrogations of him, he had several discourses with me in which I was able to note that his mind was of a sick disposition, extravagant, inflexible and capable of driving him to violent and furious actions, whose consequences could be dangerous.[4]

The last point was of the utmost importance. People were not locked up purely and simply because they were mentally ill. Most of the petitioners did not fail to emphasize that their relative was ungovernable, gave offence, caused damage to themselves and threatened to cause mishaps, both to his close relatives and to others. Their specific descriptions do not enable us to give modern psychiatric labels to their condition, any more than the medical 'diagnoses' could be put into modern-day jargon, since the doctors or surgeons did little more than support the viewpoint of the petitioners. An 'update' would not in any case be advisable, because it would all too easily lead to anachronisms: the psychological traits of modern-day people would not necessarily be applicable to societies in the past. On the basis of the information from Brussels it is possible to examine what forms of insanity were likely to lead to a request for confinements.[5]

In three out of ten cases the Brussels petitioners declared that their relative had taken leave of his senses. The person concerned was 'not only insane but furiously mad', had an 'unusually choleric disposition' or a 'natural ferocity', 'raved and ranted out of his senses', and flew into a 'blind rage' at every turn. Most medical attestations were written in the same sort of language. Some doctors, it is true, did use 'technical' terms, such as 'delirium melancholicum', 'frenzy' or 'hypochondriacal deliriousness', but that is as far as it went.

The declarations of witnesses in such cases was of great significance, especially when the petitioners were too poor to bear the costs of a confinement. 'It is no wonder that Catharina Brouette is being aban-

doned by her crippled husband', wrote her neighbours at the end of
October 1747 to the aldermen. Married life for him was a *via dolorosa*:
his wife beat him till the blood flowed, killed their cat and dog, set the
household furniture on fire and threw the burning embers at passers-by
in the street, whom she also pelted with pots and bottles. 'We can
tolerate this no longer', wrote the witnesses. After all, it is not

> ... permissible in a properly administered city that its inhabitants should
> have to be exposed to such affronts and incidents, since one of the essential
> tasks of a good magistrate is to ensure that they be free not only from the
> misdeeds of enraged persons but also from the mad, the furious and others
> who have taken leave of their senses.

The aggression of the insane person was always painted in lurid colours
and illustrated with striking examples. According to his mother, 24-
year-old Jacob Delanoydt had been behaving like a brute for more than
a year and a half: during his attacks of frenzy, which were becoming
ever more frequent, he assaulted and bit anyone coming within his
vicinity and at other times it was impossible to be under the same roof
as he, since he did nothing but 'scream, swear, sing and whistle, day and
night'. According to his wife, 68-year-old Joannes Van der Achteren
broke up the household furniture and ripped his clothes to shreds;
moreover, he had threatened her and a female cousin who was living in
the house with a knife. Antonius Hoeckhuyse too, according to his wife,
'daily went about in a complete rage': he beat her black and blue,
pestered the neighbours and uttered death-threats to all and sundry. The
sister and brother-in-law of Maria De Vliegere declared that their lives
had been made a living hell: Maria not only smashed everything up and
set fire to things, but also made one attempt after another to kill her
pregnant sister, who had been giving her a roof over her head, in spite
of everything. Theresa François, her husband declared, had been getting
into such a fury over the previous five weeks that she threatened to
murder him and their three children. The mother of 45-year-old Anne-
Marie Lambrechts also invoked preservation of life, because she had
been 'worked over' by her daughter at totally unexpected moments with
sticks, knives, tongs or spades.

Some of the petitioners stated that confinement was necessary not only
because they feared for their lives and that of others, but also – and
especially – because the insane member of their family had been
threatening to take his own life. In most cases, however, suicidal
behaviour was not associated with violence against members of the
household or other people. At any rate, the families involved in these
cases seldom made mention of acts of aggression. Whatever the case may

be, the requests show that attempts at suicide occurred frequently: in Brussels this was cited as the main motive in one out of ten petitions for the confinement of an insane person. It was always a matter of people who had several times tried to drown or hang themselves, cut their wrists, throw themselves out of windows or set themselves on fire. Thanks to the timely intervention of relatives, neighbours or casual passers-by, their attempts had until then failed, but they were still bent on succeeding in their dreadful intentions. The injuries they sustained were not sufficient to bring them to their senses. The admonitions of the parish priest were of no avail. If other members of the household let their attention slip for even a moment, then they ran the risk that the person concerned would make further attempts at suicide. 'That continuous supervision poses insurmountable problems for us', explained the petitioners: 'the mental asylum is the only place where this member of our family can be effectively protected from himself.'

Suicide as a manifestation of insanity: this was a belief which gradually took root during the period being studied, which explains why most requests involving it were made after 1740. Until well into the seventeenth century the temporal and ecclesiastical authorities in the Southern Netherlands were in agreement that anyone who tried to end his own life was committing a serious crime and a mortal sin. The person concerned had not trusted in God's mercy and by definition had no time for repentance, which meant that his soul was doomed to eternal damnation, as was that of Judas, the prototype of the 'treacherous Jew'. The aversion to this abominable infringement of God's laws was so great that the courts condemned the body of the victim to be executed and forbade that it should be buried in hallowed ground. The rule was circumvented only if the family could produce irrefutable evidence that the person who had committed suicide had shown various signs of insanity for some considerable time, so that it could be assumed that the individual in despair had not been seduced into committing the deed by the devil. The first half of the eighteenth century was a turning-point. The aldermen were increasingly less inclined to prosecute dead bodies. If they did so, then their judgement was more and more often that the person concerned had robbed himself of life because 'there was something amiss with his senses'. In Antwerp the last execution of a suicide case took place on 23 December 1752: that was when the body of Nijs Vanderneusen was dragged through the town on a sled and then impaled on a fork to public view. After that time suicide was always associated with insanity. The example of Elisabeth Pauwels, who took her own life in 1765, shows what progress had been made by the process of secularization up to that time. The woman next door testified that Pauwels had frequently cried out: 'Cut my throat, I am indeed damned because my soul has long been the devil's plaything.' 'A clear case of insanity', reads the laconic commentary of the Antwerp magistrate.[6]

The secularization of insanity is also to be seen in the change of attitude in both petitioners and aldermen with regard to all forms of religious inspiration. Whereas in previous centuries people who went about warning everyone that the end of the world was nigh or announced that they had conversed with the angels were for the most part taken seriously – whether, depending on the circumstances, they were considered prophets, the possessed or heretics – in the eighteenth century there was a growing inclination to regard them as simply insane. If in addition they behaved impulsively and the disturbance of their souls caused difficulties for others, the other members of their families had no compunction in having them put in a mental institution. This was the fate that befell the 24-year-old François De Houxte, after he had loudly proclaimed that he had been in Paradise and spoken with God and the saints. According to the brother and brother-in-law of the master-mason Joseph Philipaert, confinement was the only remedy because he refused to stop going around in public pronouncing himself the mouthpiece of God. 'Frans De Valck is quite mad', declared his sister, 'because he goes around blessing everyone – with unblessed water!' Excessive religious devotion also led to the confinement of the serving-maid Maria De Mars, who wanted to receive communion three or four times a day, continuously pestered the parish priest and every other minute prostrated herself on the church floor. This was also the case with Catharina Huybrechts, a young girl who announced that she was forced to become 'invisible' in order to consume the flesh and blood of Christ, and Martine Van de Houten, the mother of three children, who thought she was doomed to hellfire and went round all the convents seeking salvation.

It was not the religious insanity itself which gave offence and led to a confinement petition. Anyone who was mad would not know what he was doing or saying, so that moral disapproval was not the point at issue. The scandal came about from the fact that the eccentric behaviour of these religiously inspired people was a source of mockery and amusement which ridiculed the Word of God. If they had hidden their delusions and terrors of the soul from other people then they would probably not have been put under lock and key by their relatives. The latter were irritated by their ungovernable urge to give 'public performances'.

There were many other forms of non-dangerous insanity which could equally well lead to a request for confinement, because the families concerned believed that the behaviour of the insane person would cause scandal and in consequence threaten their reputation. This applied particularly to walking around naked, something done by both men and women. According to his mother, the clock-maker Marcus Van der Vinnen would have to be locked up, because he undressed himself at inappropriate times, on each occasion accompanied by streams of obscenities. For the widow Baut it was sufficient that her son Jacob had appeared once in public 'half-naked' (he had worn only a jacket and a sword!), and once without a wig and hat, for her to ask the Capuchin monks to give him two blood-letting sessions and to place him in the *Simpelhuys*. The parents of the 16-year-old Anna Baelen had more reason to worry: their daughter walked around naked through the town the whole day long and, for a piece of bread, allowed herself to be beaten with stinging nettles by soldiers. Female exhibitionists clearly had a predilection for performing in churches, where they were wont to remove their dresses – in one case, whenever the priest showed the consecrated Host to the people. If we are to believe the petitioners and the witnesses, religious services acted as a magnet for non-dangerous agitations: the afflicted wanted to take communion even though they were not capable of making confession, and they disrupted the service by incessantly making grimaces or obscene gestures, uttering gibberish, hurling the most vulgar terms of abuse at the faithful or causing havoc in other ways. Other harmless people were locked up because they made so much noise in their homes or on the street that they woke up everyone in the immediate vicinity. Thus it was that the husband of Margarita Haghen declared that no landlord would rent them accommodation any more: all too often they had had to move because of pressure from the other residents whose sleep had been disturbed by his wife's *battementen* (banging).

Anyone considered mad who did not cause scandal, had no suicidal inclinations and constituted no danger to others ran less risk of ending up in an institution, of course. Yet in Brussels such persons were involved in two out of ten requests for confinement. There was a wide spectrum of syndromes. Some of them exhibited symptoms of what today we would call senile dementia. All of them were more than 70 years of age and, according to the petitioners, had lost their powers of judgement – by which they sometimes committed 'unclean' acts, such as playing with their own excrement. Others sank into mute apathy: they reacted hardly at all to being pricked, paid no attention to their appearance and said not a word. The petitioners ascribed their apathy to severe emotional shock – caused, as in the case of one 16-year-old youth, by the death of a father, or, in the case of one young woman, by the ending of a love-affair. Doctors invariably diagnosed 'black melancholy' or 'feebleness of the nerves'. Others were living in a 'state of foolish innocence' or had 'an imbecile mind'. It is not clear whether an attempt was being made with these terms to describe differing degrees of mental weakness. From

the descriptions we have we can see only that the young men and women
– they were always children and adolescents – had had a severely
retarded development, both intellectually and emotionally. Almost all
the parents declared that their sons or daughters had been 'foolishly
innocent' since infancy. They were at a loss to know what to do. 'Not
only is our child incapable of doing any work, he cannot control himself
and does strange things – he even allows himself to be interfered with.'
Another example: 16-year-old Christiane Tielemans behaved 'just like a
five- or six-year-old child'; she was 'deceived' several times when she
went to gather firewood and had recently had a baby 'without the
slightest human comprehension', because the unfortunate girl 'just
followed the dictates of her passions, in common with the animals'.

Not all weak-minded young people, senile elderly people and those
with emotional disturbances were put under lock and key by members
of their families. With the aid of Jozef Geldhof's research we can make
a more accurate estimate of how many poor families applied to the
Bruges city council in the eighteenth century for a subsidy because they
had a mentally ill person to look after – that is, someone for whom they
were responsible, who was unable to contribute to the family income
and who in addition needed medical and nursing care. The details of
their cases indicate a spectacular increase: their number hovered between
30 and 40 up to 1757, thereafter rising to more than 100 around 1772
and to almost 200 during the Brabant Revolution.[7] It is not easy to
ascertain why one family opted for home care and another for compulsory admission. Nor can we easily glean from the magistrate's decisions
why on some occasions he refused a petition for confinement but granted
a subsidy, while on others he did just the opposite. For this we would
have to find out a great deal more, not only about the social background
of the petitioners, their relations with the 'insane' person and his mental
condition, but also about what syndromes the doctors were dealing with
and what the policy of the aldermen and the administrators of the
various institutions was. It is in any case clear that the increase in the
number of patients cared for at home did not correspond with a decrease
in the number that ended up in an institution. On the contrary, both
groups increased considerably in number during the 1770s and 1780s.

It might be assumed that only the 'hopeless' cases were locked up. The
facts also prove this hypothesis wrong. Indeed, quite a large number of
mentally disturbed people did not remain long under lock and key, as
we shall see. From this it follows that either they were very quickly
cured, suggesting a slight and/or temporary form of insanity, or that they
were not mad at all, which would imply that their relatives considered
confinement as a remedy for other 'maladies'. Indeed, there are indications that insanity often functioned as a euphemism for disorderly conduct.

Two out of ten Brussels families making an insanity declaration produced no medical attestation in support of it; instead, they handed the aldermen written testimony from the parish priest. If we add to this fact that nothing in the contested behaviour indicated any symptom of illness, it will be clear what the petitioners were up to: if the slightest damage were going to be caused to the family reputation, it was advisable that the unwanted person be placed among the insane, in the *Simpelhuys* therefore. The mother of Elisabeth Van den Huyse made no bones about it: 'In order to avoid scandal, I am asking for my unmarried daughter to be placed in an institution for the insane for a few months and for the baby to which she recently gave birth to be taken into an orphanage.' The mother of 18-year-old Jean Swyn, a shoemaker's apprentice, was just as explicit: she pleaded for confinement in a mental institution 'to avoid the dishonour that might be brought upon the parents and to the young persons who have been confined in the house of correction'; 'No problem, provided you pay the cost', ran the aldermen's response.

Not all cases are so clear-cut, and there is some doubt about the degree of insanity when people stated as their only motive the fact that their daughter was for ever quarrelling with them and had fled the parental home (a rebel?), or that their son was wasting his inheritance (a fool?) or that a married woman was keeping company with other men 'to give vent to her voluptuousness' (a frustrated husband?). If there are doubts about every individual case, we have the certainty that there was nothing wrong with many of the so-called mad people, at least that they did not demonstrate any psychological disturbances or abnormal reactions. When in 1791 an investigation was conducted into the conditions at the Brussels *Simpelhuys*, the commissioners noted that 33 persons detained at the expense of the city and 11 others maintained by relatives or people with whom they had shared a roof were completely sound in heart and mind – that is, a quarter of the total number of persons confined.[8] This was not an isolated case. In Maastricht there were numerous men and women in the eighteenth century, mostly after 1740, who were also locked up at the request of their relatives purely and simply because they would not conform to the predominant standards of behaviour; of the 277 people about whom the requests provide more or less detailed information, there were no fewer than 116, or almost 42 per cent, who could be blamed for nothing more than that they had misbehaved.[9]

'Quaed gedragh'

We should not lose sight of the fact that 70 to 75 per cent of the requests for confinement for the first time in the cities of Brabant and Flanders involved young people and adults who were declared to be responsible by their housemates or relatives. The petitioners did speak of scandalous and irresponsible behaviour, but in so doing they did not use terms which would be associated by their contemporaries with some form of insanity. Rightly or wrongly, they did not doubt the intellectual capacity of their family member. They were of the opinion that his misconduct was attributable to wilfulness and even maliciousness and that in consequence the person concerned had to be corrected and re-educated – in other words, brought to repentance through losing his freedom. The monastery or house of correction as an institution for improvement: this was the argument in a nutshell.

What did the petitioners understand by *quaed gedragh* (bad behaviour/disorderly conduct), the customary term? It is impossible to give an unequivocal answer to this question. Just as with the term 'insanity', this expression had many layers of meaning and, just as in the first case, it is a precarious undertaking to group the requests concerned into categories and thus distinguish the various forms of behaviour one from another. There are two complications we have to bear in mind.

In the first place the motive for petition was not always explained. Some petitioners resolutely refused to provide substantive information. Thus the wife of Jan Swaens wrote on 3 July 1775 to the aldermen of Antwerp that confinement was necessary for 'all the most pregnant reasons, which it is not convenient to express here'.[10] Other families restricted themselves to mentioning that it was a matter of 'scandalous acts' or 'malicious behaviour' and said nothing more. They presumably chose to go and plead their cases in person so as to avoid functionaries from the lower ranks getting to know about matters which might bring the good name of the family into question. It could be assumed that they were reasonably well-off, since almost all of them opted for confinement in a monastery.

On the other hand, we are confronted in a (limited) number of cases with the opposite problem – with requests containing an entire shopping-list of complaints. A close analysis of all the individual elements and their various combinations sometimes enables us to get to the heart of the matter with a degree of probability verging on certainty. This is not always possible however, as we can see from two examples from Antwerp.[11] On 11 December 1775 the mother of 20-year-old Cornelius Franciscus Sas declared that things could not go on as they were: her son

Table 2.1   *Categories of objectionable behaviour, Antwerp and Bruges*
(percentages)

Objectionable behaviour	Bruges 1740–64	Antwerp 1710–69	Bruges 1765–89	Antwerp 1770–89
Insanity	28.2	31.5	24.9	26.6
Unruly living	4.1	14.4	4.7	3.8
Work-shyness	19.5	8.6	23.6	21.5
Prodigality	14.4	15.4	14.8	18.6
Alcohol abuse	11.3	12.0	14.2	10.2
Immorality	11.2	5.5	6.8	9.0
Assault	4.1	7.1	4.4	3.8
Other	7.2	5.5	6.6	6.5
100% = N	195	292	365	312

refused to work, squandered her hard-earned savings, often came home
blind drunk and molested his sister. On 31 March 1778 Barbara
Jonckbloet pleaded confinement for her husband: Petrus drank from
morning till night, allowed the shop to become shabby, thrashed her and
threatened to kill her, incessantly tried to rape her daughter and
consorted with whores. It is clear that these petitioners were not
objecting to any specific acts of deviant behaviour; they considered the
way their housemates lived as wholly intolerable.

If we leave aside cases that can only be grouped under the general
heading of 'unruly living', then we can distinguish five main categories
of 'disorderly conduct': work-shyness, prodigality, alcohol abuse,
immorality, and assault and battery. Many petitioners, it is true, objected
to two or more of these 'deviations', but in general only one of the
aforementioned problems was central to their conflicts. For Antwerp
and Bruges we have investigated what were cited as the chief motives in
confinement petitions (without requests for an extension) (see table 2.1),
and here we have also taken into consideration the categories of
'insanity' and 'unruly living'. In the 1770s and 1780s the percentage
proportions among the various categories of objectionable behaviour in
both cities were largely the same. On the other hand, before 1765 and
up to 1770 we can see some striking differences: unruly living then
occupied a much more prominent place in Antwerp than in Bruges,
while the proportion of the categories of work-shyness and immorality
in the first-named city was much more limited. An explanation has to be
sought in the fact that in Antwerp before 1770 there were relatively
many more well-off families who had one of their relatives locked up

than in Bruges, as our analysis of the choice of confinement location has shown. The upper class was the least inclined to give a precise explanation of what they meant by 'unruly living'. In other words, at the end of the *ancien régime* the percentages among the various categories of misconduct paralleled each other because the social background of the petitioners in the metropolis had drastically changed; just as in Bruges, the petitioners in Antwerp came increasingly from the proletariat and the lower middle classes.

There was not only a connection between the social background from which the petitioners came and the nature of the objectionable behaviour. The latter also varied according to sex, civil state and age of the person to be confined: work-shyness was blamed mainly by parents on their sons, alcohol abuse mainly by wives on their husbands, immorality mainly by men on their wives and by parents on their daughters. The relationships between social position, family structure and objectionable behaviour will be discussed at length in the succeeding chapters. For a good understanding of the shifts that took place during the period under study, it is also first necessary to throw some light on the socio-cultural significance of the aforementioned types of 'disorderly conduct'.

Immorality is the only category that in principle bordered on the criminal. Indeed, almost every form of extramarital sex was punishable by law. According to customary Antwerp law, a married man who consorted with 'an unmarried daughter or young spinster' had to be heavily fined, the second time given nothing but bread and water for three months; recidivism would result in permanent banishment from the city. An adulterous woman was threatened with the same punishments, but her husband could also lock her up 'in a monastery or other place of confinement, there to repent or pay out a fine'. Woe to the man who 'willingly and knowingly suffered his wife to live dishonestly with another man', because he was 'banished for ever': if he did this 'for financial gain', then he would lose all his worldly goods and then be 'punished on the scaffold, or flogged or given some other punishment as deemed fit by the law'.[12]

Indeed, anyone who tolerated 'dishonest' dealings, let alone encouraged them, was considered by the temporal and ecclesiastical authorities to be as reprehensible as the prostitute herself. In most of the towns and cities of Brabant and Flanders brothel-keepers, procurers and pimps had been prosecuted since the late Middle Ages, whereby the severest punishments were reserved for men who hired out their wives or daughters for 'criminal conversation'.[13] From numerous studies, however, it also appears that there was a world of difference between theory and practice. So long as the prostitutes and those who profited from their activities gave no offence, they were generally left alone. This was

certainly the case in the eighteenth century, though 'lechery' flourished
to a much greater extent than ever before, at least according to the court
officials. It is not easy to ascertain whether their claims were well
founded, but there is no doubt that at the end of the *ancien régime* those
who consorted with prostitutes in the large towns of Brabant and
Flanders could always find something to their liking. In 1785 a Frenchman (a man who presented himself as a *philosophe observateur et
impartial*) wrote to the *amman* (government representative) of Brussels
that nowhere in Europe were there so many prostitutes to be seen as in
the capital of the Austrian Netherlands. 'It is not possible to go into or
out of an hotel, order a carriage or set foot in the mondaine districts', he
said, 'without being collared by all manner of riff-raff trying to entice
one into the temples of Venus.'[14]

It was not only preachers of morality who took such exception to
certain manifestations of paid love. If the neighbours found that a
prostitute behaved too provocatively or that her clients made too much
racket, then they did not hesitate to put in a complaint. Thus the
residents of Kasteelplein requested the Antwerp aldermen on 2 June
1788 to lock up a certain Annotje, because this woman of the streets
continually caused scandal and moreover was leading her three children
into the ways of vice, thus constituting a danger to the youth of the
neighbourhood.[15] An analysis of the criminal proceedings shows that
most prosecutions against prostitutes were instigated after a number of
'respectable' burghers had entered a complaint and that nuisance was
the reason almost always given. The nub of the offence was not paid
love itself, but its public manifestation and the annoyance the neighbours
experienced as a result. This was known all too well by the men who
had their wives locked up for immorality or the parents their daughter:
they invariably emphasized the fact that the person concerned caused
public scandal to her family and that her incorrigible behaviour –
walking around naked, alcohol abuse, making a din at night – made
good relations with the neighbouring residents impossible.

It is not surprising to learn that it was mostly men who were put
under lock and key for grievous acts of ill-treatment. What is more
remarkable is that the petitioners who cited violence as the chief motive
for confinement were considerably few in number: 4 to 7 per cent of the
total. At first sight these figures are not very impressive. Violence in the
eighteenth century was a very frequent phenomenon. At the end of the
ancien régime it even reached a high-point: from 1775 up to and
including 1784, there were no fewer than 539 registered acts of violence
in Ghent – that is an average of 11 per 10,000 residents per year, as
against six in the middle and beginning of the century. In Antwerp the
numbers were smaller, but they too shot up: the average number of

crimes of violence per 10,000 residents per year rose from 2.5 around 1765 to four at the end of Austrian rule.

Research conducted by Anne-Marie Roets sheds light on the constants and shifts in violent criminality in Ghent. In both the seventeenth and eighteenth centuries most of the offenders and victims were adult men, but the proportion of women in both groups increased considerably towards the end of the *ancien régime*. Though murder and manslaughter in the seventeenth century constituted 6 to 7 per cent of all crimes of violence, on the eve of the Brabant Revolution they came to less than 1 per cent. The extraordinary increase in light physical violence – in both absolute and relative terms – was, moreover, coupled with a decreasing use of weapons: whereas in the seventeenth century, half the men involved in affrays without fatalities incurred stab- or shot-wounds, by 1780 that number had dropped to 13 per cent; in three-quarters of the cases the men fought with bare fists. People continued to resolve conflicts by fighting in the streets, but the scene of this kind of violence became more and more the public house.[16] Is it possible to find an explanation for all these shifts in a 'democratization' of acts of violence? This cannot be excluded, since the relatively small number of occasions on which the profession of offender and victim was mentioned seems to point to a growing proportion of manual labourers and minor craftsmen in both cases. This hypothesis is supported by the fact that the outbreak in light physical violence was accompanied by changes in the social profile of the frequenters of public houses.

It was not only in public places that growing aggression manifested itself. People also came to blows at home. Before 1770 there were 'only' three women per decade in Antwerp who had their husbands locked up because of serious ill-treatment, and thereafter the number was six. In Bruges too, their number doubled: from eight in the period 1740–64 to 16 between 1765 and 1789. Was this the tip of the iceberg, or more appropriately a glimpse of hell through the keyhole? This seems very plausible, because much must have happened before a woman took this step. According to custom, a husband could chastise his wife whenever he considered it necessary.[17] This is why all the petitioners emphasized that they ran the risk of being murdered and gathered a large number of witnesses to substantiate their charge. The women involved came mainly from poor families or those with very modest means, since most of them do not seem to have been in a position to bear the costs of confinement.

Alcohol abuse, prodigality and work-shyness were the categories most likely to involve questions of money. They deserve special attention, since both in Antwerp and Bruges the number of requests in which these forms of *quaed gedragh* was the central issue rose dramatically. In the 1770s and 1780s they were cited as the main problem in more than half

Plate 1 J. J. Verhaghen, *Tavern Scene*, eighteenth century. Drinking in company with others oiled the wheels of a society in which close family ties and good neighbourliness were essential prerequisites for survival.

of all the requests for confinement. The aforementioned categories often appeared in combination with others. The explanation is to be found in the fact that alcohol abuse, prodigality and work-shyness were not formally punishable by law, so the petitioners tried to show that the unwanted person was acting on the verge of illegality and that he/she threatened to go from bad to worse.

Alcohol abuse was certainly disapproved of by the temporal and ecclesiastical authorities, but it did not in itself constitute an infringement of the law. Drunkards could be prosecuted only if they had committed legal offences – and these had to be serious, since the magistrates knew that most witnesses considered drunkenness as more of an excuse than an incriminating circumstance. From many of the criminal proceedings, moreover, it appears that a goodly number of judges shared this view. They did, however, make a distinction between *ebrietas* and *ebriositas*, chronic alcohol abuse; in the latter case there could be no talk of lenience.

It is worth noting that the terminology used by contemporaries does

not enable us to separate heavy drinkers from alcoholics as such. Before
the nineteenth century, no one spoke of 'alcoholism'. While towards the
end of the *ancien régime* more and more doctors were beginning to turn
their attention to the damaging consequences of taking alcohol regularly
over long periods, they did not consider excessive drinkers as people
who were ill and being in need of medical treatment; in their eyes they
were immoral people who had to be brought under control. From the
substantive descriptions of their objectionable behaviour we can in any
case deduce that many drinkers who were placed in an institution at the
request of their families were suffering from acute or chronic alcoholic
poisoning: they were very aggressive, did things which they could not
remember afterwards, screamed and yelled out in their sleep, and so on.
Not all drunkards, however, were alcoholics. In some cases it was simply
a question of men or women who often took to the bottle. This is not
surprising, since Bacchus could count on a great deal of sympathy in the
Southern Netherlands, at least among the masses – as many foreigners
confirmed to their surprise, or even astonishment. 'To take a glass away
from a Fleming is to cut the roots from which a tree draws its sap', was
the judgement of a French canon of the church visiting the Southern
Netherlands around 1670. During the century of the Enlightenment
there seemed to be talk of little else. The Frenchman Augustin de
Gomicourt, who under the pseudonym Derival published a detailed
account of his journey around the Austrian Netherlands in the 1780s,
could hardly say enough about *the* national vice, namely unbridled
drunkenness – by which, according to him, both men and women were
afflicted. Even if we have to look with some scepticism on these
'characterizations', there can be no doubt that Brabantians and Flemings
were heavy drinkers.

During the second half of the eighteenth century the annual consumption of beer in all the towns for which figures are available varied
between 250 and 350 litres per person. Now this impressive quantity
does not necessarily point to abnormality. Even in years of full employment and low food prices most families had to be content with a
monotonous and dry table, consisting of rough rye bread, beans and
salted foodstuffs. Clean water was rare in the towns and, where
available, was by definition tasteless. Fresh milk, because it did not
remain fresh for long, could not be transported over long distances and
because of the dreadful conditions of hygiene was often of dubious
quality. Chocolate, coffee or tea, the fashionable drinks of the eighteenth
century, could not be afforded by the large majority of people. The
lower classes therefore had to quell their thirst with beer, which
contained the greatest number of calories (as expressed per unit of
money). Moreover, the cheaper beers had such a low alcohol content

Plate 2 J. J. Verhaghen, *Card Players*, eighteenth century. The addiction to gambling was often mentioned as an additional reason for confinement during the second half of the eighteenth century.

that people had to drain several jars before they reached a state of euphoria. This took place mainly in public houses.

There were many kinds of drinking houses, ranging from large and comfortable hostelries, where people could eat and stay the night, to *cabarets* or pubs, which offered little accommodation and where only beer or brandy was to be had. It was not only thirst and lack of domestic comfort that drove the lower classes in the evenings and on holidays to the public house, where there was space, light and warmth. Public houses also functioned as a crossroads for communication, where local residents exchanged views on items of news or their problems, and doubled as relaxation centres where people could dance and play dice or cards. In short, they were the focus of social and cultural activities. Drinking in company oiled the wheels of a society in which close family ties and good neighbourliness were essential conditions for survival. Inviting all one's relatives and friends to a christening, an engagement or a wedding feast was a social obligation, whatever it cost, because the cohesion of the family and the community had continually to be re-established.

Often the jollifications at such times lasted for several days, so that it is small wonder everyone drank themselves under the table.[18]

'*Als dronkenschap het huis ingaat, de vrede spoedig het verlaat*' ('The home that welcomes drunkenness as guest, can bid with speed adieu to rest'): popular sayings are not always true, but the eighteenth-century elites were all of the opinion that the frequenters of public houses caused a great deal of mischief, both at home and in public. Although their attempts to curb visits to the inn were not dictated primarily by social concerns, their complaints about increasing alcoholism among the lower classes did have some basis in reality. Average beer consumption per capita did actually fall slightly during the second half of the eighteenth century, but this drop was due entirely to the fact that the fairly well-off burghers switched over to coffee-drinking; they distanced themselves from the 'masses' by visiting new cafés and organizing soirées at home. The lower classes, on the contrary, went even more often to the public house, since the *average* consumption of cheap beer continued to rise.[19] In fact, the number of drinking houses also rose: in Antwerp from one per 181 inhabitants in 1755 to one per 130 in 1799, in Bruges from one per 175 inhabitants in 1727 to one per 155 in 1790, and in Ghent from one per 95 inhabitants in 1756 to one per 81 around the turn of the century.[20] These figures are minima, because they cover exclusively public houses recognized by the authorities. It could be assumed that there were also illegal drinking places, particularly since the consumption of jenever was rapidly on the increase and did not need a tap for pouring.

Brandy and other distilled drinks were being made in the Southern Netherlands around the end of the sixteenth century, but their production and consumption really took off in the eighteenth century, especially after 1750. The spectacular expansion of grain distilleries brought with it a stabilization in prices, which encouraged more jenever drinking. Around 1800 in the *département des Deux Nèthes* (the present province of Antwerp) people were drinking six litres of jenever per year. If we assume that only adolescents and adults drank *borrels* (glasses of jenever), then the average quantity per consumer goes up to eight and a half litres – but it should be noted that an average in this case does not have much significance. All contemporaries were agreed that most of the visitors to the 'gin palaces' came from the lowest social classes.

It is not difficult to understand why the gin house exerted such an attraction for the proletariat. A *borrel* was a powerful drink and cost a third to a half less than a pint of the cheapest beer. Visiting a brandy house (often illegal), moreover, strengthened mutual solidarity and thus promoted the creation of a social and cultural identity – to which the 'civilized' burghers indirectly contributed by continually railing against the scandalous behaviour of the jenever drinkers.

The lower classes nonetheless condemned alcohol abuse, as the requests for confinement show. One in ten undesirables ended up in an institution because of alcoholism. If we add to these the people locked up who, according to their families, regularly hit the bottle without being addicted to drink, then the figure comes to almost 30 per cent of all cases. From the place of confinement we can deduce that a number of hardened drunkards came from the 'better' circles of society. At the same time, they also constituted a very small minority. Nine out of ten alcoholics were put under lock and key at the expense of the city, and from the mention of their professions it appears that they were partly from labourers' families and partly from the lower middle classes. The overwhelming majority consisted of adult men who were prosecuted by their wives, where the latter generally laid emphasis on the animal behaviour of the alcoholic towards those who lived under the same roof: every time he came home blind drunk, which happened with increasing frequency, he would burst into a rage at the least provocation, wreck everything in his path and beat everyone up, even the children.

Another sign of the times: in a growing number of requests, prodigality was given as the chief motive for confinement. Indeed, the more or less stable proportion of this category (14 to 19 per cent) should not prevent us from losing sight of the fact that in the 1770s and 1780s many more requests were entered than previously. At the end of the *ancien régime* twice as many people in Bruges were accused by their relatives of excessive extravagance as in the middle of the century, and in Antwerp it was almost three times as many. They were a mixed group, both as far as their social position was concerned and as regards their relationship with the petitioners. Some of them were the children of rich families who, according to their parents or relatives, led debauched lives that cost them a fortune. Others belonged, as appears from their professional status, to the middle classes: master craftsmen, small traders and practitioners of the liberal professions were the most strongly represented. Most of them were dubbed by their wives as ne'er-do-wells who brought little money into the house and spent a great deal, by which they threatened to ruin themselves and thus reduce their families to penury. Since the women involved knew that prodigality was not punishable by law so long as the debts were settled, they contended either that fraudulent bankruptcy was one of the risks or that their husbands were gambling money away from the business.

It was not purely by chance that an addiction to gambling was increasingly cited as an additional reason for confinement during the second half of the eighteenth century: from the 1740s onwards the town and city administrations tried to check the tide of gambling fever, which in their opinion was taking an ever stronger hold. Their assertions cannot be verified. It is possible to calculate what the lotteries organized by the central government brought in and how many people took part in them, but an investigation of this nature would not provide a definite answer, since there were many illegal gambling games. There is much qualitative information to suggest that in the Austrian Netherlands there was a passion for gambling in all sorts of ways and that people from all social groups were thoroughly involved. While the coffee-houses, the foyers of theatres and above all the private salons teemed with professional gamblers à la Barry Lyndon, the inns and gin palaces were the setting for more modest gambling. Nonetheless, the stakes in such public places could proportionately be very high: from the trial reports we can see that in each game people gambled three or four *stuiver*, or a third to a half of the average daily wage. During the second half of the eighteenth century most labourers and members of the lower middle classes continually tried to improve their fortunes by running high risks, but the growing production of cheap printed playing-cards also encouraged them to gamble their savings at *basset, faro, lansquenet, brelan, passedix, rafle* and other card-games.[21]

Whereas most gamblers who ended up in an institution around 1750 at the request of their wives came from the better social circles, by the end of the *ancien régime* the overwhelming majority of them were manual labourers. This can be deduced not only from the place of confinement and the person's profession, but also from the numerous substantive descriptions of the poverty in which the families involved were living. The desire to gamble among the lower classes was closely linked to the precarious circumstances of their lives: gambling did after all offer a chance to make a big profit easily and quickly. It is for this reason no paradox that more and more money was being gambled as the material conditions of the proletariat declined: the smaller the income, the greater the temptation to gamble.

The increasing number of cases of work-shyness is also an indication of changes in the social climate. During the 1770s and 1780s this category exceeded all other forms of *quaed gedragh*: a fifth to a quarter of the petitioners labelled their relative as an incorrigible idler. There were a number of adults among the loafers, but nine out of ten were children or adolescents, youths in particular, locked up by their parents. Most of them came from the lower classes, because in three-quarters of the cases the petitioners confirmed that the family income was not sufficient to keep supporting a 'sponger'.

In the towns and cities of Brabant and Flanders, parents had a duty during the *ancien régime* to 'maintain their children until they were able and knew how to earn their own bread, board and clothing', according to Antwerp custom. In practice this *momborie* continued so long as the

Plate 3 L. Defrance, *Couple Playing at Dice*, second half of the eighteenth century. The upper classes also gambled, but they did this in coffee-houses, in the foyers of theatres and especially in private salons.

children were unmarried and under-age – that is, until the age of 25. On the other hand, parental power implied that children owed a duty of obedience to their father and mother – both of them, in the cities being studied – otherwise the latter could 'reasonably chastise them' and even keep them prisoner at home 'for a certain time'. If the parents wished to lock up their rebellious son or daughter elsewhere, then they had to request the permission of the magistrate.[22]

If the aldermen sometimes refused to lock up a minor on the grounds of mental illness, in the case of idling the request was always honoured.

This is hardly surprising, since the urban elites were, on the one hand, constantly trying to curb disguised beggary and, on the other, to mobilize young workers. But in fact most confinement requests for minors included other complaints to which the authorities were sensitive: the work-shy son fell into bad company, spent his whole time in a drinking house, stole the housekeeping money – in short, he threatened to come up against the law unless, according to the petitioners, he was firmly taken in hand in time. Possible damaging consequences: note the keywords. The parents realized that matters to which they objected were not punishable by law, but they also knew that the aldermen did worry about the dividing-line between immoral and illegal conduct.

A society under stress

Disapproval by the community of objectionable behaviour, particularly by neighbours and acquaintances, played an important role in the decision to have a family member locked up. We shall give examples of petitioners who held their unsullied reputation in such high esteem they considered anything that might besmirch it as sufficient grounds for taking drastic measures. The available information, however, suggests that the families for whom financial considerations were of primary concern were much more numerous and that the proportion of them increased considerably towards the end of the *ancien régime*. We have already noted that work-shyness, prodigality and alcoholism were the most frequent complaints during the 1770s and 1780s. It seems probable that money in such cases generally tipped the balance when weighing up the family honour – in particular because the petitioners involved came from the proletariat and the lower middle classes, and they ascribed their material problems to the misbehaviour of their housemate or relative. This is why it makes sense to see if there was any connection between the rising number of requests for confinement, the increasing use of cheaper institutions and the growing proportion of the financially precarious categories on the one hand and the changes that took place in the material conditions of the less well-off population-groups on the other. Given the current research situation it would be hazardous to make general statements about the social context in Brussels. The socio-economic developments in Antwerp and Bruges are well known though, at least in broad outline.

The second half of the eighteenth century was for Antwerp a period of industrial expansion. Some branches in the textile industry languished or even disappeared, but others rapidly flourished, especially the production of mixed fabrics and cotton-spinning. Towards the end of the *ancien régime* Antwerp had developed into a textile centre of the first rank. From figures taken in 1789 and 1800 it appears that half of the working population was involved in textile manufacture. Apart from the clothing trade, which accounted for 15 per cent of registered jobs, other industries were of little significance. The growth of the textile industry went hand in hand with the proletarianization of numerous craftsmen. Among some 17,500 people working in this sector around 1800 there were barely 800 independent producers and most of them had few employees, if any. The overwhelming majority of textile workers was in other words dependent on a very small number of entrepreneurs. Although the second half of the eighteenth century was characterized by a general rise in the cost of living, the workers were not able to obtain any wage increases at all, so that their purchasing power dropped considerably. The explanation has to be found in a combination of two factors: firstly the employers were able to keep the pay of adults down by taking on large numbers of youthful workers, and secondly charity was organized in such a way that its recipients could always be forced to work for the entrepreneurs at the lowest possible rate. In short, industrial expansion created a lot of employment but brought with it little in the way of general welfare. Some contemporaries were well aware of this, as can be seen from the bitter judgement pronounced in 1785 by the charity administrators: 'how could Antwerp have thought of establishing factories where the pay is so low that the craftsman, were he to have some family difficulty, yea even the slightest accident, would be in no condition even to subsist?' Indeed, textile workers constituted a particularly vulnerable proletariat, since more than 80 per cent of them possessed absolutely nothing apart from their labour. They escaped penury only if all the members of the family had continuous work and contributed to the family income.[23]

Just as in Antwerp, textile manufacture in Bruges was the most prominent economic sector and its restructuring was accompanied by the proletarianization of a mass of skilled craftsmen. However, there was a crucial difference: in Antwerp increasing production of mixed fabrics and the expansion of cotton-spinning amply compensated for the loss of jobs brought about by the decline in the traditional branches, even though the new jobs were taken mainly by women and children, while the restructuring in Bruges confronted numerous families with structural unemployment. The proportion of textile-workers in the total population of Bruges dropped from around 21 or 22 per cent in the period 1729–38 to 11 or 12 per cent during the 1760s, and by 1800 this figure had fallen to 10 per cent.[24] New sources of employment had been created, it is true, especially in trading and the service sector, but these could not make good the catastrophic loss. This can clearly be seen from the enormous proportions that pauperism assumed. In the middle of the century 20 per cent of the population was on public relief, and the nadir had yet to be reached: in 1775 the number of people in need was estimated to be about 14,000, or 46 per cent of the total population.[25]

At present little is known about the economic development of Ghent in the eighteenth century. There can be little doubt, however, that the expansion of export industries, in particular linen-weaving and the manufacture of mixed fabrics (which began about 1750), did not much benefit small master-craftsmen and wage-earners. Research into shifts in the average value of moveable goods which parents left to their children indicates that the gap between the highest and the lowest social group in the period 1737–87 became much greater. This polarization was the result of three processes: a minority acquired considerable wealth, while most people from the middle strata on the social ladder dropped back and the purchasing power of the proletariat greatly decreased. Needy families in 1741 still represented only 13 per cent of the Ghent population; in 1784 that proportion came to 18 per cent and over the following years it continued to rise, to 21 per cent at the end of the *ancien régime*.[26]

In no way do we wish to suggest that there was a direct connection between poverty and confinement, let alone that the people who were confined at the expense of the city came exclusively or even predominantly from destitute families. Such a hypothesis is all the more improbable, because out of the hundreds of families in Antwerp who received charity around 1780 there was not one that entered a request for confinement during the 1770s and 1780s. While there were people on poor relief under lock and key who had committed no offence formally punishable by law, that was mainly at the instigation of the charity administrators. It seems plausible that the process of proletarianization and impoverishment, on the one hand, led to a greater frequency of all manner of 'misconduct' and, on the other hand, a growing number of 'respectable' workers' families and those from the lower middle groups goaded members of their ranks into disciplining those who had stepped out of line, for fear of social degradation. Or did they attach more importance to the view of others as their material well-being declined? Did their urge to lock up an 'uncontrollable' member grow precisely because they had nothing more to lose, except for their respectability? We shall try to reach a conclusion by taking a closer look at the conflicts first between parents and their children and then between married couples.

3

Rich Kids, Street Boys
and Little Whores

At first sight it seems hardly surprising that most of the conflicts that led to a confinement request arose between parents and children. As far as the age pyramid is concerned, it is possible to compare European society during the *ancien régime* with the present developing countries: an extraordinarily broad base and a very narrow top. Just as in the metropolises of the Third World today, the street scene in the towns and cities of the Austrian Netherlands was dominated by young people. At the end of the eighteenth century almost half the urban population in the duchy of Brabant and the county of Flanders was under 25 years of age, a proportion which differed little from the figures calculated for England and France.

The numerical preponderance of children and adolescents was not a new phenomenon, though. Fragmentary information suggests that the percentage proportion was even higher at the beginning of Austrian rule. Yet more and more young people were being placed in an institution as the Age of Enlightenment came to an end. Whereas in Antwerp 'only' two per year were confined up to 1770, in the following decades the average came to six per year. In Bruges their numbers also rose: from three per year before 1765 to five thereafter. Did parents have less understanding of the sins of youth? Was their authority being defied more often? Did their patterns of expectation change and was it difficult for young people to adapt to them?

Frustrations

In all the cities being studied, three-quarters of the parents who put in a request for confinement were complaining about the unruly life of their son. The sons' ages could vary greatly. Jan Frans Van Zeebroeck was the youngest we came across: although he was still only 11 years old, his mother, a widow, besought the aldermen of Brussels on 29 June 1741 to put him under lock and key because he was disobedient; the boy was placed in the house of correction for two years at the expense of the city.[1] While he was certainly the Benjamin among the prisoners whose ages we know, many other 'uncontrollable' sons ended up in an institution before they had outgrown their children's clothes. In Antwerp 15 per cent of them – and in Bruges 28 per cent – had not yet reached the age of 15. It is doubtful whether they were sexually mature, because puberty arrived later then than at present, especially among children from the lower classes, whose growth was greatly retarded owing to their very limited diet. However, the overwhelming majority of the sons confined were older. In Bruges nearly four out of ten were aged between 15 and 19, and in Antwerp as many as half were in the age-group 20 to 24. The number of daughters locked up is too small a basis for calculations, but it should be mentioned that none was younger than 15 and that most were from the 20 to 24 age-group.

We shall return to the preponderance of boys, as well as to the differences in age between those from Antwerp and those from Bruges on the one hand, and between the sons and daughters on the other. Attention should, however, be drawn here to a socio-demographic change that greatly increased the chances of parents and children coming to blows, namely, the restrictive pattern of marriage that quickly took hold towards the end of the *ancien régime*. Figures for the towns are not as yet available, but it could be assumed that developments there were paralleled by those in the country, since the urban wage-earners were also faced with a decline in their material conditions, which meant that it became more difficult to start a family. In other words, as time passed more and more young men saw themselves obliged to delay their marriage, and a growing number of men and women even had to remain celibate for the rest of their lives. Towards the end of the *ancien régime* the average age at first marriage in Flanders was to increase to about 27 for women and about 29 for men.[2]

The postponement of starting a family was obviously very frustrating, particularly as quantitative and qualitative information suggests that both boys and girls were becoming sexually mature at an earlier age during the eighteenth century. The frustrations resulting from the ever longer

Table 3.1 *Percentage distribution of petitioners according to their relationship with the child to be confined: Antwerp, Bruges and Brussels*

Petitioners	Antwerp	Bruges	Brussels
Both parents	19.9	14.2	11.0
Stepfather and mother	2.9	2.8	2.8
Mother (widow)	38.2	37.7	44.3
Father (widower?)	27.0	35.3	39.0
Guardians	12.0	10.0	2.9
100% = N	241	247	246

'waiting-time' between the onset of puberty and starting a family was reflected in the growing numbers of premarital conceptions and illegiti- mate births: in Ghent the former rose from less than 15 per cent around 1760 to almost 45 per cent around 1800, while the latter rose from about 3.5 per cent to 7.5 per cent. Neither phenomenon could in any way be ascribed to greater permissiveness. The changes in premarital sexual behaviour were brought about by the processes of impoverish- ment which made it more difficult for young men from the lower classes to make an economically sound marriage. Because they had to wait longer than their predecessors, there was more chance that they took the decisive step only when they were confronted with a pregnancy. Nor was the rising illegitimacy synonymous with 'moral corruption'. Sexual relations led increasingly to the birth of an illegitimate child because as time passed more and more proletarian couples were anticipating a marriage which had to be postponed for economic reasons. It seems probable that engaged couples who were faced with unemployment avoided a legal union and in many cases simply lived 'in sin', a social union that was often much more stable than is generally assumed.[3]

On the other hand, many unwanted children presumably had to contend with problems of an emotional nature caused by dramatic events in the parental home. A crucial moment in their development was the premature death of their mother or father. Death indeed struck very early during the *ancien régime*. Average life-expectancy did rise slightly during the eighteenth century, but the mortality rate remained terribly high: two out of three children lost one or both parents before they became adults.[4] There is no confirmation needed of the fact that within a broken family other patterns of relationship come into being. For this reason we have investigated how many sons and daughters to be confined came from one-parent families (see table 3.1). The small number of 'uncontrollable' children and adolescents against whom charges were brought by both biological parents is striking: 11 per cent in Brussels, about 14 per cent in Bruges and about 20 per cent in Antwerp. In all places the behaviour of the son or daughter concerned was in four out of ten cases exclusively objected to by the mother, who was invariably a widow. It is not possible to know whether the mother was still alive when the father was the only petitioner. If only the definite cases are considered, then widowers represented in Antwerp a total of 22 per cent and in the other cities about 30 per cent of all the petitioners who requested the aldermen to lock up a son or daughter. In short, the majority of unwanted young persons – 60 to 70 per cent – came from one-parent families. It should be noted that in this respect there were no appreciable differences between the social groups: comparatively speaking, there were almost as many widows and widowers among the petitioners who opted for the monastery as among those who were able to draw on government support for the financial burden of confinement. Family structure thus played a very important role, regardless of social background. This is not surprising, because the premature death of a parent not only put members of the family under emotional pressure, but also impelled them to a revision of role-models and patterns of authority, which could easily lead to tensions and conflicts.

Among the lower classes the consequences were particularly serious, both for the surviving partner and the children. The loss of the main breadwinner almost automatically plunged the family into penury, while the death of the mother meant among other things that the father had to step in and bring up the children, which was very difficult for someone working away from home. In both these cases it was, for pragmatic reasons, desirable for the survivor to get married again as soon as possible. Indeed, this happened very often. Increasing poverty during the second half of the eighteenth century, however, made it ever more difficult for widows to remarry. It is quite possible that some of them locked their children away for reasons of their unruliness in order to better their chances on the marriage market: no one wanted to run the risk of confrontations with a rebellious stepchild. Two findings lend weight to this hypothesis. In the first place, complaints usually concerned an only son or the eldest child. In the second place, it can be seen from the petitions for extensions made by some petitioners that they had in the meantime remarried.

The petitions to have children locked away show that a second marriage could indeed lead to tensions between a son and his stepfather. In Antwerp and Bruges a total of 14 boys had come to blows with their mother's new partner. In a number of cases they were blamed not only for openly defying their stepfather's authority, but also for making a

Table 3.2 *Distribution of 'uncontrollable' children in Antwerp, according to place of confinement, 1710–89*

Place of confinement	1710–69			1770–89		
	Boys	Girls	Total	Boys	Girls	Total
Monastery	84	11	95	29	7	36
Public institution, at the expense of						
– the family	2	0	2	4	3	7
– the city	14	15	29	55	17	72
Total	100	26	126	88	27	115

misery of the lives of his younger child (or children). Establishing a balance of power in the new family was always a source of strife, as can be seen from the descriptions of objectionable behaviour patterns, the main feature of which was rebelliousness. This most probably explains why not a single stepdaughter was ever put away and why stepmothers never featured as petitioners in confinement cases: women were no threat, no matter what position they occupied in the household.

As far as the social profile of the petitioners is concerned, we can see striking differences between the towns and cities in this study, especially between Antwerp and Bruges. Until about 1770 it was mainly the well-to-do families from Antwerp that complained about the unruly lives of their children. This can be seen from looking at figures on the place of their confinement (see table 3.2). In the period 1710–69 some 77 per cent of the 'uncontrollable' sons and daughters were put under lock and key at the expense of their parents or guardians; three out of four of them ended up in a religious house. The spectacular rise in the number of requests for confinement in the 1770s and 1780s was also coupled with a dramatic change in the choice of place of confinement: the proportion of monasteries dropped to 31 per cent. Considering that the parents of almost all the boys and girls who ended up in an insane or penal institution had to appeal to the authorities to cover the costs, there is but one conclusion: towards the end of the *ancien régime*, conflicts between parents and children took place to an increasing degree in families which had little or no property. Such was the case in Bruges as early as the middle of the century. From 1740 to 1764 only one out of 15 unwanted children was placed in a monastery. If we add to this portion all those who were locked up in public institutions, then we get to about 12 per cent of the total. After 1765 the proportion of those who were more or less wealthy dropped to 9 per cent, so that there still continued to be a considerable difference between the situation here and that which obtained in Antwerp.

It could be assumed that the well-off in general had different reasons for locking up a son or daughter than those without means. The former always had family property whose inheritance had to be made safe, while the latter badly needed any source of income, however modest. Although they did not have to foot the bill for the 'accommodation', proletarian families nonetheless suffered a considerable drain on their financial resources unless the child concerned was completely unsuited for or refused to work. That is why in a study of unruly behaviour we have to take account of the social background of those who were locked up.

Troublemakers from among the *jeunesse dorée*

Since the actual return on capital investments in the eighteenth century was relatively low, the preservation of the family fortune was a principal preoccupation for the privileged classes of the time. That is why they tried as far as possible to keep the number of children down and imposed a very restrictive policy with regard to marriages – which in substance meant that some of the offspring, voluntarily or not, remained celibate or entered the Church. Marriages were as a rule arranged by the parents. It was always a question of finding a spouse who was of equal (financial) worth for a son or daughter or, in the absence of a large fortune, at least came from a family with standing in society. Of course not all the young people agreed with their parents' choice. The partners they chose for themselves, however, very seldom had the approval of their parents. If they had attained their majority and were not to be shaken from their resolve, no one could hinder their marriage. But the couple could expect financial reprisals in such a case: from their parents they received only their 'bare, legitimate portion' – that is, one-third to a half of what they would have inherited under normal circumstances – and they were cut out of the will by the other members of the family.

The upper classes had formidable weapons to bring to heel a son who had not attained his majority, behaved badly and could not be reasoned with. They could call upon the aldermen to make him a *stadskind* [a 'ward of the city' – approximately equivalent in English to a ward of court]. This arrangement arose out of the necessity to have mentally ill children kept under guardianship after they were of age. The customary law also stipulated that someone 'of evil and weak-minded or profligate disposition' – thus a debauched and extravagant person – could be held under legal guardianship indefinitely. It was a drastic step to take and one which did not do any good for the family's reputation; the official announcement proclaimed to people everywhere that there was a black sheep in the family. The fact that the number of such wards of the city increased in Antwerp in spite of this, especially after 1770, shows that more and more of the *jeunesse dorée* were finding it difficult to bow to the will of their parents and relatives.[5]

Marrying beneath his station was always sufficient reason for the aldermen of Antwerp to proclaim a young man from good family as a ward of the city and put him under lock and key, as happened to Joannes Andreas Peytier. On 22 September 1790 he was placed with the monastic order of *Cellebroeders* (Alexian Brothers) in Lier at the request of his guardians, because he wanted to marry the 'ignoble' Anne-Marie Verstraeten from Brussels. Joannes Andreas was not under age. He made a counter-petition, in which he contended that he had absolutely no plans for marriage and that above all he 'could in no way be said to have lost any part of his wits'. His protest obviously made some impression, because on 25 November the aldermen set him free. The reaction of his guardians was much more severe. On 17 January 1791 they wrote indignantly that Joannes Andreas 'is still consorting with the female of easy virtue, to the extent that the latter who now cohabits with him, has so cleverly been able to mislead him that he . . . is once more resolved to proceed with said marriage, whose only end will be his ruin and destruction, as well as the scandal brought upon the petitioners and their family.' The result: Joannes Andreas was sent once more to Lier. He caused such havoc there that the monks threw him out, after which he was lodged in an Antwerp monastery. What happened next we cannot know. At the end of 1791 Joannes Andreas Peytier concluded the marriage which his family had so detested and the couple left Antwerp, never to return.[6]

'All's well that ends well' was the exception to the rule. On 16 May 1793 the father of Jan-Baptist Beeckmans had him put in a monastery of the Alexian Brothers, where he was supposed to stay for a year, because he had allowed himself to be seduced by a serving maid called Maria Nelissen; he had left home and was not only living with this 'bad' woman, but had dreamed up an 'insane' plan to marry her. Jan-Baptist had to meditate for a full 12 months, after which he did what his father expected of him: he entered into marriage with a woman of standing.[7]

Although the petitioners in such cases stressed the dishonouring character of the proposed marriage, there is no doubt that financial considerations weighed most heavily in these matters. So long as there was no talk of marriage, well-to-do parents had not the slightest difficulty with the fact that their son was having a relationship with a girl from a lower social class. The only condition was that such a relationship should not lead to excessive expense. Woe betide the young man who endangered the family fortune, however. Gerard van Wangen was proclaimed a ward of the city because he led a 'very lavish, unruly and debauched life'. He had no fewer than four residences, of which one was in Louvain, where he was supposed to be studying law, and another in Brussels. He rode in his carriage 'every day from one city to the next, without going to church or attending to his studies, spending entire days and nights drinking, gambling at dice, cursing and swearing.' Living like this he had parted, in the space of one year, with 10,000 guilders, in addition to a large amount of silverware. When Gerard ignored the warnings of his guardian and set himself up in the capital to continue his 'lascivious and unruly life', things could go no further: on 15 May 1778 he was incarcerated with the Alexian Brothers in Antwerp. According to his mother, a wealthy widow, the 23-year-old Josephus De Heuvel was also an unbridled profligate. He seldom if ever came home before the grey streaks of dawn appeared in the sky – and when he did, he was dead drunk. His escapades cost large sums of money, particularly since he was forever running up gambling debts. When he left Antwerp and began to lead a Bohemian life, his mother delayed no longer and had him put in a monastery for two years.[8]

The preoccupation of the wealthy classes with preserving the family fortune was not a new phenomenon, any more than their drastic actions against any of their offspring who squandered their money. During the first half of the eighteenth century parents from Antwerp's upper classes entered confinement petitions whenever a son was careless with his inheritance and ignored their reprimands. Thus, at the request of his mother in 1723, was Theodoor Guilliam van Roosendael, Lord of Bouwel, locked up after he had thrown away a small fortune, and a year later proclaimed a ward of the city because he still continued to be unreasonable.[9] Such cases could nevertheless be counted on the fingers of one hand. It is not until the 1770s and 1780s that we see numerous families of high social standing falling over themselves to complain about the 'libertine' way of life and the unruliness of their male descendants. The number of troublemakers from among the *jeunesse dorée* increased to such an extent that people began to talk of a generation conflict, as we can see from the debates conducted in 1784 and 1785 on the so-called Theatre Question.

At the beginning of 1784 the central government gave authorization that thenceforth theatrical entertainments could be given during Lent. Although two-thirds of the subscription-holders in Antwerp were delighted with this measure, nothing changed, since the vicar-general of the bishopric and the mayor had granted the theatre managers a

Plate 4   J. A. Garemijn, *Youth*, eighteenth century. At the end of the *ancien régime* urban youth was becoming an increasing problem, which started talk of a generation conflict.

considerable sum of money on condition that no performances would be given during the period of Lent. The new military commander, the brilliant and cosmopolitan Prince Charles Joseph de Ligne, a great theatre-lover and author of essays on the art of acting and staging, brushed aside the conservatives: during the Lent and Easter periods of 1785 the theatre bustled with life. The opponents, who included many prominent people, tried to get round it by other means and set about reorganizing the subscription system. The principal complaint: 'a spirit of divisiveness is thereby set between older and younger persons, the latter appearing nowadays to want to lay down the law.'[10]

For young people from the social middle orders the room for manoeuvre was even more restricted. Their parents were certainly not prepared to accept extravagances. Some of them were trying to get closer to the upper classes, prompted by the continual need to accumulate capital. Others belonged to what sociologists call the 'middle middle-class'; since connections with the top stratum were out of the question, they attached great importance to anything that distinguished them from the 'common people'. Others still had so little in the way of savings that they lived in permanent uncertainty, and the risk of impoverishment was very real. In short, it was a very heterogeneous social category – but, however different their positions, interests and aspirations, married couples from the middle stratum of the population generally made very high demands of their children. A son, according to them, had to be obedient, honourable, thrifty and industrious. Those who did not practise these cardinal virtues would not be able to count on much tolerance, as the petitions for confinements demonstrate.

In Antwerp the overwhelming majority of under-age sons who were put under lock and key by their parents up to 1770 came from the middle classes: 74 out of a total of 100. We might also deduce that most of them were considerably well-off, since 60 of the 74 had opted for a monastery with the Alexian Brothers. As the misbehaviour was some-times described in very vague terms, it was not always clear what they were complaining about. If we consider only the petitions provided with sufficiently substantiated information, however, then it is quite clear that it was financial considerations and worries about the family reputation that formed the core of the problem. This applied especially to the numerous requests in which parents accused their sons of having relations with a 'wicked' woman. In 1726, 24-year-old Cornelis Francis-cus Van Oudenhoven was put away in a monastery at the request of his father, a notary, because he had quit the parental home and gone to live with a maidservant. The same fate befell the 19-year-old Isaac Joseph Janssens in 1730: he had been rebellious since childhood but his antics were finally stopped when his guardians learned that he wanted to marry a serving girl. The 22-year-old Louis Smulders was also placed with the Alexian Brothers because he had been consorting with a 'dishonest' woman from Holland, who according to his parents was only out to press him into marriage. The same was true of 23-year-old Philippus Carolus Batkin, who ran away with a maid in 1744, and of 22-year-old Arnold Emmanuel Michielssens, son of a gingerbread baker, when he spent entire nights with a 'bad' woman, left for Paris and there tasted forbidden fruits with such dedication that Papa feared the worst.[11]

A forced marriage indeed had to be avoided at all costs: not so much because the birth of an illegitimate child caused a scandal as because prosperous burghers expected that their sons would marry a girl from the same social class or if possible from a higher one. In this way the family could consolidate its social standing or even move up a rung on

the social ladder. The mere thought of a marriage with someone who
was less well-off – or worse, who had nothing – was a nightmare for
middle-class parents. This can be seen from the innumerable works of
fiction which were produced by and for the bourgeoisie. Here, the
authors of the little stories that appeared in almanacs continually
hammered home the fact that a difference in class between marriage
partners was something sinful. In a Ghent almanac of 1749 this principle
was clearly set out:

> Die wil trouwen sonder rouwen
> Neemt met god eerst zijn beraet
> Door gebeden, trouwt met reden
> En met raet, gelijck van staet.[12]

> (Those who'd marry without sorrow,
> First with God should think upon it,
> Then through prayer wise counsel take –
> And a spouse of equal state!)

Requests for confinement demonstrate that the members of the middle
classes proudly flew the flag of diligence and sobriety. They considered
work as the foundation of morality, the cornerstone of order in the
family and society at large, the essential condition for improving one's
lot. A son who did not bother to study, refused to carry on his parents'
business or made no effort to learn a useful profession was locked up
without pardon. The examples are legion. In 1739 the diamond polisher
Petrus Borremans was placed in a monastery at the request of his mother
because he spent his days in taverns and persistently ran up gambling
debts. In 1742 the 16-year-old Joannes Swaen endured the same fate
because he refused to train as a surgeon. In 1747 18-year-old Michiel
Neel ended up behind bars because he had run away from college several
times and stolen from his mother. In 1748 the guardians of 22-year-old
Jacob Sira declared that this eternal student was quite beyond their
control: he persistently lied and cheated and was always getting into
debt. In 1755 23-year-old Joannes Franciscus De Bie was locked up by
his mother because he did nothing but consort with whores. In 1760 the
apothecary Ignatius Van Wamel complained about his 24-year-old son
Joannes Franciscus, who did nothing constructive and squandered all his
money in Brussels. In 1767 Dominicus De Backer was placed in a
monastery because he parted with all his savings and even sold his own
clothes so that he could go drinking. In 1769 the vintner Jean Lefèvre
contended that confinement for his son Petrus was the only remedy left
to him: he had sunk a fortune into his business, but Petrus' extravagance
was inevitably leading to bankruptcy.[13]

58   *Rich Kids, Street Boys and Little Whores*

Until about 1770, many well-to-do parents ascribed the irregular behaviour of their sons to insanity. Some of them were probably acting in good faith, but the substantive descriptions of unruly behaviour warrant the assumption that this was mainly an excuse. This is all the more probable since very few families in the 1770s and 1780s had their sons declared insane, while comparatively more rich men's children ended up in an institution for being wastrels than ever before. Did the greater frequency of the phenomenon finally enable the petitioners to call a spade a spade, and tell the unembroidered truth? This seems likely, since the growing extravagance of the younger generation led to heated discussions in the better circles. And these were not limited to words. In 1777 the central government issued an ordinance which stipulated that loans taken out by persons under age without the written authority of their parents would thenceforth be declared null and void. The reason: 'the disorder which reigns more than ever before among the young, where we see the number of them reduced to idleness increasing day by day, without religion and without manners, capable of bringing contagion to entire families and imperceptibly to all classes of citizen.'[14]

Rogues and scoundrels

The generation conflict manifested itself not only among the upper and middle classes. Fights between parents and children were more frequent towards the end of the *ancien régime* among the more modest social groups. From 1770 up to and including 1789 no fewer than 55 wage-earners (male and female) requested the aldermen of Antwerp to have their under-age sons locked up for the first time – that is, about three a year – and in Bruges between 1765 and 1789 the number actually reached 99, or an average of four per year.

Just as was the case with the nobles and well-to-do burghers, most of the proletariat laid emphasis on the scandal that the unruly son brought to the family. The neighbours were outraged at his behaviour, so they contended, especially as the pastor had admonished him repeatedly in public:

We are obliged to take drastic measures for the sake of our reputation, since tongues are wagging about us: people are holding us responsible for his vandalistic behaviour and for the bad influence he is having on other children. We have nevertheless done our utmost to set him on the right path. As good parents we have not only shown him patience and love, but also done everything we could to get him taught a trade, but he always caused such problems as an apprentice that he was thrown out time after time. We sent him to Sunday school, but he systematically played truant and hardly ever went to Mass, in spite of all the parish priest's admonitions. Despite the sadness he causes us, we still love our son. It is precisely because we have his future at heart that we have taken recourse to having him confined. Willingly or unwillingly, the boy must be brought to repentance – otherwise perdition awaits him.

We cannot really know whether such words were intended to be taken literally. It is possible that the petitioners had genuine affection for their son and that they were concerned about what would become of him. However, the requests cannot be interpreted as reliable accounts of deep-rooted feelings without some reserve, as Arlette Farge and Michel Foucault have rightly pointed out.[15] The sharp contrast between the 'good' parents and the 'degenerate' son, whose misbehaviour was painted in the most lurid colours, gives the reader some cause for scepticism as far as the sincerity of the proclaimed affection and the accuracy of the portrait given is concerned. We cannot escape the impression that there are a considerable number of well-tried and generally recognized rhetorical formulas being used – in other words, that the petitioners painted their feelings and attitudes in colours which would be acknowledged by everyone as manifestations of fatherly (and motherly) love. It is worth mentioning in passing that almost six out of ten proletarian petitioners, because they were illiterate, engaged the services of a public scribe, who of course encouraged the use of stereotypes. Whatever the case may be, the fact that most parents from the lower classes placed a great deal of emphasis on their affection and care shows that such notions were very closely linked to their sense of honour.

It does not follow from this that the purity of the family reputation was the prime consideration. The central point was, in nine cases out of ten, that the son made no contribution to the family income. The boys concerned were not only depicted as incorrigible loafers, who persistently sought any pretext to get off doing regular work, but also as 'rogues' or 'scoundrels', because such terms in the *ancien régime* had criminal connotations. They did not hesitate to steal from their parents and to spend the money in the tavern, where they spent their time playing dice. 'Our 15-year-old son Albert is an ill-behaved and work-shy boy' – so wrote his parents, the Valcks, on 7 September 1786 to the aldermen of Antwerp:

> though he is clever and strong he does nothing constructive, wasting his time from morning till night walking abroad upon the streets, playing dice and gambling anything he could lay his hands on one way or another with his cronies or similarly ill-behaved youths, so that the predilection for such ruinous gambling drives him to get up at night while his parents are asleep and empty their purses; even when he was staying with other people, with whom the petitioners had placed him as a guest or apprentice, though for

but a short time, he stole from them – which the petitioners had to make good, so that now no one will tolerate having him in his house.[16]

Work-shyness was always illustrated thoroughly. The parents referred to numerous employers who could bear witness to the fact that their son cut corners. Franciscus Denoost, aged 14, was placed by his mother as an apprentice with a cotton-spinner, a silk-winder, a pattern-cutter and a wool-weaver, one after the other. Not only had he let each of these employers down in a short space of time, but in addition he had been leading an unruly life. 'Considering that as a poor widow I am scarcely able to maintain myself', declared his 49-year-old mother on 18 November 1780, 'I must rid myself of a son who does nothing but eat me out of house and home.' The 15-year-old Benedictus Claukens had reached such a pitch of misbehaviour that during a period of three or four years he had been through at least 20 masters to teach him a trade so that he could earn a living. 'Put him under lock and key', pleaded his parents on 3 June 1785, 'because he ignores both our warnings and those of the parish priest and for some time now he has sought the company of other *kapoenen* [scoundrels] so that we fear he will commit violations of the law in the streets.'[17]

If we are to believe the petitioners, then laziness and deceitfulness went hand in hand. In both Antwerp and Bruges almost half of the wage-earners who made confinement petitions accused their sons of dishonest practices. In most cases it was a question of theft at home: the boy had dipped into the savings pot of his father or mother, systematically said he had spent more than he actually did when he went shopping for them, or secretly sold or pawned household objects. Did the miscreants consider themselves as thieves or were they – in their own eyes – merely trying to get back what was owing to them? Did the petitioners really feel so strongly about the thieving antics of their sons as they gave the impression of doing, or did they add a criminal dimension to a few peccadilloes in order to convince the aldermen of the sons' wicked dispositions and dangerous tendencies? The petitions do not give us a definite answer. Only when the petitioners also made mention of thefts outside the home, for which they were held to account – as in the case of Albert Valck – can we be certain that the sons willingly and knowingly had broken the law and that their confinement was advocated in order to prevent worse happening. On 2 April 1778 the widow Michielsens, mother of six children, put it very succinctly: 'Not only do I not have the money to pay people with, because it has been stolen by my 14-year-old son Hendrik, but I fear moreover that he will likely end upon the gallows.'[18] This was not a unique case. Several youths had filched raw materials from their employers, committed small shoplifting offences or misappropriated items belonging to the public domain. Although they had been caught, no official complaint was made, because their parents had settled the matter amicably – they had paid up.

The great majority of dishonest sons had not committed any offence punishable by law, however – at least, according to the petitioners, they had only stolen housekeeping money or items from the house. Yet the petitioners often insinuated that the objectionable behaviour bordered on the criminal. They substantiated their accusation (or rather, imputation) with a whole litany of arguments, of which the most prominent was the dissolute life of their son: he stayed out for nights at a time without their knowing where he was, though he doubtless resorted to dirty tricks, because how could someone who seldom worked continually come home blind drunk unless he obtained the necessary 'drinking-money' by devious methods? Indeed, his friends were notorious street-rogues, some of whom had already been prosecuted in the courts.

Were the parents merely trying to put their son under suspicion, or did they know much more than they wanted to let on, and did they consider confinement on request as a means of avoiding prosecution, as a preventive measure? Although the first possibility cannot be excluded, there is a justifiable suspicion that most of the petitioners were opting for confinement because they feared that the problem-child would otherwise end up in jail sooner or later. Their descriptions of his objectionable behaviour contain so many significant details, which could easily be checked by the authorities, that it is difficult to doubt their sincerity. Take the case of the De Smet couple. On 28 June 1785 they wrote to the aldermen of Antwerp that their 16-year-old son Herman had to be put under lock and key to protect him from slipping into bad ways. As far as they knew he still had not committed any legal offence, but he led such an unruly life that they could no longer vouch for him. Not only had he 'given himself over for four years to such a sluggardly and flabby life that ... during this time he had had twenty shops [employers] and been thrown out of all of them', but moreover he truly behaved as a vagabond. A year ago he had gone to Mechelen together with some other 'scoundrels', where the 'gang' had roamed about for several days. What did they all get up to there? A three-week stay in the boys' orphanage on bread and water had not brought Herman to his senses. On the contrary, his 'agitation' had got worse. At the end of 1784 he had secretly gone off to 's-Hertogenbosch, where he stayed for five weeks; he came back in 'rags and tatters', without wanting to give any explanation about what he had been doing. After that he ran away from home dozens of times. His last escapade had lasted 18 weeks:

together with some other 'rascals' from Antwerp and a number of demobbed soldiers he had roamed about the county of Flanders, by which – in his own words – he had been reduced to begging: but was the word of such a youth to be believed?[19] Was this an open question or a half-truth? We are inclined to opt for the second alternative, because in the spring of 1785 the Antwerp court functionaries rounded up a gang of young ruffians, a number of whose members had been operating in the polders of the Waasland; they did not mention Herman De Smet as their accomplice, it is true, but they did say he was a good friend . . .

Parents from the lower classes in the 1770s and 1780s had good reasons to harbour suspicions about the comings and goings of a work-shy son. An analysis of criminal proceedings in Antwerp shows that as time went by more and more youths were forming gangs who black-mailed people into giving alms, went shoplifting and broke into houses to steal. This was a new phenomenon, as the aldermen themselves remarked. Criminality among the young, according to them, was taking on such alarming proportions that public order was being threatened by it. They were not exaggerating at all, because the community at large was being increasingly startled by mischievous youths who roamed the city at night in groups committing all sorts of acts of vandalism or who started fighting with each other. The sources do not always make it possible to make a distinction between, on the one hand, district or neighbourhood associations of young people who, because of the lack of a responsible position in society sealed by marriage, were inclined to behave like animals now and then, and, on the other, youth gangs specifically engaging in criminal activities. However, there can be little doubt that numerous youths from poor neighbourhoods hung around with each other for mutual protection and benefit.

In March 1770 the 13-year-old cotton spinner Frans Rooms was arrested, together with his 15-year-old brother Gerard and the 15-year-old cotton-washer Peter Masso, alias Masocken. According to several witnesses, the three of them had gone on a shoplifting spree. Gerard and Peter swore till they were blue in the face that they were innocent, but they could not explain where the money they had in their pockets came from; both had been unemployed for some time and their respective mothers, single women, were penniless. When their younger partner, Frans, gave in, at last they were found out: together with four other street boys, they had not only pinched food to eat, but had stolen handkerchiefs from market stalls and then sold them. To the question what adult was their leader, Masocken answered that 'he never went around with adults, nor had he committed any thefts'. The other ruffians gave similar explanations. However much the court officials pressed them, the youths kept repeating that they had acted alone and that they managed very well without adults. On this point they were indeed telling the truth, as the further course of events shows.

Despite their tender age, the brothers Rooms and Peter Masso were sentenced to 12 months in the *Steen*, the city prison. In the year 1771 on Shrove Tuesday, Masso and Frans Rooms managed to escape – Gerard was physically too big to crawl through the little window. No attempt was made to track them down. Did the authorities consider it not worth the trouble, since they had served most of their sentence? Whatever the reason, Peter Masso took up service on an East Indies trading ship and disappeared for ever from Antwerp. Frans Rooms on the other hand started a new gang. Since he did not dare to return to the parental home and could find no relative to shelter him, he had to sleep rough. He tried to earn his living as a washer of cotton yarn, but his daily pay was not sufficient to still his hunger, let alone rent a room. It will therefore come as no surprise that he returned to thieving. Picking pockets seemed to be so lucrative that Peter's 13-year-old brother, Hendrik Masso, nicknamed Klein Masocken, also opted for a quick profit in place of hard labour and teamed up with Frans Rooms. Three other youths did the same: 14-year-old cotton-spinner Toontje Blommaert, 18-year-old tailor's assistant Peter Martens, alias Madameken ('Little Madam'), and a certain Janneke. Gerard Rooms too, who was released at the beginning of March 1771, joined the group, because he 'didn't know what wood to make arrows from', as he later explained. The gang specialized in thieving from shops, which was so cleverly done that some victims did not notice the loss until some time afterwards. The booty consisted mainly of cash, but in addition the youths stole fabrics and items of clothing, which they sold, and expensive foodstuffs, such as candy-sugar, plums, figs and flans, which they consumed themselves; most of the booty was fenced in hostelries, where they sought lodgings and bought the comradeship of soldiers. When, at the beginning of April, Klein Masocken, Toontje Blommaert and the Rooms brothers laid their hands on two books with silver locks they thought it safer to palm these costly objects off in another locality. Through Temse they walked to Ghent, where they found a receiver and committed a number of thefts in shops. Shortly after their return to Antwerp they got into trouble and all four of them ended up in jail.

The arrest of the 'big guys' in no way meant that the Masso–Rooms gang had been uncovered. Madameken made himself the leader and in a very short time recruited a large number of new members: 13-year-old 'farm-worker' Jan Baptist Delaet, the brothers Karel and Jan Depuie, two blacksmith's assistants aged respectively 15 and 17, Hendrik Poppel (nicknamed Domine), a 17-year-old locksmith, Peter Jacob Van de Wal alias Peken, a 17-year-old pipe-maker, Joannes Sechele, alias Pastel, a 20-year-old cotton worker, Jan-Baptist Claessens alias Magere Tist ('Slim Tist'), a 21-year-old dock worker, and six others whose ages and professions have not been ascertained. For six months they succeeded in living almost exclusively from shoplifting. In November 1771 they were caught red-handed by a watchful tradesman and brought before the courts. Jan-Baptist Claessens received the severest punishment. The aldermen sentenced him to four years' forced labour because it appeared from the investigation that he had not only committed 'wicked misdeeds', but that he had also indulged in 'lewd' acts: he had prostituted himself on various occasions and had incited numerous boys to commit sodomy with adult men for money.

Slim Tist did not have to serve out his full sentence. Shortly after Pentecost in 1775 he was released for good behaviour, but he soon returned to his old ways. How could it be otherwise? He was penniless, was not welcome with his family and could not find a job. During his wanderings in and around Antwerp he made the acquaintance of other marginalized people, among whom was 24-year-old Jozef ('Seppen') Cloots, an unemployed painter, who was alone in the world. They teamed up together and scoured the city looking for shops which could be robbed without too much difficulty. Neither of them knew much about breaking and entering, though. For this reason Slim Tist turned for help to Joannes Jonar, a 27-year-old locksmith whom he had got to know during his time in prison and who was still behind bars. 'If you help me to escape, you can count on my assistance', Jonar reassured him. Slim Tist needed no second telling: he smuggled a small metal file in through the latrines of the prison and within a few days they met in a drinking-house. Together with Seppen Cloots they formed the 'hard' nucleus of the gang, which was further expanded to include a number of 'messenger-boys', among whom was an old acquaintance, Klein Masocken, whose zest for making a deal was all the greater for not having earned a penny after being kicked from pillar to post. But crime did not seem to pay. After the gang had broken into three premises and taken only fabrics, linens, items of clothing and a number of decorative objects of little value, Jonar let the cat out of the bag when he was drunk. He was reported and made a full confession in the hope of saving his skin. Slim Tist and Seppen, who were arrested on his instructions, denied everything, but after hours of torture they had to admit their guilt. The final scene was played out on 14 December 1775: Claessens, Cloots and Jonar met their end on the gallows in the *Grote Markt*; they had not yet breathed their last when Masso and another accomplice, the mason's apprentice Jacob Floor, were dragged to the scaffold and, with the hangman's noose above their heads, flogged until the blood flowed.

Thereafter Masso went to 12 years' hard labour and Floor was banished for ever from the duchy of Brabant.

If the aldermen thought that these exemplary punishments were going to encourage youths to stay on the straight and narrow, then they were deceiving themselves. During the winter of 1777–8 complaints poured in about thefts from shops perpetrated by young 'scoundrels' – of this those in authority had no doubt, since all the victims declared that money and goods had gone missing after a gang of youths had been making a commotion near their place of business, or had distracted their attention in some other way. On 16 March 1778 passers-by recognized the 15-year-old cotton-spinner Guillielmus Feber, alias Luutje, as he stormed out of a shop with a bundle of stockings under his arm. One week later he was picked up at midnight at his sister's house. He protested loudly: 'A long time ago I stole some apples from my late mother, but that's not a hanging matter! Why am I still not abed at such a late hour? Why, I suffer from sleeplessness! Me, hiding! Not at all, my sister and brother-in-law took pity on me, because father constantly beat me and for no reason.' After three weeks of solitary confinement, he gave in. Yes, he had indeed committed theft with some other young men. He named 14-year-old Cornelis Cardon, alias Drolleken ('Little Turd'), 15-year-old Benedictus Van Dyck, alias de Dikke ('Fat Boy'), 15-year-old Lieven ('Lieveke', or 'Sweety') Van Ham, 16-year-old Hendrik Dorens, 16-year-old Peter ('Peerken', or 'Little Pete') Rousseau and 17-year-old Peter De Ridder, all of them cotton-spinners. What had they stolen and from where? From shops and markets they had taken loaves of wheat bread and other expensive foodstuffs as well as handkerchiefs, stockings, hats and shoes. They had passed the items of clothing on to female fences, mainly to 'Mevrouw', who lived on the street known as Vuilrui, and the profits were spent partly in the gin houses and partly in gambling, in which they indulged on Sundays. How many 'tricks' had they managed to pull off and how much had this brought in? Luutje could not remember: they had been at 'the game' for so long. To the question who their boss or captain was, he answered that they were all equal and that stealing depended on the toss of a coin which they also all took part in equally; they tossed it several times to decide who would do the stealing, keep watch, carry off the stolen goods, hide them and finally sell them. 'Mevrouw' was arrested on 13 April: Theresa Verschueren, a cotton-spinner aged 30, was married but deserted by her husband, which was why she had to supplement her income mainly by begging and running a clandestine drinking-house. Nothing else? 'No by all the saints!' Never seen Luutje and Drolleken? 'Well, they used to come with their mates now and then for a *borrel*, but that was all.' Unfortunately, the declarations of some 20 youths put paid to her account. On 21 April she made a full confession and one month later she was flogged in public and banned from Antwerp for 20 years. The members of the gang were let off with a stern admonition. Their youthfulness was considered as a mitigating circumstance. The authorities, moreover, were of the opinion that the public thrashing of Theresa Verschueren would be a good lesson for them.

Cornelis ('Drolleken') Cardon and his friends did indeed try to earn an honest living – some as cotton-spinners, others as 'factory weavers' and yet others as peddlers. When in the winter of 1780–1 they found themselves out of work, they chucked it in and took up their old handiwork again. They had so much success with snatching and pick-pocketing that their example caught on: in March 1781 the gang had more than 30 members, of which the eldest was 18 years old. They had no leader as such, but the words (and fists) of Drolleken were decisive. He had gathered a group of young boys – he himself was 17 – around him who obeyed him unquestioningly. He tried to make money from everything. He was not averse to putting his sister in men's clothing and passing her off for a couple of *rijksdaalders* (five guilders) in the town of Bergen op Zoom on a 'buyer of souls', recruiting sailors for the [Dutch] East India Company; the deception was discovered some days before the ship set sail. When the members of the gang got into trouble towards the middle of April, things got too hot for Drolleken. He fled to Mechelen, where he unsuccessfully tried to find work. It was to be the beginning of a whole odyssey. He went to Lille via Brussels and Ghent. Because he was not much good at French, he had to retrace his steps. He committed successive acts of theft in Kortrijk, Bruges and Ghent, after which he decided to try his luck in the north. But he never reached his destination. A few kilometres from the border he was picked up by a patrol, grilled and taken to Antwerp, where the curtain fell on his activities: on 30 June 1781 Cornelis Cardon was sentenced to two years' hard labour in the penitentiary at Vilvoorde.

Over the next few years new gangs of thieves formed up. The biggest and most successful, at least as far as the gangs that were finally caught were concerned, consisted of children aged about 12 to 13. They were led by two 17-year-old youths, Jan Franciscus Thijs, alias De Boer ('The Farmer'), and Jan Van den Hoeck, alias Kersekop ('Cherry-Head'), who collected up the stolen goods and delivered them to a professional fence. The latter, Hendrina Josina Sas, nicknamed Moeder Cato ('Mother Cato'), cannot, it is true, be compared with Charles Dickens's Fagin, who tried to ensnare Oliver Twist in his net, but she did have great powers of persuasion, insight into human nature and organizational ability. She provided a wide circle of 'customers'. She taught the children the tricks of the trade: how to pick pockets, to distract the attention of market stall-holders or shopkeepers, to communicate by gesture, and so on. She praised anyone who brought in valuable objects and scolded the poor unfortunate who managed to grab only worthless junk:

> What will the others think! You always come back with rubbish. Why can't you procure some silverware? If they were pieces worth a hundred guilders I could sell them. Seek to bring me linenware, silver snuff-boxes and watches. My youngest son [the 12-year-old Jacob] is also a thieving dog. My boys thieve like magpies. Get out to the country and take the residents' linenware as it hangs out on the line after washing. Just bring it to me, wet or dry. And if you can get the coverings off wagons, bring them in for me to sell – but they must be of fine cloth, because the rough brings in no money.

Her advice was heeded. The children stole not only groceries, raw materials (flax, cotton, iron and lead), fabrics and items of clothing, but also small valuables such as tin dishes, porcelain water jugs, copper candlesticks, silver snuff-boxes and pocket-watches. Under Thijs's direction they hired themselves out as farm labourers in the polders, where they committed several break-ins. Their share in the profits was not particularly large: in general they received a quarter to a third of the amounts Mother Cato brought in. But the cash flowed in regularly and there were also little extras to which she treated her pupils: a glass of jenever, a sandwich with butter *and* cheese, a herring, biscuits. Thanks to her expertise the children made a welcome supplement to their incomes from snatching. Success also led to recklessness. At the end of January 1785 the mother of one of the gang's members pawned a stolen snuff-box. On a chance visit to the *Berg van Barmhartigheid*, the public pawnshop, the victim recognized his property and reported it, which finally gave the court officials some hard evidence. It was not until the middle of April that the whole gang was caught: Sas, Thijs, Van den Hoeck and 17 children. Mother Cato paid for her criminal career with a public flogging and 15 years' hard labour in Vilvoorde. In 1786 she received a reduction in her sentence, but she could not benefit from it because she died in her cell on 11 October 1792. Her funeral was attended by Thijs and Van den Hoeck, who still had another year to go in jail.[20]

Of course, the transcripts of the trial contain information only about thieves who got caught. It is, however, striking that the gangs concerned were able to operate for quite some considerable time. The organizational ability of a fence like Mother Cato does not provide sufficient explanation. There were groups of youths who had no leader as such and did not turn to adults to sell the goods they had stolen. The absence of an extensive and professional police force undoubtedly made it difficult to prevent crimes and catch the criminals, but why did broad sections of the population remain so complacent? Why were so few crooks reported? Did the neighbours and buyers of the 'goods for sale' have no suspicions? This seems highly unlikely, since most gangs consisted of boys who lived in adjacent streets and alleys, which implied close social contacts, and everyone knew that pauper children were not in a position to buy luxury goods, unless ... For this reason we are inclined to look for an explanation in the social background from which the members of the gangs came. Their neighbours and acquaintances were labourers who had the greatest difficulties imaginable making ends meet. We can make no definite pronouncements on the existence perhaps of some proletarian solidarity or a sense of shared identity, but it is clear that the law could not count on the cooperation of the lower classes in tracking down young thieves. They kept silent when they were summoned as witnesses and they even openly expressed sympathy for the lads who had stolen from the wealthier burghers and been severely punished for it, as can be seen from the fierce reactions to the sentence passed on Anna Vervaeck. This 17-year-old serving-maid had stolen a pair of shoes and some items of clothing from her employer, a merchant by the name of Cobens. He reported her to the authorities, and the aldermen passed a severe sentence on her. On 5 November 1767 Vervaeck had to climb the whipping-post for a flogging. If the assembled crowd greeted this 'spectacle' with a great deal of murmur, their indignation rose to a crescendo when it was announced the girl was to be banned from Antwerp for ten years. Hundreds of voices called for Cobens to be lynched. He narrowly escaped and barricaded himself inside his home, all the windows of which were smashed. The magistrate issued an order forbidding all assembly, but it had no effect. The angry crowd refused to leave Cobens in peace, called him inhuman and tried to break down the door of his house. The vigilante patrol had to be called out and they arrested several 'rioters'.[21]

Account should also be taken of the fact that the lower classes had an interest in the flourishing trade in stolen goods. Fencing provided men's hats worth three to three and a half guilders and leather shoes worth one and a half guilders for half to a third of the normal price. Small traders were asking 14 to 17 *stuiver* for a new cotton handkerchief dyed Turkish red; on the 'black market' people paid five to seven *stuiver* for it. A piece of *siamoise*, a mixed fabric with a linen warp and cotton weft, in a shop cost an average of ten and a half *stuiver* per ell (about 0.7 metres), but from a fence it was three to five *stuiver*.

It was not purely by chance that the demand for cheap textiles, items of clothing and accessories rose rapidly during the 1770s and 1780s. On the one hand the purchasing power of most wage-earners was falling, which meant they could afford fewer 'luxury' items. On the other hand they were attaching increasing importance to their outer appearance, as can be seen from the greater variation in their clothing. Their need to 'keep up with the fashion' was growing as the socio-cultural differences became more pronounced. Towards the end of the *ancien régime* profound innovations were taking place in the material culture of both the elites and the middle classes, and changes in fashion followed rapidly one after the other.[22] The symbolic aspect of the new consumer pattern – different kinds of fabrics, clothes, jewellery and decorative items – did not escape the wage-earners, especially the young. Within the narrow confines of their spending power they too strove after a certain degree of 'luxury', which came down to the acquisition of cheap replacement products, second-hand goods or . . . stolen objects.

But how was the growing supply of stolen goods to be explained? In other words: why did so many youths commit crimes against property? Domestic factors doubtless played their role. Many gang members came from one-parent families. Four out of ten were brought up by their mother, who was either a widow or a divorced/abandoned wife, and two out of ten by their father, who tended mainly to be a widower. From the statements of the youths involved it is possible to deduce moreover that they did not associate their parental home with feelings of affection and security. They would probably not have understood the term 'unhappy childhood', but this could certainly be applied to them. Take the case of the Masso brothers Peter and Hendrik. Their parents Guillielmus and Petronella Daelemans, were married in 1750. Eleven years later Petronella sought official sanction through the ecclesiastical court for a separation because Guillielmus was a hopeless drunkard and terrorized the whole family. The man was put under pressure by the clergy and promised to improve his ways. These were idle words, because in 1768 Petronella had once more to turn to officialdom: Guillielmus mistreated her and the four children horribly; the eldest son often spent the night on the roof in order to avoid his father. Petronella finally got her way – providing that the two oldest children, Peter and Hendrik, were put in the care of their father. The consequences we already know. The cotton-spinner Philip Cassou, a member of the Sas gang, had also accomplished much for his tender years – he was 13 when he was first arrested. His father died in 1779. One year later his mother, Joanna Van Dijck, got married again, this time to the ribbon-weaver Peter Brouckhoven, who disappeared into the night four weeks later. Joanna subsequently had a relationship with a starch-maker who abandoned her shortly after the birth of her illegitimate daughter. She tried to earn her living as a cotton-spinner, but her income was insufficient and this is why she began to consort with soldiers; when her son came before the courts she was three months pregnant. Another tragic case was the 13-year-old cotton-spinner Joannes Meulenbos, who was made fatherless in 1785. His mother, No De Gijger, a peddler, lived with Koben Hens as his mistress (his legal wife actually lived in the same street!). There was no love lost between Joannes and his 'uncle', who continually took to the bottle and committed all manner of brutalities. The atmosphere got so bad that No took her son away to Bergen op Zoom, where she sold him to a ship's recruiter; when he came to sign on the boy was found to be too small and sent away, which sent No into a fit of rage. Was it any surprise then that Joannes and Koben's 12-year-old son, nicknamed Sus Pandour, eventually joined a gang of youths?

Family and emotional problems are not the whole story, however. During the first half of the eighteenth century there would also have been youths who experienced no affection at home, and at that time there was no mention of gangs committing acts of theft from shops. The testimonies of relatives and neighbours suggest, moreover, that many parents from the lower classes who pleaded for their uncontrollable son to be confined had done nothing for which they themselves could be blamed. The question thus remains: why did increasing numbers of proletarian youths flout parental authority and why were they reproached mostly for work-shyness?

During the second half of the eighteenth century in Antwerp there were shifts in the employment structure that had a profound effect on both the composition of family incomes and relationships between parents and children. We have already seen that the restructuring of the textile industry was accompanied by the proletarianization of numerous skilled craftsmen and the impoverishment of most wage-earning workers. Since the new sectors were not subject to corporate regulations, the most wealthy entrepreneurs soon gained the upper hand. They were able to exert pressure on the wages of adults by hiring young employees. Children were taken on mostly for cotton-spinning and this sector expanded to an extraordinary degree as a result of the growing demand for mixed fabrics. In 1789 there were 4,000 cotton-spinners; ten years later they numbered more than 6,000. Most of them were youths. 'For a confirmation of this', wrote the merchant François Paul De Meulder in 1778, 'one has only to walk through a few streets in Antwerp: everywhere there are cellars filled with those poor children spinning cotton yarns till the sweat pours off their bodies from morning till night.' Their labours were badly paid. Around 1780 a ten-year-old cotton-spinner received a maximum of one and a half *stuiver* per day – enough for a little over one kilogram of rye bread; 15-year-olds who had sufficient experience could earn two to two and a half *stuiver* per day, or 1.4 to 1.7 kilograms of rye bread.[23] It will therefore come as no surprise that the 'cellar-farmers', as the supervisors came to be called, had their work cut out for them. The children were recalcitrant and ran away if they were hauled over the coals or spanked because of some fault in their work. Thus, according to the almoners, 15-year-old Leonard Hooremans, whose parents' plea was upheld, 'changed cotton-spinning cellar almost every day whether by running away after the slightest correction, or by being thrown out by his employer because of his laziness or maliciousness.'[24] Such cases were legion. Many youths were on the lookout for alternatives. Some went begging without their parents' knowledge to escape working for such wages. Others tried to make counterfeit chits to enable them to receive charitable benefit. Others still went as far as thieving. It was no accident that most of the petty crooks arrested used to be cotton-spinners!

Child labour was of course not a new phenomenon. Manual workers in the past had often employed children, and no one thought it unusual that they worked long hours and earned very little. After the middle of the eighteenth century, however, this practice grew enormously and changed in character: increasing numbers of young people were no longer apprenticed to a master, but thrown together in cellars or other rooms where they had to work under the supervision of the *loonbazen* (wage-bosses). The problem was that proletarians could not afford to protect their sons from this new, hard world. They were confronted with the paradox that child labour meant permanent low-wage competition, while they themselves desperately needed the meagre earnings of their offspring. Material need forced them into setting their children to work as quickly as possible, even if it led to exploitation.

Here was the tragedy: the labour of a young son constituted a potential source of conflict in proletarian families because the parents had little choice but to let him contribute to his own upkeep, and the youth himself was often not prepared to accept the employer's conditions. The chances of coming to blows were very considerable in one-parent families, because the son in such cases was inclined to question role and authority models, especially as he grew into adolescence. Many widows and even widowers not only blamed their sons for work-shyness, but also accused them of violence: a typical allegation was that at the slightest admonition their son would smash up the household effects, set the linen on fire, molest his father/mother – in short that he exercised a reign of terror at home. Ill-treatment of parents seems unbelievable, but it was a sad reality. Most of the perpetrators came from the 20 to 24 age-group, but some of them were much younger; one widow even declared that she feared she would be struck dead by her 14-year-old son.

Social and economic changes thus increased the chances of conflict

between parent and son in Antwerp. As time passed, more and more
youths were growing up in families where material conditions constituted a permanent source of worry. They had to contribute to the family
income as soon as possible, which for most of them meant they had to
spend the entire day under the supervision of a *kelderboer* (cellar-farmer)
spinning cotton – in other words, doing work that was poorly paid and
offered little chance of improvement; considering that the work required
little in the way of skill, adults earned only 30 to 40 per cent more than
they had when they were 15 years old. Dissatisfaction with his own
economic position (and what that implied socially and culturally)
increased as the son approached the threshold of adulthood, especially
since the 'waiting-time' between sexual maturity and being in a position
to marry was getting even longer. The loss of one or both parents
increased the inclination of the young adult to protest and rebel through
a lack of sense of belonging in the community combined with problems
of an emotional nature.

The competitive power of the textile industry in Bruges also supported
to an increasing degree the use of cheap child labour, but there was a
crucial difference between the situation here and the one pertaining in
Antwerp: the economic transformation that was taking place in Bruges
from the second quarter of the eighteenth century was accompanied by
a dramatic drop in employment, which enabled employers to pay even
lower wages. This explains why the number of 'work-shy' youths in the
middle of the century was much greater than in Antwerp, both in
absolute and in relative terms. Growing unruliness among pauper
children was the reason why the magistrate of Bruges set up a fishing-
net manufactory at the expense of the city, where, from February 1767
onwards, unemployed youths had to present themselves. The parish
priest and the almoners had to see to it that parents on charitable relief
sent their sons to the 'manufactory'; if they did not, then their names
were removed from the poor list. On 1 July 1768, there were more than
80 youths working there, 'the greater part of them being of the class of
unruly and idle youth'. The intention was to encourage pauper children
to work for private enterprise for the lowest possible wages. This is why
they received no more at the manufactory than they would on charity
and they were subject to a regime of iron discipline. Since many of the
youths were trouble-makers or ran away, the city administration gave
the police the order in October 1768 that thenceforth all 'rebels' and
'deserters' should be arrested and incarcerated in the house of
correction.[25]

This policy perhaps encouraged proletarian parents to take the initiative themselves – that is, to request the aldermen to put their 'work-shy'
son under lock and key. Nonetheless, we cannot ignore the fact that the

social bonds of a growing number of youths were becoming effectively weaker, as can be seen from the numerous accusations of theft, vandalism and other forms of criminality.[26] The explanation has to be sought in the deterioration of their economic position: many of them were faced with partial or total unemployment, and anyone who was lucky enough to find employment had to be content with starvation wages. Small wonder then that the number of youths who committed petty crimes in Bruges was far greater than in Antwerp or that the proportion of 15- to 19-year-olds incarcerated was much higher in the former city than in the latter.

If we take all this into account, we can understand why so many wage-earners turned to the authorities to have a juvenile disciplined: they were held responsible for his 'misdeeds' and they had to bear the consequences of his 'idleness' – namely, loss of income. A few months of forced labour would bring the youth to his senses, as the petitioners declared; a longer period in custody was not desirable, because that would cause more harm to themselves. On 28 August 1782 Isabella Gobbaerts pleaded with the Antwerp aldermen to release her only son, Joseph, from the provincial penitentiary at Vilvoorde before his sentence was up, where he had been immured at the behest of his parents because of his laziness and violence. The argument was that he had been brought to repentance, and she needed the extra income because her husband had just died.[27] Her statement sums it all up: the intention of proletarians was not primarily to punish their uncontrollable sons, but rather to force them to contribute to the family income. Confinement on request was purely and simply a survival strategy.

Were there no alternatives then? Yes and no. From the requests it appears that many parents had first tried to dispose of their sons by 'selling' them to a military recruiter. The national regiments in the Austrian Netherlands were, just as in most Western European countries, part of a standing professional army consisting exclusively of volunteers. By 1787 the number of men had increased to more than 17,000 – which is three times as many as in 1725. In spite of this considerable expansion, military leaders were struggling with a chronic shortage of recruits, which meant they were not inclined to refuse the services of recruiters who employed dubious methods for finding 'volunteers' and to incorporate these into their armies. It was simply a matter of having a sufficient number of soldiers; how this was achieved was of little importance, even if the recruiters committed fraud or permitted some form of 'pressing' – putting pressure on the candidate or his family. Parents who declared that their son was 'prepared' to go into service were consequently welcomed with open arms; the youth had only to have reached the age of 18 and be not less than 1.63 metres tall. What was attractive about this strategy was not so much in the premium that the recruiter paid as in the fact that the parents had got rid of a sponger for three years. They might also nourish the hope that the 'pest' would learn discipline in the army. It is not possible to work out how many soldiers came into the army in this way or to what extent military service fulfilled the expectations of the fathers and mothers involved. The overwhelming majority of recruits were from the lower classes in any case, and the largest contingent consisted of adolescents and young adults. This is not surprising, since a common soldier earned such little money that he simply could not get married, and the possibilities for advancement were very few. Add to this the strict discipline and it becomes quite under-standable why the recruits took the first available opportunity to desert, as we can see from the enormous number of orders for their recapture.[28] For that matter, the requests for confinement point in the same direction. Among the 18 former soldiers locked up at the request of their parents in Antwerp during the 1770s and 1780s there were seven who had fled their regiments. In Brussels the proportion was even higher in the decade 1770–9: 11 deserters out of a total of 17 ex-recruits. However, whether the youth had completed his service or not, he still continued to behave badly, according to the petitioners. Since the army had failed as a method of exerting pressure, there was nothing left but confinement.

It might be argued that the long period of peace between 1763 and 1789 had an indirect influence on the 'youth problem'. For more than a quarter of a century the national regiments did not take part in active service, which spared the lives of thousands of young men. In contrast, the Seven Years' War had taken a heavy toll: in 1758 and 1759 the government had to enlist no fewer than 9,200 men just to replace the soldiers from the Austrian Netherlands who had fallen in battle in Bohemia. Until the Brabant Revolution and the wars against France there was no further mention of military losses. The demographic consequences were all the greater because the natural death rate fell, which meant that more and more children were reaching adulthood, while the processes of impoverishment made it more difficult to start a family, with all the attendant frustrations. In short, the new generations were not decimated in war and their dissatisfaction with their own position was growing. The combined action of both factors perhaps explains why youths from the towns played such an active role in the revolutionary events of 1789 and the following years. Of course, the available information suggests that the protesting and fighting youths from the lower classes were often 'rebels without a cause'; in Antwerp, for example, some of them chose for the Patriots and others for the Emperor, the preference clearly being based on solidarity with the other youths from the same neighbourhood.[29] Yet it is difficult to shake off the impression that many adolescents of the time were turning against those who in their eyes represented 'authority', however vague and mixed up their attitudes to it were. Could the Brabant Revolution be considered up to a point as a generation conflict?

Debauched daughters

Girls represented only a small proportion of the minors who were locked up at the request of their parents: about one-quarter in all the cities in this study. This is not surprising, since it was much easier to control the comings and goings of a girl than of an adolescent boy. The daughters of the well-to-do were generally brought up by nannies or governesses who constantly chaperoned them, and they often had to spend many years in an Ursuline monastery or other religious institution in order to complete their education; this gave them little or no freedom of movement. The *petite bourgeoisie* sent their daughters to schools where the emphasis was not so much on intellectual development as on the acquisition of accomplishments considered appropriate for a woman. The entire pattern of upbringing in the higher ranks of the middle classes was designed to instil into girls the qualities of willingness to please, humility and obedience so as to increase their chances on the marriage market. Men certainly did not want to be confronted with an independently minded wife, because a reversal of the traditional role-model was socially unacceptable. Pedagogic treatises, fictional texts and illustrations made it clear that a woman could not under any circumstances wear the trousers. This does not mean that she had to be childish and incapable of doing anything. A girl with backbone, with *esprit*, was much appreciated – but she had to be very careful to know within what limits such qualities might be displayed; she had to learn where and when a certain independence of mind and action was valued, tolerated or, conversely, disapproved of. The home and family circle, the school, literature for the young: the whole environment of the middle and upper classes taught a girl one golden rule: 'know thy place'.

The available information suggests that rebellious girls in eighteenth-century high society were the exception. From Karel Degryse's study it appears that Cornelia Brigitta de Witte was the only daughter of a wealthy Antwerp family who during the period under consideration disobeyed her father and married beneath her; the marriage, which took place in 1716, did have the blessing of her mother, however and, though he was not rich, the husband was the commanding officer of a military garrison and did have a certain prestige.[30] Among the minors to be confined there were only two girls – one from Antwerp and the other from Bruges – who came from the better social classes; both of them ended up in a monastery because of mental illness.

Insanity was also given by most parents and guardians from the middle classes as the chief reason for locking up an under-age daughter. Only three exceptions came to light, all of them in the Antwerp *Requestboeken*. Two girls were immured because a 'bad' man threatened to lead them to ruin – in other words, there was a danger that they might enter into a *mésalliance*. According to her guardians, 22-year-old Joanna Maria Jacobs had to be protected from herself because she wanted to marry a 'lunatic'; and 20-year-old Petronella Van Coekelberghe had, according to her doctor father, to be wrested from the clutches of a 'libertine', who had enticed her to Louvain, where the couple were living a dissolute life. Another 20-year-old, Anna Maria Carpentiers, was placed in a monastery for two years at the request of her guardian, a priest, because she ran away time and again from the boarding school to which he had sent her to learn French and handicrafts.[31]

Most 'uncontrollable' daughters came from the lower classes: 90 per cent in Bruges and 60 per cent in Antwerp – though it should be noted here that their proportion in the latter city rose towards the end of the *ancien régime*. Nevertheless, they were very small in number: 23 cases in Bruges in the period 1765–89 and 17 in Antwerp between 1770 and 1789. Why did wage-earners complain less often about a daughter than a son? Greater tolerance seems hardly probable, since proletarian parents attached much importance to their reputation, and an absent daughter's income was as great a loss to them as that of a son. It might therefore be assumed that fewer girls from the lower classes were locked up at the request of their parents or guardians because in general they did what was expected of them. However, this brings us no closer to an explanation: why were girls more obedient than boys? Two factors might have played a role here.

In the first place girls did different work from boys. The decline in the traditional branches of the textile industry during the second half of the seventeenth and first half of the eighteenth centuries was accompanied by a spectacular growth in lace-making. Though exports to Spain, France and England were repeatedly interrupted by political crises and embargoes, Brabant and Flemish lace triumphed on the international market thanks to its superior quality and low price. In Antwerp the number of women engaged in making lace rose from 2,000 in 1650 to 10,000 in 1738, and in Brussels the numbers of women and children working in this industry were the same shortly afterwards. We lack statistical information for Bruges and Ghent, but a great deal of qualitative information suggests that lace production expanded there too. Though this industry encountered difficulties after the middle of the century, it continued to offer more employment at the end of the *ancien régime* than any other sector of the urban economy.

In the second place the work of the lace-makers was organized quite differently from that of male employees, and this applied to both children and adults. Girls learned to make lace at an early age. This took place first at home: the mother or an elder sister demonstrated how to make simple braiding on a rush-bottomed seat in the absence of a cushion. From their seventh or eighth year the girls went to a *spellewerkschool* (a school where they learned the trade) to get proper training. The teaching was often free of charge, but the parents had to agree to let their daughters work for the 'headmistress' for several years without any pay. In 1747 there were 47 lace-making schools in Bruges and during the third quarter of the eighteenth century some 120 to 150 in Antwerp; in both cities, moreover, there were charitable institutions and monasteries where orphans and/or pauper children could learn the trade. After their training most of the girls found themselves back home: together with their mothers, sisters and/or female relatives, they went on to produce work for the agents of the lace wholesalers.

The saying 'no lace without blood and tears' is perhaps an exaggeration, but the working conditions in this sector were hardly enviable. The pupils, depending on the season, had to work ten to 12 hours a day. The rate of output was high and the treatment certainly not kindly; in Bruges there were even court cases brought against mistresses who mistreated their 'pupils'. As long as someone was still in training, that person earned absolutely nothing and thereafter had to be content with very low pay. Around 1780 the average income of a skilled lace-worker in Antwerp came to two *stuiver*, or 1.4 kilograms of rye bread, per day; only a small minority who could make unusually complicated patterns were able to draw higher wages.[32]

Nevertheless, a girl's life as a lace-worker was utterly different from that of a young cotton-spinner. She did not work under the supervision of a 'cellar-farmer' or 'wage-boss', but in a school or in the parental home – which meant not only that she enjoyed a certain degree of security, or at least remained in familiar surroundings, but that she could also be more easily influenced and controlled. She also remained dependent on her parents for her living for some considerable time and after her training often worked together with her mother, which perhaps promoted the development of emotional ties.

It is, however, striking that there was not a single girl younger than 15 who ended up in a correctional institution. Both in Antwerp and Bruges, two-thirds were aged between 20 and 24; most of them were actually on the threshold of adulthood. The request was generally made by the father, who was almost always a widower. His accusations could cover a wide spectrum of behaviour, but some categories of unruly living were never cited and others were given very frequently. As regards the first point: not a single girl of proletarian family was ever put under lock and key for violence or because the father did not accept her choice of partner. Some of the petitioners cited work-shyness, prodigality or alcoholism as the chief motive. Most of them, however, complained of the 'immoral' life their daughter was leading, labelling her a *publicque hoer* or *canaille* (trollop): the girl (or rather, the young woman) went after married men, frequented places of ill-repute and sought the company of soldiers, with whom she sometimes spent the whole day without anyone knowing where she was.

Some girls had made prostitution their profession. That was at least suggested by the substantive information provided by the witnesses. The neighbours of 22-year-old Anna Dewilde, of Bruges, declared that the girl had 'been living for some time with Madame Lecomte, whose house is well known as a bordello'. Such cases were rare, however. Almost all the daughters requested to be confined by Bruges wage-labourers denied that they were prostitutes; they admitted that they had occasionally provided sex for payment, but in their opinion that was not enough to brand them as a whore; they had tried to earn their living as lace-makers.[33] Although their argument made little impression on the alder-men (at least it did not stop them from giving permission for a confinement), they were probably touching on the truth. Of the 190 young women – three out of four of them were under 30 – who were thrown out of Brussels by court officials because they had given themselves over to 'criminal conversation', only 44 declared that prosti-tution was their only source of income; the 146 others stated that it was merely to supplement their income and that they did have a specific job.[34]

Considering that lace-workers, (female) cotton-spinners, seamstresses and knitters earned too little to save any money, it is quite understand-able that they should be on the lookout for means of earning a little extra. In years when food prices were low and there was full employment they would have been able to make ends meet, but in less prosperous periods that was certainly not the case. The brothel-keepers knew this only too well, as we can see from the enticing words of a *madame* from Ghent: 'My dear, if you wish to spend time in the company of a gentleman, or seven or eight of them, you shall eat tarts, drink wine and have as much money as you will . . ., and, my dear, no harm shall come to you and you shall earn it all so quickly . . .'[35] Castles in the air? Yes, and for two reasons. In the first place, sex did not pay so well. Of course the price varied greatly, but for the day's pay of an unskilled worker it was possible to find something to one's liking. In the second place, prostitution brought with it all sorts of risks. Some girls to be locked up had contracted 'the Venus sickness' and others had brought one or more illegitimate children into the world – but what alternative had an unmarried woman who came from the lower classes and was hard-pressed for money?

Whichever way it was, the petitioners did not so much take offence at the fact that their daughter was prostituting herself as at her performance in public, her lack of discretion. The point was that the girl made no secret of making love for money. She walked abroad with her lover for a day, spent the whole evening in a drinking-house, continually hung around the barracks and not only offered her services to the soldiers, but – worst of all – was not averse to following the troops when they were stationed in other places. The scandal lay in the fact that the whole neighbourhood knew about it. 'We are obliged to intervene for the sake of our reputation', declared the petitioners, 'for we are being spoken to by our friends and acquaintances about the improper behaviour of our daughter.'

Take the case of the Van Laer family. The father, Joannes Baptist, a widower, was almost blind and as a result was not able to keep watch over his youngest daughter, Catharina, who was 23 years old and unmarried. The watchful eyes of his oldest daughter, Joanna, and his son-in-law missed nothing: Catharina's debauched life brought scandal upon the family. On 21 July 1785 her father put his cross on the bottom of the petition for confinement that Joanna and her husband had drawn up. The accusation stated that Catharina had

> for a long time now not only consorted with riff-raff and other persons of dubious character, but that she even works openly as a whore, to the extent that last year she became tainted with the Venus sickness and was gravely afflicted thereby; that since that time she had proceeded to Brussels and Mechelen and now being returned once more to this place she continues in her licentious life and public scandal.

Confinement was not only necessary to keep the family reputation safe, but also to protect society, since there was a risk that the girl would 'go on to further excesses, yea, even thieving, to the greater scandal and anguish of the signatories.' This viewpoint was supported by the Antwerp almoners, who declared that Catharina had 'for more than two years now been leading a licentious and publicly scandalous life ... approaching men upon the streets at night and seducing them into impropriety, and thus the aforementioned person should be collocated at the earliest opportunity.' Thus it was that Catharina Van Laer was sent to the provincial penitentiary at Vilvoorde for a year.[36]

Although every case had its own specific history, the public nature of the objectionable behaviour was always the central feature of father–daughter conflicts. From the requests we have studied it seems clear that the proletariat adhered to the dictum 'what you can't see can't harm you', which in substance meant that a whore could not cause scandal. But woe betide the girl who brought embarrassment upon her parents. It did not matter whether it was done deliberately or unintentionally. If the wider social environment found that certain limits had been exceeded and this was openly acknowledged, then the others living in the same house and her relatives had to take drastic measures. It is no accident that Catharina Van Laer left the city of her birth after she had contracted a sexual disease, nor that her father entered a petition for confinement shortly after her return to Antwerp: if there was going to be scandal, then departure or confinement were the only options. The same probably applied to most of the proletarian girls who were put under lock and key by one or both parents, since three out of five of them had tried in vain to earn a living elsewhere.

4

Marriages Made in Hell

Although descriptions of relationships within a marriage are by definition coloured by the persons giving them, sociological studies show that
the relationships themselves are influenced to a large extent by financial
circumstances, education, religion and other factors that apply to
different social groups and that men and women view a cohabitational
relationship differently. Historical research has revealed that relationships between spouses during early modern times have undergone all
sorts of changes. There is a great difference of opinion, however, as to
their periodization, intensity and significance, as well as to the question
of how they are to be explained. If the current research situation does
not enable us to come to definite conclusions about countries such as
Britain, France and Holland, where the history of the family enjoys a
great deal of interest, when we come to the Austrian Netherlands we are
completely in the dark.

Of course, certain aspects of the problem have been studied fairly
thoroughly. This applies particularly to legislation and moralistic literature. Both sources show that households during the *ancien régime* were
ruled over by the husband. He exerted the marital power, which among
other things meant that he had the right to punish his wife. From this it
does not follow that married women were assigned a totally subservient
position. Both the temporal and ecclesiastical authorities stipulated that
the rule of the husband had its limits. From sermons, catechism
commentaries and books on confession it can, moreover, be seen that
during the second half of the eighteenth century the clergy placed
increasing emphasis on mutual love. According to Father Petrus Mas-
semin a woman could not actually refuse a husband's will – but he
always had to bear in mind that 'it had to be the love of a human being

Table 4.1 *Sex of the persons wanting their marital partner locked away, Antwerp and Bruges*

Sex	Antwerp		Bruges	
	1710–69	1770–89	1740–64	1765–89
Wife	49	69	34	71
Husband	30	35	25	52
Total	79	104	59	123

and not that of an untamed beast.'[1] The author of another tract, the *Catholycken Pedagoge*, published around 1775, went one step further:

> The duty of a husband is to treat his wife with courteous love, honestly and gently, and to respect her, remembering that a woman is given him as a help-mate and companion, and for this reason, although the husband is the head of the family, the woman is nonetheless not his slave.[2]

But to what extent did theory match up to practice? Does an analysis of the confinement requests enable any light to be thrown on the daily conduct of affairs between marriage partners? Can we test, on the basis of this material, the social ideal against reality?

Complications

There is no lack of information. Conflicts between husbands and wives were certainly less numerous than those between parents and children, but they did occupy second place in importance. Both in Antwerp and Bruges about a third of the confinement petitions involved fights between marriage partners. This general average does, however, mask important chronological variations in the number of petitions and the large differences in the proportions of both sexes (see table 4.1). Once more it appears that the end of the *ancien régime* presents an abnormal picture. From 1765, and/or 1770, up to and including 1789 there was an average of five persons per year seeking to put their marital partner under lock and key as against one or two in the previous period. Both men and women used confinement as a means of discipline, but the latter did this much more frequently: in Bruges they amounted to 58 per cent of the total and in Antwerp their number actually rose from 62 to 66 per cent. Why was it mainly women who took the initiative and why did they turn to the aldermen more and more towards the end of the period? Were the fights between spouses really becoming more numerous or were the various forms of *quaed gedragh* becoming less acceptable than they had been in the past? Several factors make it difficult to answer these questions.

In the first place not every man or woman who suffered mistreatment at the hands of his/her partner turned to the civil authorities for help. While the Roman Catholic Church considered marriage to be an inviolable bond, it did make provision for couples to separate. Married couples could just go their separate ways without further ado if they wished, of course; or one partner could desert the other without the deserted party's necessarily making a complaint. Finally, account should be taken of the fact that a hellish marriage could be continued for the sake of the children, family honour, the financial situation or other considerations.

In the second place it should be borne in mind that the petitioners wanted to convince the aldermen at all costs of the seriousness of the case, which meant that their requests were by definition 'coloured'. It does not follow from this, though, that they tried to have their partners locked up under false pretences. There were of course dubious cases, mainly involving declarations of insanity, but these were in the minority. The rectitude of the petitioners can be seen not only from the numerous testimonies on which they were able to draw, but also from the fact that they were not talking about a one-day event. From the cases of 61 Antwerp couples we know how long they had been married before one partner confined the other: it was an average of 12.5 years – six months longer than the Parisian couples studied by Farge and Foucault.[3] Obviously variations were noted: eight couples lived together for less than five years and two others had passed their silver wedding anniversary. If we leave these extremes out of consideration, then we reach an average of 12 years. The petitioners did not therefore take this step lightly, particularly because most of them – seven out of ten – had children to look after. The heart of the matter was, in their words, that 'he/she had made both my life and that of the children such a misery that we are now near to despair; confinement is the ultimate recourse, the last opportunity we have to bring him/her to repentance and thus to prevent the total dissolution of our marriage.'

Though the basis for the charges can seldom be doubted, the actual descriptions of the objectionable behaviour do sometimes give rise to questions. The problem is not so much that they painted the relationships within the family in black and white, as that they were clearly inclined to put forward arguments to which they knew the aldermen would be susceptible, and thus to lay emphasis on forms of *quaed gedragh* which

bordered on the criminal or which were at least considered to have
seriously exceeded the bounds of the morality of marriage. A close
analysis of the texts shows that the real origins of the domestic disputes
were often mentioned only in the second place because the petitioners
believed that the aldermen would not see in this type of evidence
sufficient grounds, if any at all, to grant the request. However, it is not
always possible to find out the true circumstances of the case, or at least
the actual motives of the petitioners.

Yet the confinement requests do, despite those shortcomings and
complications, constitute a valuable source for studying relationships
between marriage partners. Of course, it is a question of extreme cases,
of desperate people reaching for a life-raft – but it is precisely for this
reason that we can assume that such cases were the tip of the iceberg.
Considering the individuals concerned had lived together for such a long
time, their stories have a very great deal to tell us.

Their accounts are doubtless constructions that cannot simply be
accepted at face value. Through their selection and presentation of the
facts they were striving after a very specific aim: all the sins of the world
had to be laid on the shoulders of the opposing party – especially those
which would be unforgivable in the opinion of the public, otherwise
their request would come to nothing. This does not detract from the fact
that their stories give us a picture of the way they regarded domestic life,
of their expectations of it and their views of the role-models, mutual
rights and obligations – of the 'good' marriage partner.

Obviously attention has to be paid to the social environment from
which the petitioners originated. It can be assumed that ideals of
marriage, standards of behaviour and emotional experiences are differentiated socially – more specifically, that there is a certain connection
between the circumstances of a person's life and the opportunities open
to him/her for affection. Social background also has another role to play.
Confinement for a person's marital partner would for most of the
petitioners have been a painful experience, regardless of their wealth and
social standing; but this radical step confronted proletarians with quite
different problems from those of the better-off, both as regards the
family income and the care of the children. This is why we have looked
into how many men and women in Antwerp were locked up at the cost
of their spouse or the city administration. We have calculated the
numbers of payers and non-payers for two periods to find out if there
were any changes in the choice of place for confinement (see table 4.2).

The parallels with parent–children conflicts is striking. Until about
1770 it was mainly the well-off who came to blows with their marriage
partner and had him/her put under lock and key. Thereafter their
numbers fell dramatically: from 82 per cent to less than 35 per cent. The

Total 4.2 *Distribution of 'uncontrollable' marriage partners in Antwerp according to place of confinement, 1710–89*

Place of confinement	1710–69			1770–89		
	Men	Women	Total	Men	Women	Total
Monastery	39	16	55	25	9	34
Public institution, at the expense of						
– the family	4	6	10	1	1	2
– the city	6	8	14	43	25	68
Total	49	30	79	69	35	104

spectacular rise in the number of confinement petitions during the 1770s and 1780s must be ascribed almost entirely to the proletariat and lower middle classes. This was also the case in Bruges, it being understood that most of the petitioners in the middle of the century belonged to the lower strata of society: from 1740 up to and including 1764 non-payers represented almost 72 per cent of the total and thereafter their numbers rose further to 81 per cent. How are these differences and shifts to be explained? Let us look at the motives that the men and women involved gave for their petitions.

Desperate men

It comes as no surprise that relatively few men complained to the aldermen about the 'improper' behaviour of their 'other half'. A man who did not seem to be able to exercise his marital powers, even though he had the right to punish his spouse, made himself an object of ridicule. He was to be pitied. Since the early modern period countless illustrated stories had made it clear that women could under no circumstances wear the trousers. If this did happen, then men would find themselves in a 'mistaken' world, one which was turned upside-down and thus simply wrong. The attractive thing about these prints is not so much in the teaching they depict as in the amusement they provide, as Lène Dresen-Coenders has remarked. The comedy lay in the fact that *bazige Griet* (approximately, 'Bossy Betty') held the reins in the household, while in accordance with the ecclesiastical and civil attitudes of the time her husband should do this.[4]

To be amusing, the reversed role-model had of course to have some

Plate 5 J. J. Verhaghen, *Woman Drinker*, eighteenth century. Foreign travellers could not say enough about the unbridled addiction to drink in Brabant and Flanders, which affected both men and women.

basis in reality. The confinement requests show that 'infernal wives' did indeed exist, at least women who rode rough-shod over the accepted norms of behaviour. Before 1770 we came across only two such figures, both women from Antwerp. On 20 February 1731 the grocer Peter

Geens petitioned the magistrate to place his wife Martina, the mother of two children, in a monastery: 'Not only does she drink like a fish and swear like a trooper, which threatens to lose me all my customers but she also thrashes me in the presence of others; recently, she beat me up so badly that I still bear the wounds.' 'With Barbara it is impossible to keep house', wrote the schoolmaster Philippus Van der Meiren on 10 September 1755: 'I am giving up after twenty years of marriage because all she does is continue to run up debts, and if I make the least remark about it she sets about me, even attacking me with her kitchen knife.'[5]

Towards the end of the *ancien régime* increasing numbers of men were labelling their wives as hellcats: six in Antwerp during the period 1770–89, five in Bruges between 1765 and 1789 and four in Brussels during the decade 1770–9. All of them were from modest or poor backgrounds, since they were not able to bear the costs of confinement. Some of them declared in no uncertain terms that they feared for their lives. Such was the statement of Jean-Joseph Bacheli from Brussels, whose wife had tried to murder him, according to several witnesses. Gaspard Heckart, from the same city, felt himself threatened because Maria-Catharina, mother of two children, had repeatedly stabbed him with a knife.[6] From Bruges, Peter Eyerick was so afraid that he no longer dared to sleep in his own home: Marie beat him about the head at night with sticks and other objects.[7] The petitioners had no doubts about the reasoning abilities of their other half. They made not a single attempt to have her declared insane. The witnesses equally used no terms that could be associated with insanity. Did the aggression of these women stem from disappointments and frustrations? We can only guess, because the husband and witnesses limited themselves to an account of the facts, with no interpretations.

However, we should not limit our view to the most extreme cases. The other women who wore the trousers in the house were accused of a whole range of misbehaviour. A single example will suffice here. Anna Catharina De Bru from Antwerp, the mother of four children, had tried to make trouble right from the beginning of the marriage. She scolded her husband for being a 'rogue' and a 'scoundrel', refused to do the housework and squandered her money on 'coffee, milk, sugar and bread rolls'. He himself had to be content with dry food since Anna Catharina took possession of his pay. She was, moreover, a bad mother. When he recently urged her to wash their youngest child, who was covered in filth, she threatened him with a piece of wood 'in such manner that he once more had to flee the house'. Indeed, Lambertus was always the weaker of the two. His wife hounded him out of the house in the mornings with a broom, threw a scalding hot saucepan at his head, gave him nightmares by continually playing with knives, and so on and so on.

A single 'detail' tells us something about the state of mind of his wife. 'When I was chopping wood', Lambertus tells, 'she came and stood next to me, covered her eyes with an apron, laid her head on the block and said: "now chop off my head, I am tired of my life".'[8]

Another indication that the so-called weaker sex was asserting itself to an increasing degree during the second half of the eighteenth century was that, as time went on, more and more women in Ghent were coming up against the law because they had inflicted bodily harm. Whereas their numbers were negligible around 1760, in the period 1775–84 they rose to 68. Almost all of them were married women who had quarrelled with neighbours, acquaintances or employers, against whom they had not only deployed a sharp tongue but also, and principally, their fists. Four out of ten fights took place in a drinking-house, but most acts of violence were committed in the home of the victim, who was generally so badly injured that the court officials could still see the results for themselves; half of the people wounded were men.[9] The beefy wives who were the butt of so much comedy did therefore truly exist. It is rather striking that the theme of the 'battle of the sexes' enjoyed the greatest success in the eighteenth century among the less well-off section of the population. Can we deduce from this that 'Bossy Betty' was a familiar figure in just that environment – or, rather, was becoming so? This seems very plausible, since both the confinement requests and the legal prosecutions indicate a growing number of violent female wage-earners.

All this should not make us lose sight of the fact that most of the men put forward quite different arguments for having their other half locked up. Setting aside a number of exceptions, they depicted her as being either insane or a whore.

Insanity was the chief motive for committal in the better-off circles: 25 of the 32 Antwerp women who were confined at the expense of their husbands had, according to the latter, lost their reason. Twelve petitioners stated that their wives were so 'furious' that they threatened to cause injury, both to others living in the house and to third parties, and three others stated that she was showing suicidal tendencies. Their declarations were confirmed not only by a doctor, but by numerous witnesses as well. Four confinement requests involved women who had sunk into total apathy: they did not react to pricks, stared motionlessly before them, did not care for themselves and could be fed only with the greatest difficulty. 'Isabella has, since the birth of her last child, been afflicted with a great weakness of the nerves, which increases more and more, so that the doctor knows of no other remedy . . . to change her humour', wrote a desperate notary by the name of Melchior Theodorus Colins, to the alderman on 23 November 1782. 'I sent her last month to Sint-Niklaas in the hope that the Sisters would be able to help her, but it came to nothing. On the advice of the physician I am asking you to have her placed in the hospital at Herentals for a year.' The magistrate had no objections.[10]

There are six cases which give rise to doubts as to the basis of their diagnoses. Was it proof of insanity that Jacoba Van Bortel scolded her husband and (adult) children in public and that she remained 'until the time of writing in the company of bad people to the scandal and dishonour of the petitioner and her friends', or that Catharina Robijns refused to do the housework and preferred to indulge in the brandy her husband produced? What are we to think of the merchant Philippus Begoden, who requested the magistrate to arrest 'his' Theresa and lock her up in a monastery: together with her two youngest little girls she had deserted the marital home. Was she completely mad because she led a 'dissolute' life in Brussels and had given birth to a child sired by a Jew?[11] Is it not much more the case that the ego of the men concerned had been severely dented and that the insanity of their partner had to function as a balm for their wounded pride and as an explanation for their weak behaviour?

The proletariat and the lower middle classes were less 'delicate'. Only two of the 33 married women who were confined at the expense of the Antwerp city administration were not, according to their husbands, in possession of all their faculties. All the others were of sound mind and body, but ... the petitioners were quite blunt: six of them referred to their wives as shrews or vixens and 25 as public whores. This loaded term served to describe widely differing patterns of behaviour. Two categories of 'dishonourable' women come to the fore in the requests.

The largest group consists of women who, according to their husbands, sold 'love' for money. They frequented 'places of dubious reputation', consorted with 'suspicious men', walked 'naked by day and by night and drank in the streets', squandered a great deal of money though they earned but little, and caused scandal through their continuous fighting and swearing – and all this 'to the detriment of young, innocent children'. Some of them were prostitutes in the real sense of the word: they worked in bordellos, rented a bed in a tavern or systematically bribed soldiers for the purpose of gaining access to the barracks. Figures cannot be given, but there can be little doubt that the presence of a garrison was beneficial to 'the world's oldest profession', however much the authorities tried to keep the 'street-daisies' (*sic*) out of the barracks. Thus the sentence of a military judge passed in 1735 on Anna Catharina De Vos because of 'the foul, unclean trade which she had exercised with soldiers in the barracks in the castle here' [in Antwerp] was that she spend 'an entire day upon the stocks there and thereafter be chased from the aforementioned castle as an infamous whore to the

accompaniment of drums and whips and rods about her neck.' This did
not deter her and she continued to visit the *corps de garde* in secret. Her
husband had had enough of this and put in a request for confinement,
which was promptly granted.[12] This example shows where the breaking
point lay: prostitutes were accused only when it came to a public scandal.
The same applied to women who considered paid sex as supplementary
earnings. The essential point was never that they prostituted themselves
every now and then. The petitioners did not neglect to mention the
principal profession exercised by their wives – lace-worker or cotton-
spinner. The point was that third parties – the neighbours in particular –
took exception to her activities and pressurized the husband, directly or
indirectly, to keep her under control.

The 'man-hunters' formed a second group. These were eight women
who, it is true, were held up as whores but who, from the substantiated
descriptions of their behaviour, had simply had enough of their husbands
– actually because another man had stolen their heart, which they took
no pains to hide. 'Everyone knows about her infidelity', wrote the
husband of 41-year-old Anna Catharina Masseau, a flax-spinner by
profession, on 9 June 1780,

> and she is so depraved that she does not even keep it a secret from our
> children – quite the contrary: she receives her lover, a married man, in their
> presence. I have several times chased him from the house, but this achieves
> nothing but quarrels with the neighbours who are heartily sick of the
> squabbling. Add to this that my wife prefers to act the whore rather than
> to work and you will understand, Noble Sirs, that I am at my wits' end:
> perhaps a sojourn in the house of correction at Vilvoorde will bring her to
> her senses.

The aldermen did not prevaricate: they put her under lock and key at
the expense of the city. If a husband insisted on it, they were even
prepared to request colleagues from abroad to detain and extradite an
unfaithful wife. The tailor's journeyman Franciscus Van Haver made
just such a request on 28 November 1780. His other half, Anna
Catharina, 43 years of age and the mother of seven children, of which
four were still alive, had pawned her linen at about the beginning of the
new year in order to run away with 22-year-old Peter De Weers to
Amsterdam. 'Six weeks ago she came back completely penniless and
pregnant: but I did not make accusations', declared Franciscus,

> for I still held her dear and the children moreover had need of their mother.
> How could I have thought that such love, or at least fondness, was mutual?
> Now I realize she had no intention other than to put Peter De Weers to the
> test, because when he also came to Antwerp, she at once forgot her good
> intentions, stole the clothes the children had received from the almoners

and returned once more with her lover to Amsterdam. I am a poor man, but I have my sense of honour. For this reason I earnestly beseech you to arrest her and lock her up.

As the Antwerp magistrate took the necessary steps and engaged the cooperation of the city fathers of Amsterdam, Anna Catharina did indeed end up in a correctional institution.[13]

Women fight back

It has already been noted that women had to be able to put forward decisive arguments in order to convince the aldermen that their husbands ought to be put under lock and key, even though they had committed no legal offence. It is all the more remarkable that a growing number of them took this decision and that they almost always had a sympathetic hearing. Whereas 'only' 34 men were locked up at the request of their wives in Bruges in the period 1740–64, during the succeeding quarter-century their number rose to 71 – that is, more than twice as many. In Antwerp the phenomenon took on much greater proportions: from eight cases per decade before 1770 to almost 35 per decade thereafter. What patterns of behaviour were considered so intolerable that they led to imprisonment? Just as for all other private confinement requests, the response to this question in fact requires a twofold investigation. On the one hand we have to examine what accusations the petitioners made, and on the other why their requests were granted. It cannot be assumed that the decisions of the magistrate were taken on the basis of humanitarian considerations. We shall come back to this. At this point we shall limit ourselves to a discussion of the objectionable behaviour as it was described in the petitions.

Women from the better-off population groups were less inclined to have their marriage partner declared insane than men from the same background. In both Antwerp and Bruges the average came to 52 per cent, while the reverse was true in almost 80 per cent of cases. Were the 'thresholds of shame' not only determined socially, but did they also vary according to sex? Given the attitudes of contemporaries driven by machismo, it seems reasonable to assume that men were more worried about their reputations and in consequence reached more quickly for a remedy to salve their wounded pride. Their female counterparts did this much less often. Whereas 28 out of 43 Antwerp women (thus two out of three) who paid the cost of confinement in the period 1710–69 declared their husbands insane, after this time only eight out of 26 (thus barely a third) made use of this argument. Given that the accusations

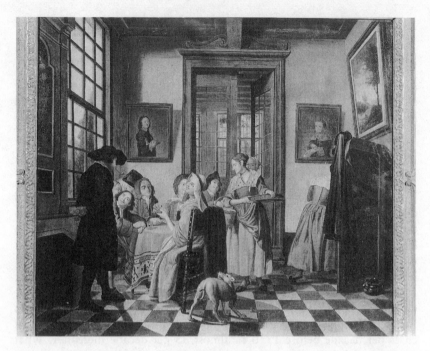

Plate 6 J. J. Horemans II, *The Card-Game*, eighteenth century. Is the fact that the woman is holding all the aces in her hand an indication of a shift in the traditional role-model?

remained largely the same, the explanation will most probably have to be found in the greater frequency of misconduct: as more women from well-off families had to cope with the same sort of problems, so grew their willingness to give all the details.

The petitioners involved had sufficient financial means to be able to choose between care at home and committal. Why did they opt for the second, most radical possibility? In just one case it was because the husband threatened to take his own life. The declaration that Maria Gilliams signed on 8 August 1782 runs as follows: her husband, Joannes, a well-to-do shipper, had several times tried to do away with himself; with the help of the children she had always been able to prevent him, but the family could no longer bear the tension. It is doubtful whether this was the only motive, because the 'insanity' of Joannes also manifested in the fact that he had had intercourse with 'dishonourable' women and that these 'affairs' cost a great deal of money.[14]

All the other declarations of insanity had aggression as their central theme, which was usually accompanied by or resulted from alcoholism. Most of the petitioners recounted their *via dolorosa* in detail, but with much discretion. They gave numerous examples of the mistreatment which they had had to suffer – often for many years: punches, kicks, stabbings and a great deal more, whereby the torrents of abuse and destruction of furniture and clothing served to act merely as an 'introduction'. As for sexual assaults and humiliations we can learn little, although we may imagine with a deal of accuracy that men who behaved like animals, as some were depicted in the requests, were not averse to indulging in such acts. Could such intimate details not be set down on paper? This seems plausible, since almost all the petitioners who wrote that it was a matter of 'scandalous events', without giving further details, were women who had accused their husbands of acts of violence; or was there such a taboo about sexual 'deviations' that they simply could not be spoken about? To this we have no answer.

There are good reasons to doubt the reasoning capacities of some of the bullies. For example, Joannes Franciscus de la Tombe used to become so frenzied that his wife had to summon the Alexian Brothers almost every day to restrain him and/or tie him up. Peter Hertoch also behaved like a savage. Not only did he beat his wife black and blue, but he also attacked everyone else; in a fit of rage he had recently poked out the eyes of his own horse.[15] In many cases, though, there is some doubt about the diagnoses of the petitioners, even if they were confirmed by a doctor. This being said, there is no doubt that the women concerned had been terrorized by their husbands. Most of them listed so many acts of violence and substantiated them with such convincing proofs that the truth of the matter was beyond dispute. Whether they really believed that the aggression of their marriage partner could be ascribed to 'madness', and thus had to be considered as a symptom of insanity, is somewhat problematical, however. Take the case of the vintner Joannes Baptist Hendrickx. On 31 May 1780 the aldermen of Antwerp supported the conclusion of his wife and that of the surgeon she had consulted: Hendrickx was insane because he drank like a fish, beat his wife, caused havoc everywhere and cursed and swore at respectable persons, both laymen and clergy, if they dared reproach him. Two factors support the assumption that the label 'madness' was used here in order to prevent further damage being done to the family reputation. In the first place the wife and relatives acting as witnesses emphasized that Hendrickx's misconduct was bringing their good name into disrepute and that his confinement would serve to clear them of all blemish. In the second place they considered that a forced confinement of three months in a monastery would be more than sufficient, which appears to indicate something more in the nature of a detoxification cure than the internment of a dangerously insane person. The wealthy Jacob Emmanuel Van Lancker was declared insane on 31 October 1788 for the same reasons. In this case, too, the wife emphasized that a scandal had to be avoided at all costs, and a short period of detention clearly sufficed to cure her husband of his 'madness'.[16]

However cautiously they have to be interpreted, the confinement requests do serve to throw some light on the expectations that women from the better-off population groups nurtured with regard to marriage. Of course, the requests contain exclusively negative judgements, since the accused is being presented as a brute, but from this sombre portrait gallery we can deduce *a contrario* what sort of ideals the petitioners had, what standards and values a husband should in their opinion adhere to and to what attitudes and manners they attached the greatest importance. Their pattern of expectation can be summed up in two words: mutual respect. The general theme is that both partners have rights and obligations, considering that they were dependent on each other; that they had to decide on matters concerning the whole family together; that both husband and wife had to honour their respective beliefs – in short, that mutual understanding was the foundation of a good marriage. A number of petitioners made allusion to affection or the lack thereof, but they are the exception. Most women kept silent about their emotions and feelings, except when it came to the children. As mothers they speak in the bitterest terms about the loveless selfishness of their husbands. An individual was not only a heartless father because he treated the children badly, even hurting them physically, but also because he neglected their upbringing and education and threatened to set them on the wrong path by his immoral behaviour.

Proletarian women took the same stance, it being understood that the emphasis in this social environment lay on mutual material responsibility. The associative character of marriage had to be expressed in the area of productivity: the family constituted an economic partnership, whose stability could be guaranteed only by mutual cooperation, which in concrete terms meant that all of its members had to occupy their time usefully. Almost all female wage-earners who turned to the Antwerp aldermen during the 1770s and 1780s accused their husbands of work-shyness and/or profligacy. Cornelia Matthijs declared that her other half, Bernard Joseph, had 'for years on end abandoned working many times', that he spent more time in the tavern than at work and 'that she and her children were obliged under protest to earn his living for him.' The cotton-printer Jacob Lauwers, nicknamed Zat Lauwken ('Drunken Lauwken'), did nothing but drink; he even sold household effects so he could continue drinking. The weaver and slater Engelbert Bal also lived off his wife and children, whom he beat if they did not give him their earnings. Petrus Van Dyck reduced his family to penury because he not only refused to work but sold the raw cotton that the merchant-entrepreneurs provided for his wife to spin. The linen-weaver Joannes Baptist Van Evenbroeck hit the bottle day in and day out; he had recently pawned his tools, so that he could no longer exercise his profession. This anthology can be supplemented with many other examples. The crucial point is still that the accused let his housemates do all the work and that they earned too little to continue maintaining a sponger, let alone pay his drinking bills.

Many women from the lower classes complained about the brutality of their husbands. In 31 out of the 43 requests mention is made of acts of violence, of which as a rule both the wife and the children were victims. Gommarius Van Den Eynden, a journeyman painter and decorator, regularly chased the customers out of a tavern his wife Maria kept and emptied the jug of jenever himself, after which he turned into a beast; 'I can show you my wounds and those of the children', wrote Maria to the aldermen. The 50-year-old journeyman weaver Joannes Baptist De Meyer got into such a rage when he was drunk that those living under the same roof as him were forced to flee for their lives. Another journeyman weaver, Franciscus Van De Velde, who was also branded an alcoholic, had on many occasions taken a knife to his wife; he used the weapon, moreover, to rip the clothes from her body and to slash the marital bed to shreds. He was no exception: 11 of the 31 violent wage-earners had, according to their wives, destroyed, sold or pawned the bed and bedding. This accusation should not be considered as a point of secondary importance.

Beds were the most expensive items of furniture proletarians had in their houses. From studies of household inventories made following the decease of a parent to protect the interests of under-age heirs, it appears that the expense of beds and bedding was the ultimate for which wage-earners (male and female) saved. Despite their progressive impoverishment in Ghent at the end of the *ancien régime*, they still set aside as much money for the purchase of beds as they did half a century earlier, which meant that the proportion of bedding rose to 50 per cent of the total cost of their household effects.[17] This is not surprising since, given their very cramped housing, a bed was the only form of domestic comfort to which those of very modest means could aspire. It should also be borne in mind that no single item of furniture had such great symbolic value: it referred both to the intimate contact between the partners and to the fruits thereof – thus to two forms of love: that of the couple as lovers and that of the couple as parents. The combination of both elements explains why so many proletarians preferred to vent their rage on this item of furniture and why the petitioners felt so strongly about it. The destruction, selling or pawning of beds and bedding was not only a heavy material loss, but also a sign of contempt that no woman could accept, since it affected her as a wife *and* as a mother.

It should be emphasized once more that the confinement requests were just the tip of the iceberg. From an analysis of the crime figures for Ghent it appears that, as time went on, more and more men were venting their frustrations on people and/or property. From 1775 to 1784, 440 men committed acts of non-grievous bodily harm as against 175 in the period 1755–64, although the population growth barely reached 13 per cent. Male aggression, moreover, was increasingly directed against the opposite sex: the proportion of female victims rose from 14 to 30 per cent. Their relationship to the perpetrator cannot always be determined for certain, but the available information suggests that a growing number of conflicts were fought out within the family and between neighbours.[18]

Just as we saw from the wives of the well-to-do, female wage-earners were very discreet about matters of sexual intimacy. In contrast to the former however, they did not hesitate to expose and denounce the escapades of their husbands. Thus Maria Catharina De Clijn wrote on 12 September 1778 to the Antwerp magistrate that her husband, a boatman, was not only a 'choleric' good-for-nothing, who terrorized her and the children, but that he was also 'favourably disposed towards womenfolk, to the extent that he was almost constantly tormented by gonorrhoea' or the Venus sickness. Another example: on 26 March 1789, 78-year-old Joanna Berdevel declared that her husband, a 49-year-old journeyman weaver with whom she had been living for almost a quarter of a century, refused to give her a single penny even though her own pay did not suffice to cover all the costs of the bare necessities of life; he referred to her as an *oude tere* (approximately, 'old tart') and preferred to spend his money on another woman, by whom he had recently had a child. But, however indignant she and other proletarian women were, however much they complained about their husbands, they kept quiet about sexual misconduct within the family. The only exception was Barbara Jonckbloet. On 31 March 1778 she requested the aldermen of Antwerp to put her husband, a butcher's assistant, under lock and key because he did not contribute to the family income, spent his days in the drinking-houses, molested everyone in the house *and* would not leave their eldest daughter in peace – that is, continually attempted to rape her.[19]

Brutality, whoring, adultery and even incest: the accusations were harsh. The petitioners of course could not set down every little detail for the magistrate. One could speculate whether the various forms of 'bad behaviour' mentioned were the real origins of the conflicts. It is not possible to pass judgement on every individual case, but a systematic comparison of the requests indicates that financial considerations occupied centre-stage. Not only did all the female wage-earners who put in a confinement request accuse their husbands of alcohol abuse and/or laziness, the most financially sensitive categories, but in addition they portrayed this misbehaviour in the most lurid colours. It is, moreover, striking that most of the women who made other complaints concluded their account with material considerations. Phrases such as 'to her ruin and actual impoverishment' occur time and again. It does not follow from this that the petitioners were prepared to accept ill-treatment and humiliation, nor that they considered the besmirching of the family reputation unimportant. The fact that the husband literally left his wife and children in the cold (that is, refused to fulfil his primary function as the breadwinner) was decisive, however. After all, he made himself redundant and, which was much worse, he sponged off the others in the house, who were already finding it difficult enough to make ends meet without this additional burden. In short, private confinement was a question of survival.

Yet the question remains: why did increasing numbers of female wage-earners have their husbands confined? The factors contributing to the increase in the numbers of parent–child conflicts also played a role in the fights between husbands and wives. The restructuring of the textile industry confronted a growing number of men with loss of income and status. In all the large towns of Brabant and Flanders numerous master-craftsmen were reduced to becoming wage-earners, which for them meant social degradation, particularly since most male employees had to be content with lower wages than their predecessors. After all, they ended up in sectors where less training was required and in which the labour of women and children was being brought in to an increasing degree. In Bruges the consequences of the proletarianization process were more dramatic than in Antwerp, given that the arrival of new industries provided insufficient compensation for the decline in the traditional textile branches, which made it very difficult for male workers to get a job. For women, things were quite the contrary. The lace industry and the clothing trade continued to offer a great deal of employment. It is possible that the number of jobs in the former lessened towards the end of the *ancien régime*, but the latter enjoyed an extraordinary expansion, from which seamstresses profited in the main, since both the big master-tailors and the traders in fashion articles had need of cheap labour. The new textile industries, such as cotton-spinning and cotton-printing, also offered relief. In Antwerp more than half the people over the age of 12 earning their living from cotton-spinning around 1796 consisted of women. In the textile printing-presses, which mushroomed from 1777 onwards, they were able to get work as a 'schildermeid' (approximately, 'colouring-maid'); we cannot give total figures, but there is little doubt that the women in this branch of industry constituted a considerable portion of the labour force.[20]

Thus industrial reconversion weakened the position of men on the labour market but offered many more women the opportunity to make a contribution to the family income. It should be noted here that we are in no way claiming that the latter did no productive work before this time. While the current situation of research does not make it possible to assess their role in economic life during early modern times, the available information does suggest that women in the Low Countries had a long tradition behind them of working relatively independently. The point is that more and more urban women during the course of the eighteenth century were drawing wages. As is the case of the children, who had also been integrated into the labour market, they earned too little to keep up the purchasing power of the average family income, since most men were making a more limited contribution than in the past and the cost of food and accommodation was rising. Proletarian women were, however, becoming responsible for a growing proportion of the family income. Since they now had cash themselves, they were able to be more independent from their husbands *and* they considered that they had the right to bring him to order if he did not make his own contribution – if he did not work on a regular basis or if he squandered his money.

Structural shifts in the balance of power between marriage partners easily led to tensions. This is why the question of whether it was that more men were becoming increasingly aggressive or whether fewer women were prepared to accept the brutality of their husbands is not really the problem. Everything indicates that changes occurred in both instances. From present experience we know that the consequences of economic crises – in particular, long-term unemployment and social declassification – make themselves felt in the smallest recesses of society. Sociological and psychological studies make it abundantly clear that male frustrations can be so great that they seek to disburden themselves in aggressive behaviour, which is often directed against their own wives and children. This was also the case in the past. In eighteenth-century Leiden there was a clear connection between industrial decline and social deterioration on the one hand and an increase in domestic disputes and violence on the other. In nineteenth-century London proletarianization and impoverishment went hand in hand with increasing tension within the family: when men, even though family incomes were dropping, continued to demand as much money as before for their own personal requirements, this led to fights with the others in the household, which again provoked aggressive reactions from the husband/father, with all their attendant consequences.[21]

'Poverty is a solvent', to paraphrase Olwen Hufton's expression: 'it eats into human relations and often dissolves bonds.'[22] The conflicts between proletarian marriage partners have to be seen in that light. It is possible that there were sadists among the men who were locked up at the request of their wives. However, it seems more likely that most of them turned to drink and/or brutalized the rest of the family because they felt frustrated by their social degradation and the changing balance of power within it. Loss of income and status was a painful experience for everyone, but it struck home particularly among wage-earners, because in their view they lost out on two fronts: on the labour market and in the family. So long as their function as (chief) breadwinner remained, they had little to fear from their wives. Ill-treatment or adultery was not sufficient reason for proletarian women to seek redress in the courts. They saw marriage above all as a contractual relationship, in which the emphasis lay on social and economic obligations. Love and passion were not necessarily absent, but such emotions did not play a decisive role, either in the ending of a marriage or in making the decision on whether to continue with communal living or not. It was only when the husband reneged upon his most essential obligation, when he refused to bring the money into the household, thus breaking his initial contract, that the whole situation came under review. In that case the wife no longer felt herself obliged to play the humble and obedient spouse. Drastic intervention was necessary in such circumstances, because the man involved constituted a threat from all points of view: economically speaking, he was just a burden to the family; socially, he undermined the necessary reciprocal relations with the neighbours by his misconduct, while emotionally he did nothing but smash things up. Was confinement in such a case not the best solution?

Separation: an alternative?

Of course, confinement did not bring an end to the marital relationship. It was a question merely of a short-term break in the couple's communal living, since most of the people being objected to did not remain long in an institution. Did the petitioners opt for this procedure precisely for this reason? Did they hope that their partner would repent and finally behave as a good spouse should? Or was there no choice left to them, so that they had to act in this way in the absence of alternatives? From a present-day perspective it seems incomprehensible that some of the aforementioned husbands and wives did not press for a separation. During the *ancien régime* the possibilities in this respect were very limited, however, at least in the Catholic countries. This point requires some explanation.

Although as regards marital legislation there were large differences between the Protestant countries, legal separations generally came within the domain of civil jurisprudence. This, among others, was the case in the United Provinces, where the Reformed Church accepted both divorce – *divortium* – and separation from board and bed (in English law *a mensa et thoro*) – *separatio* – though it should be noted that in practice they 'censured' the members involved – they excluded them from taking communion, which implied that once they had moved house they would not be able to receive a certificate of good conduct. Divorces were allowed in the North on two grounds: when one party could prove that the other had committed adultery or had disappeared without trace for a long time, the so-called malicious desertion. The most important consequence was the right for the innocent party, the claimant, to remarry. If neither adultery nor malicious desertion could be cited, and if people still wished to end communal relations, then separation from board and bed could be applied for. In this case it sufficed to prove the incompatibility of the characters of both parties – which had to be demonstrated from the continuous 'domestic quarrels' which could take many forms, from relatively harmless differences of opinion to severe physical ill-treatment. Such cases were generally quickly dealt with by the aldermen, since most couples first went to a notary to have an Accord of Separation drawn up, which only needed to have an official stamp of approval. The consequences of a separation were of course less drastic than those of a divorce. With separation from board and bed, the marital bond was not broken and thus remarriage was not possible. From an administrative and judicial viewpoint there were also important changes to the position of the wife: not only did the obligation to live together lapse, but marital power was also given up, which meant that the wife was no longer dependent on her husband, that she could freely exercise authority over her share of the property and that (for the most part) she could make a claim for maintenance.[23]

In the Austrian Netherlands things were quite different. Although the civil and ecclesiastical authorities differed on many points, and differences of opinion increased further during the reign of Joseph II, divorce officially remained forbidden until the end of the *ancien régime*. The new legislation on marriage which the emperor promulgated on 28 September 1784 made an exception only for non-Catholics – Protestants – and these constituted a very small minority.[24] Separations from board and bed were possible in principle, but they were not easily obtained. Given that the Catholic Church until 1784 had exclusive power to act in settling marital affairs, people had to enter their petitions to its officialdom: only when judgement approving separation had been pronounced could they turn to the aldermen, who were empowered to settle only the material matters of the case.

The ecclesiastical courts did not often give approval for separation. Complaints of adultery and ill-treatment were taken seriously because the clergy believed that the salvation of a person's soul in such circumstances was in danger; people threatened to bring eternal damnation upon themselves. If lesser (in their eyes) reasons for separation were put forward, then the church officials strove in the first instance to effect a reconciliation between the parties, by which the 'guilty' party, as the case may be, was put under the pressure of the parish priest. If the marriage did not improve and the partners (or one of them) insisted on a separation *a mensa et thoro*, then the process could take a very long time, as Maria Anna Buens from Ghent, the wife of Judocus Matheus Du Bois, found out during the first half of the eighteenth century. However much proof of her husband's objectionable behaviour she was able to produce, and however many witnesses came forward to confirm her account, the ecclesiastical authorities kept postponing her case. In addition, in expectation of a judgement she had to go and live in a monastery in Deinze, and the guilty party in fact dragged things out as long as possible. The 'confinement' of the unfortunate wife lasted almost 20 years and the happy end she had so long awaited, her separation, came only with her own death.[25] This is probably an exceptional case, since its protagonists came from very influential families and as a result there were many vested interests involved. A suit for separation was never a sinecure, however. Not only did the ecclesiastical judges take their time to investigate the petition; they very often refused to grant it.[26]

Joseph II secularized marital legislation in the Austrian Netherlands. The first article of the edict of 28 September 1784 stipulated quite clearly that marriage was a civil contract whose realization came exclusively under the jurisdiction of the civil courts; the Church could only perform the ceremony. There was something else that was new: persons under age – that is, persons aged less than 25 – thenceforth had to have the permission of their parents or guardians in order to marry, which implied that the Church could no longer put its own viewpoint in this matter. In contrast to the other parts of the empire where Joseph II introduced the possibility of dissolving the marriage bond and thus of marrying again, divorce in the Austrian Netherlands still remained forbidden. In accordance with the prevailing legal practice, mistreatment and extramarital relations remained, moreover, the most important grounds for requesting a separation from board and bed: 'When one of the spouses is grievously maltreated by the other or exposed by the other to seduction, whether to crime or to a perversity of *mores*, the offended party shall have the right to turn to the civil courts to obtain assistance and security through the ordinary channels of the Law.' However, withdrawing power from church officials afforded the opportunity for a wider interpretation. Article 46 stipulated furthermore that the spouses could first divide up their possessions in accordance with the provisions of the marriage contract and thereafter present themselves before the judge 'to confirm to him that it was of their own free will that they were separating one from the other, and that they were content with the arrangements agreed between them'. The legislators were aware of the fact that the clergy would vigorously protest against such a simple procedure, which came down to separation by mutual consent. For this reason they added that 'the judge would not hear the spouses if they did not produce written testimony from their parish priest, their minister or [in the case of the Orthodox Churches] their pope.' Both parties had to present themselves in person to the local cleric, who had to do everything in his power to persuade them to change their minds; were his advice and admonitions to fail, then he had to draw up a written declaration, after which the aldermen could separate the spouses *a mensa et thoro*. The clergy were thus not entirely excluded; in principle they could always hinder a separation.[27]

Nothing is known as yet about the effects of the edict. We do know the reactions of the ecclesiastical authorities, but the question remains whether their fears were justified – in other words, whether the number of separations from board and bed really did increase after 1784. If this were the case, then the Brabant Revolution put an end to it all. Married couples who wanted to separate with or without mutual consent had to wait until December 1796, when French law took effect in the Belgian *départements*, which made divorce – and thus remarriage – possible. Here it should be noted that this liberal legislation did not survive long: in 1807 the *Code Civil* introduced so many restrictions that the road to separation was once more littered with obstacles.

It could be argued that it was really much easier to abandon a marriage partner without formality when he or she made life impossible, when one party felt attracted to someone else or if the couple simply got tired of each other. Some marriage bonds were indeed dissolved in an informal manner. Obviously figures cannot be given, but the confinement requests and the criminal trials suggest that such cases were certainly not unusual and that their number increased towards the end of the *ancien régime*. Whatever the case may be, both sources show that it was not exclusively a male decision. Women also left the marital home, and some of them remained adamant about not returning, even when they were threatened with legal prosecution. Abandonment without formal separation was a risky business, however. Married couples were legally obliged to live together. A woman had, moreover, to take account of the marital power which made her dependent on her husband, which among other things meant that she owed him a duty of obedience. Finally, sight should not be lost of the fact that both partners remained responsible for each other's debts, which, given the economic undertone of most conflicts, was no small risk. Anyone who moved abroad did not need to worry about all that, of course, but then a great deal had to be given up. In short, mutual consent *and* trust in the other partner were, if not necessary, at least desirable preconditions for ending cohabitation informally. However, the archives yield no trace of information about such cases. The only sources we have are the complaints of the ecclesiastical authorities about the increasing numbers of unmarried people living together among the lower classes in the large towns and cities. If we assume that such pronouncements had some basis in truth, then we are confronted with the paradox that it was precisely the clergy's unshakeable attitude to divorce which drove increasing numbers of proletarians to opt for that communal living against which the Church had so rigidly set its face.

There can be no doubt that separation and divorce in some countries functioned as an alternative to confinement, at least up to a point. In Neuchatel, which belonged to Prussia after 1707, the number of divorces and separations rose from 16 in the period 1707–16 to 77 in the period 1777–86. In the Dutch towns the phenomenon took on even greater proportions, especially at the end of the eighteenth century. In Leiden more than twice as many marriages were dissolved by the aldermen in the 1780s as in the 1750s. The same trend can be seen in Alkmaar and Delft. Given that the populations of the towns under scrutiny either remained constant or dropped, and that there are no indications of any radical shifts in the demographic structure, it could be concluded that the increase in the number of separations and divorces was both absolute and relative. Johan Joor, who has made a thorough analysis of divorces and separations in Alkmaar, draws a connection between social and economic adversity and the break-up of marriage: at the end of the eighteenth century material conditions deteriorated considerably, which increased the chances of fights between husbands and wives. This reasoning also applied to Leiden, because activity in the textile business fell sharply and this caused many families to get into financial difficulties.[28]

Material conditions can certainly not be seen as the only cause of divorce and separation; socio-cultural and personal factors also played their part. However, the economic aspect took centre-stage in the proceedings. This is not the only parallel with the petitions for confinement. Just as with private confinement, divorce or separation was generally applied for after many years of marriage: in all the towns for which figures are available the average period came to 11 years in the case of divorce or separation and 12 to 12.5 in the case of confinement on request. Furthermore, in both cases it was mainly women who took the initiative. This is not surprising, since *within* the marriage they were simply not able to offer much in the way of response. Given that the traditional laws on marriage were based on the natural superiority of man over woman, it was the husband who dominated in the eyes of the law and government. He had the right and even the obligation to keep the 'innate' weaknesses of his wife in check and if necessary to exercise the 'appropriate correction' to keep her in submissiveness, obedience and tolerance – which meant among other things that *she* was not considered fit to correct the faults and mistakes of her other half. The Age of Enlightenment brought no changes in this respect. Insofar as the philosophers of the time paid any attention to the position of the wife, they simply repeated the traditional viewpoints. For Voltaire it was a foregone conclusion that the fair sex had to bow before the stronger:

> Il n'est pas étonnant qu'en tous pays l'homme se soit rendu maître de la femme . . . Il a d'ordinaire beaucoup de supériorité par celle du corps et même celle de l'esprit.
>
> (It is not surprising that throughout the world man has made himself master of womankind . . . Ordinarily, he has much superiority over her in body and even in mind.)

Jean-Jacques Rousseau was also of the opinion that the education of women had to be directed towards comforting and satisfying her future husband:

> Leur plaire, leur être utile, se faire aimer et honorer d'eux, les élever jeunes, les soigner grands, les conseiller, les consoler, leur rendre la vie agréable et douce: voilà les devoirs des femmes de tous les temps et ce qu'on doit leur apprendre dès leur enfance.
>
> (Pleasing them, being useful to them, making themselves loved and honoured by them, bringing them up as children, caring for them as men, advising them, comforting them, making their lives pleasant and easy: these have been the duties of women throughout the centuries and they must all be taught them from their infancy.)

In exchange for all this, all the husband had to do was earn the money and/or manage the finances well, thus look after the material well-being of the family. A wife could expect no other forms of reciprocity.[29]

A comparison of the developments in the United Provinces and the Austrian Netherlands indicates an inversely proportional relationship between separations on the one hand and petitions for confinement on the other. Both in Leiden and Alkmaar many more couples opted for a separation *a mensa et thoro* than for divorce. The reasons for this do not matter, since divorce in the South was simply forbidden. It is worth noting, however, that the annual average number of separations in the North was significantly higher than the petitions for confinement by one or other of the marital partners and that this discrepancy grew during the course of the eighteenth century. Although there are parts missing from the church archives and the available information must be interpreted with the necessary degree of circumspection, there is no doubt that the number of board and bed separations in the Austrian Netherlands remained very limited; in most of the bishoprics investigated, it even dropped during the second half of the eighteenth century.[30] In other words, the growing tensions within marriage resulted in a spectacular rise in the number of confinement requests because the opportunities for a couple to separate were extremely limited.

The question still remains as to which were the factors that determined the choice between separation and confinement on request. The second of these strategies certainly offered much more chance of success in the Austrian Netherlands, but the first was also utilized. Objectionable behaviour does not constitute an adequate explanation, since a comparison of the divorce suits and the confinement petitions shows that the complaints were often similar in nature. Although personal motives undoubtedly played their part, there are reasons for assuming that other factors, namely financial considerations and preoccupations with the family reputation, were in general the deciding ones, whereby the attractiveness of the chosen strategy was in addition most probably determined by the social provenance of the opposing parties.

There has until now been no research into the social background of the people in the Austrian Netherlands who requested a separation from board and bed. Their professions were not often mentioned in the transcripts of the cases and such information is, moreover, difficult to interpret. In addition, all we have to go on is a number of lists of well-to-do families from Antwerp and Ghent which permit us to find out whether or not they had been involved in separation proceedings. Obviously it is not possible to make thorough-going judgements on the basis of this material. The only certain conclusion is that separation was a phenomenon to be found among all classes of society, but that the elite seldom made use of it for resolving marital conflicts. The available information appears to indicate that the largest contingent in board and bed separations was from the middle classes.

At first sight it seems remarkable that separation was an exceptional phenomenon at the top of the social ladder. Rich married couples could always permit themselves to separate, given that both partners had sufficient financial means at their disposal, whether they were married with a community of property or with a contract. The claimant could even have an interest in a separation simply to prevent the other party getting all the property. However, the family inheritance constituted a stumbling-block when the division of property threatened to damage the interests of the near family members or relatives. The example of Buens–Du Bois shows that in such a case everything was done to prevent separation. Fictional texts suggest, moreover, that the elite in the Austrian Netherlands considered separation *a mensa et thoro* as a dishonourable solution to domestic difficulties. The combination of both factors explains why so many men and women from the upper classes placed their other half in a monastery. The purpose of confinement in a religious institution was precisely to hide their problems from the outside world; it was sufficient to have one's marriage partner declared insane to keep the family inheritance safe.

Both separation and private confinement confronted many people from the middle classes with material problems. There was a price to pay for both strategies. Fragmentary information, however, indicates that it was much cheaper for couples to go their separate ways than to pay for the maintenance of a partner in a monastery or public institution, even if he or she were put under lock and key for but a short time. Of course separation meant a radical reorganization of business interests, since the couple usually had a family firm; a division of property could, moreover, weaken the financial basis of the business. Skilled craftsmen and shopkeepers formed the largest group involved in board and bed separation cases, according to the records of people's professions. This comes as no surprise when two additional elements are taken into consideration. In the first place it can be deduced from the proceedings that the claimant ran the risk of being reduced to penury by the misconduct of the partner. In the second place separations were more often initiated by the wife than the husband: division of property enabled the former to have control of her own possessions and to set up her own business entirely independently.

Although separations *a mensa et thoro* do appear among the lower classes (where it was almost always the wife who took the initiative), most proletarians considered confinement on request as the best solution to unbearable tension within a marriage. The explanation has to be sought in the precarious social and economic position of female wage-earners. The costs of separation proceedings were not a hindrance, since the ecclesiastical judges offered the possibility of dealing with the case 'Pro Deo' – thus, free. The problem lay in the financial consequences of separation. It has already been noted that increasing numbers of women were providing additional income for the family and that as a result they could be more independent from their husbands. Just as the children, however, they earned so little that the total loss of the main breadwinner almost always resulted in dire poverty. From a material point of view, separation made sense for a female wage-earner only if there was the certainty, or at least the hope, that another man would care for her. It is not purely by chance that in the United Provinces more divorces than separations were sought by women without means: divorce offered the possibility of marrying again. It is true that the deed of separation generally obliged the husband to pay maintenance, but what was to be done if he 'neglected' to hand over a part of his wages? The aldermen would certainly have had other more pressing problems to deal with. Even less help could be expected from other members of the family, since proletarian households could not afford to take on any additional burdens, let alone make themselves responsible for the upkeep of a divorced woman. Finally, it should also be remembered that the removal of the obligation to live together did not necessarily deliver the claimant from the other party. Proletarians had little choice as regards living and working conditions, so that there was a considerable probability that the partners were literally stuck with each other, which could often lead to painful confrontations. Philippus Stienon of Antwerp, for example, turned into a savage after judgement for a board and bed separation had been given, according to his wife; he intimidated her so much that she petitioned the aldermen to have him put away. Maria Van Diest turned to the magistrate for the same reasons: her husband, Theodorus Van Kleymve, had moved in somewhere else on the orders of the ecclesiastical court – but he pestered her almost every day, hurled such terms of abuse as whore, bitch and trollop at her in public and even threatened to kill her.[31]

Incarceration on the other hand not only offered the advantage that there was nothing more to be feared from the uncontrollable person for the time being, but also held the possibility that they would come to their senses and that after their release from the house of correction they would go on to live a decent life – in other words, a husband would fulfil his obligations as breadwinner and head of the family. We shall give further examples of men (and women) who did not give up their bad habits and who were locked up once more at the request of their housemates. They did, however, form a minority. It is doubtful whether the others who were incarcerated came back meek as lambs, but their behaviour did not give rise to new complaints. Or should the small number of requests for prolongation of sentence be ascribed instead to the material problems with which the rest of the family were faced and which were simply too great? This cannot be excluded, since some wives asked the aldermen to release their husbands before their sentence was up because their wages were not enough to cover all the essentials of life. 'The Director of the Provincial Penitentiary can bear witness to the fact that my husband has improved his life', stated a woman from Antwerp on 11 May 1785, 'and I do not earn enough to feed my children: help me and set him free.'[32] Do such statements indicate that proletarian women had to choose between the devil and the deep blue sea?

Finally, the fact cannot be ignored that the question of guilt in a separation case was generally less explicit than in a case of confinement of the partner, in the eyes of both the judges and the outsiders. If in the one case relatives, neighbours and acquaintances harboured any doubts about the basis of the complaint, the motivations of the claimant and the legitimate character of the action, in the other everything appeared perfectly clear: anyone who was behind bars was either guilty or insane. This absolute judgement was of the greatest importance in a community in which Catholic morality pervaded thought and behaviour and in which deviations from the accepted norms and values quickly led to social isolation. Almost everyone had to suffer the ill-effects on his or her reputation, but for proletarians the consequences were especially serious, since their reciprocal relations with relatives and neighbours were undermined by it and they constituted an essential element in their survival strategies. By locking up the 'bad' partner, the position of the 'innocent' claimant was made safe in the social network – and even strengthened. People were after all acting in the general interest, as can be seen from the support received from third parties. A courageous deed had been done. Private confinement was not only permissible, it was justice itself in the opinion of both witnesses and aldermen. If the claimant in the case of confinement were able to assume an aura of guiltlessness and social commitment, which was not at all easy in the case of separation, the possibility of punishment provided additional satisfaction. With confinement on request the keys to the whole business lay in one person's hands: the description of the objectionable behaviour – and thus the choice between a house of correction and a mental institution – the duration of detention and both release and prolongation. This psychological aspect should not be underestimated. For women in particular it must have been tempting to be able to act both as the claimant *and* as judge. In the end it was she, the wife, who was in control of the situation: she could speak, she was listened to, she was agreed with, she determined the sentence – in short, she succeeded in reversing the roles.

Talking of punishment, why did so many women request the aldermen to confine their violent husbands instead of bringing formal charges against them and thus try and get a prosecution in court? Did they really hope their husbands would come to repent in the 'House of Improvement' or did they have (still) other motives? In the lower income groups financial considerations could have played a part, since a court case cost money, but there were also well-to-do women who had been severely mistreated by their husbands and who opted for confinement. For this reason we are inclined to look more for an explanation in psychological and social factors. Now, whether a husband ended up in an institution at the request of his spouse or as the result of a legal sentence, he was in the course of time set free (at least in most cases) and the couple had to live together again. However, private confinement was considered as a form of correction while imprisonment was associated exclusively with criminal activities, and that made a vast difference. In the eyes of the law there were complications, moreover. In general the acts were not committed in a criminal context, not even in public, but in a domestic situation where the husband by definition occupied a dominant position. There was no consensus on the question of where marital 'correction' ended and brutality began. Since the husband had the right to discipline his wife, he could beat her. On this (almost) everyone was agreed, laity as well as clergy, the governed and the governors. The chastisement had to be just and moderate, since neither of the partners could exceed the limits of the acceptable – but where did the borderline lie? No one knew. Some contemporaries postulated that the stick used for beating should not be thicker than an inch. Others were of the opinion that certain parts of the body should under no circumstances be touched. The fact that such 'criteria' were put forward is an indication of the acceptance of the phenomenon as such.

It is possible that the ideas that caught on in the United Provinces about the exercise of marital power influenced legal practice in the Austrian Netherlands. Dutch jurists and commentators published treatises in which they openly spoke out against physical discipline and where they stated that a woman had the right to seek redress if her husband thought differently; in some towns such punishment was even officially forbidden.[33] The stricter prosecution policy seems to indicate that sensitivity on this matter was changing things for the better in the South as well: at the end of the *ancien régime* 49 per cent of the men in Ghent who were guilty of mistreating their wives were effectively prosecuted, as against barely 25 per cent in the middle of the eighteenth century.[34] Given that most victims were from the same neighbourhood or were acquaintances, it cannot be deduced from the figures that violence within a marriage evoked disapproving reactions more often; they show only that anyone who assaulted a woman outside the home could count on tolerance less often. The annexation of the Southern Netherlands to France did not signify any reversal in this respect. Mistreatment of women was thenceforth considered as a criminal offence and severely punished, but the violence between married couples remained unmentioned and clearly unmentionable. In no way did private

Plate 7 J. J. Horemans II, *Tea-Time*, eighteenth century. Towards the end of the *ancien régime* many changes came about in the material culture of the wealthier sections of the population, which were accompanied by greater value being placed on privacy.

life constitute a point of discussion. Women who made complaints about their husbands were told that all they had to do was apply for separation or divorce; the procedure here was made so pliable that anyone could in principle embark on this course to put an end to domestic misery. Just as was the case with the traditional elites, the revolutionaries did not consider it desirable to intervene directly in domestic disputes. Both partners had to assemble a *tribunal de faimille* which could be composed of both relatives and neighbours and acquaintances: the court had only to examine whether the judgement of these *arbitres* complied with the law.[35]

The limited amenability of the legislative body to take measures to control marital violence, both under Austrian rule and during the French administration (and thereafter), was connected with the trend towards upgrading private life. From numerous contemporary writings we can see that the better-off population groups were increasingly inclined, from the middle of the eighteenth century onwards, to consider any outside interference as an intolerable invasion of privacy. The dimensions of public and private, open and intimate, had according to them to be kept strictly separate. In concrete terms this meant that the family from the social upper crust became more closed and more domestic, which probably meant that emotional ties between housemates were strengthened. The other side of the coin was that acts of violence within the family were presented as private events in which the outside world should not become involved; other members of the family had to intervene and settle the dispute in such a way that all the court had to do was confirm their 'sentence'. It is doubtful whether such an approach enabled mistreated wives to improve their lot. Current research abundantly demonstrates that it is precisely that legal no-man's land – that is, the powerlessness to bring matters to court – that lies at the heart of so much distress for women.[36] We can assume that such was also the case two centuries ago, especially since everything indicates that community life in the towns of Brabant and Flanders during the second half of the eighteenth century gradually lost out to power, which had very serious consequences for proletarian women in particular. We shall presently see why.

5

The Eyes of Others

Although most of the conflicts that led to a petition for confinement occurred in the setting of the nuclear family and the petitioners were almost always the housemates of the unwanted person, private confinement could be defined – up to a certain point – as a form of collective action. This is no paradox. It has already been noted that the decision to put someone under lock and key, even though for only a short time, was not lightly taken. Not only did the petitioners often have years of torment behind them, but they had also sought the advice of third parties. Some of them had gone to relatives, others to neighbours, friends or colleagues; yet others had gone to the priest, the almoners or their employer. The admonitions of these intermediaries had come to nothing, however. 'We are quite ashamed', wrote the petitioners, 'for we must daily suffer their look of moral disapproval, and even contempt, and we can understand their attitude all too well.' 'Il n'existe pas de scandale sans regard d'autrui', to quote Farge and Foucault ('There is no scandal except in the eyes of others').[1] The view of other people was indeed of the greatest importance in a society in which good relations with members of the family and others in the neighbourhood were essential conditions for survival. The argument of 'fear for our reputation', which was employed by so many petitioners, should not therefore be dismissed merely as a figure of speech. On the contrary, the declarations of witnesses show that the pressure of the wider social environment played a very important role.

Neighbours

Neighbours were often involved in cases of private confinement, although they seldom took the initiative themselves. As principal claimants they appear only 19 times in Antwerp throughout the whole period 1710–89, and the accusations in such cases always concerned an isolated, aged person, so it can be assumed that there were no relatives. The predominance of the nuclear family can also be seen from the limited frequency with which the neighbours acted as secondary or subsequent signatories to the petition. In Bruges this occurred 21 times and in Antwerp 24 times – in other words, barely 4 per cent of all the requests for confinement entered in both cities. Nevertheless, the neighbours were active participants in the drama. Almost 60 per cent of the petitioners from Antwerp and no less than 75 per cent of those from Bruges let it be understood that those living in the vicinity were heartily sick of the behaviour of the person to be confined and that they threatened to lose the respect and friendship of their fellow citizens if action was not taken. They were not exaggerating at all. More than half the witnesses who submitted a written declaration were neighbours and most of them substantiated not only the account of the petitioners, but also added revealing details, by which they made quite plain their disgust for the objectionable conduct of the person concerned.

The significance of the informal bonds between near residents cannot sufficiently be emphasized. Town-dwellers did not constitute an anonymous mass but were members of neighbourhood or district communities, which were much more than the sum of the houses and their residents. Every neighbourhood or district had a fairly intense social life, which held a high place in the affections of the families concerned. It was a hierarchical network of relationships, since the differences in financial circumstances and status, however small they might be, had to be taken into consideration, but community residents derived a feeling of collective identity from their informal social connections, by which they were as attached to their part of the town or city as country-dwellers to their own village.[2]

Good neighbourliness was of the greatest importance to the less well-off sections of the population in particular. It was not only because their precarious material conditions made them dependent on others at crucial moments in life and in crisis situations – the birth of a child, unemployment, illness, the death of a breadwinner – but also because, as a result of their cramped housing conditions, they had to get on with their near neighbours. There was no question of privacy in the poorer sections of a town. Proletarians were continuously confronted with their fellows, literally and figuratively, which implied both helpfulness and meddle-someness. There was not much that escaped the eyes and ears of the neighbours. Rumours and gossip spread like wildfire and could grow into a scandal against which little or nothing could be done. Reputations were continually made and destroyed again. Respectability had to be established every day. It is in this context, in this socio-cultural environment, that the struggle for existence was played out – which in concrete terms meant that the chances of survival, both emotionally and materially, were determined through the honour of the family. Families who came into discredit through the objectionable behaviour of one of their members ran the risk that the neighbours would in the course of time avoid them and even refuse to help them in cases of emergency. Who could respect the parents of a daughter who conducted herself as a public whore or a married couple whose 'squabblings' threw the whole neighbourhood into an uproar? Who would give any more credit to the wife of the artisan who squandered his money building up debts at the tavern? Who would be inclined to put up with the fact that a man was making life hell for both his wife and the neighbouring residents? The need to maintain and strengthen social ties – thus, keep reciprocal relationships going – explains why the less well-off sections of the population attached so much importance to 'respectability'. The interpretation doubtless differed from that in the 'better' circles, but the positive or negative appraisal of society – the approving or disapproving view of the neighbourhood community – had so many consequences for families of modest means that they were just as preoccupied with their reputations; in this milieu, too, there were hierarchies that were not based purely on differences in income.

In some towns in the Austrian Netherlands neighbourhood communities were more or less institutionalized, which does not detract from the fact that they enjoyed a considerable degree of autonomy. Just as today district committees are set up to give expression and form to communal complaints, mostly in a spirit of collective opposition, so too in the thirteenth century in Ghent *gebuurten* (neighbourhood associations) were established which had nothing in common with other groupings such as brotherhoods or guilds. It was a matter of territorial units, which in general were very small: a *gebuurte* usually covered a single roadway or part thereof, with the adjoining small streets and alleys. The number of neighbourhood associations grew considerably during the late Middle Ages and especially after the Renaissance. In 1777 there were no fewer than 211 of them, together forming 19 districts (*wijken*) or principal quarters, which came down to an average of about 210 inhabitants or 45 to 50 households per neighbourhood. Their origin is not to be sought in the extension of urban areas or demographic expansion, but in the growing number of functions the *gebuurten* took upon themselves *and* were allocated. The aldermen realized that they could render many services, both administratively and legally, and for this reason involved them in public works – fire-fighting, maintaining order and numerous other tasks concerning the urban community as a whole and which would be difficult to carry out without the cooperation of the residents.

All adults living in Ghent were full members of a neighbourhood association, regardless of financial circumstances or position. They met regularly at an inn at the invitation of the dean. This man was not appointed by the town council, but democratically elected by the residents of the neighbourhood, usually for a period of three years. He was the link with the authorities: on the one hand he represented the members in dealings with the aldermen and on the other he had to inform the members of the orders made by the authorities and to make sure they were carried out. The 'democratic' character of the voting was of course relative. Women were not allowed to vote. They could only appoint the 'lady-dean', whose role was limited to presiding over community dinners. Since the dean and lady-dean each had to pay a sort of deposit greater than their share in such festivities, the so-called *jonste*, we can assume that they were fairly well-off; in particular, they were allowed under no circumstances to accept money or gifts for their services, and the former, moreover, had to have a lot of spare time at his disposal. The dean was assisted by a man called a *baljuw* (also unpaid), whom he could choose from among the neighbouring residents himself and who played the role of a living newspaper, as it were (for which he did draw payment); but the tasks were so many that a full-time job was quite impossible. Together with the *baljuw*, the dean was responsible in the first instance for the collection and management of the contributions and fines the members had to pay. With the exception of the poor on relief, the residents had to make a certain contribution to the community chest for all sorts of affairs: for removing house; for every birth; for the weddings of children (even when they became a beguine, nun, monk or priest, the ceremony involving a symbolic 'marriage' to Christ); for silver and golden jubilees; for every death (the 'death-debt'); on the purchase or sale of a property situated in the neighbourhood. The members could also be fined: if they were absent from general assemblies, the neighbourhood festival or the funeral of a fellow-member; if they neglected or refused to carry out the tasks allotted to them; if they disturbed the peace. At this point we come to a crucial aspect of this institutionalized social life.

The dean of a neighbourhood association had extensive administrative powers. He had to organize the night-watch, take command of fire-fighting, supervise the maintenance of the roads and waterways (which he had to have cleaned or repaired when necessary), take care of the street lamps, encourage the residents to decorate them on the occasion of processions, solemn pageants or other ceremonies, check how much grain each family had in case of hardship, draw up a list of houses where soldiers could be billeted when they arrived, and so on. His legal authority was much more limited, but nonetheless important *and* time-consuming. He had to ensure that the residents of the neighbourhood lived 'in peace, love and friendship'. He was the *peismaker*, the peace-maker. He functioned as intermediary in disputes which today would be cases for the police or a Justice of the Peace. He had to calm down the *krakeelmakers* (squabblers) and fine them, a fine which was increased according to how abusive the insults or how violent the fights were; if a person was wounded they could be very steep. The dean also had to act when one marriage partner accused the other of adultery or when someone accused one of the neighbourhood residents of whoring. If he did not succeed in resolving a conflict (and thus deal with the matter amicably) then he had the obligation to inform the court officials, who summoned him as a witness if the accused were to be tried. It was above all in quarrels between neighbours that the deans seem to have been irreplaceable. This was why the French authorities quickly decided to reverse their decision of 1795 to dispense with the neighbour-hood associations in Ghent. In 1804 they gave them the green light again because the deans were in a position to make an important contribution:

> to the prevention and impediment of disputes and fights and, moreover, in the reconciliation of persons quarrelling over matters concerning their interests or feelings, and to bringing peace and quiet by reconciling households and families where there is disharmony.[3]

So far as we can ascertain, there existed no similar organizations in the other cities in this study. While each of the 13 districts of Antwerp were divided into *kwartieren*, these smaller geographic units had no form of autonomy; they came under the leadership of representatives of the 'Borough' – that is, the well-to-do burghers – who were appointed by the city administration. It does not follow from this that neighbourhood life in Antwerp was less intense than that in Ghent. From contemporary commentaries, fictional texts, trial documents and other qualitative information it can be deduced that the residents of adjoining streets held all kinds of celebrations, contributed to funds for decorating and lighting 'their' part of the city, jointly sent petitions to the aldermen for favours or making formal complaints, opposed certain government regulations as a community – in short, giving expression to a feeling of 'togetherness', which rested rather more on proximity than on social homogeneity. Such informal bonds must not be idealized or romanticized, of course. A number of samples taken at random from civil and criminal trials suffices to persuade us that the harmony within a neighbourhood community was highly relative and that, moreover, there was a high price to pay for it. The thresholds of tolerance were so low that even small deviations from the acceptable norms could lead to great tension and completely poison interpersonal relationships. Anyone who wanted to live in peace with his fellows had not only to be cooperative, but also to subject himself to the tyranny of public opinion.

Just as in Ghent, people from the same neighbourhood in Antwerp used informal – though no less repressive – means to make a person's life miserable, cause material damage and even ostracize him to the extent that there was nothing left for him but to move away. The inhabitants of Antwerp could not, however, resolve their conflicts by appealing to a neighbourhood intermediary whose judgement had the force of law behind it, or at least was sanctioned by the magistrate. They had instead to turn to the judicial apparatus. Only the aldermen and the commissioners appointed by them were able to settle disputes. If the opposing parties lived in the same house and were relatives and/or neighbours, and if the accused were likely to incur a fine of no more than 50 guilders, then the case was heard without the *Openbaar Ministerie* (Public Ministry), which made it possible to settle matters quickly. The judge-commissioner in such cases functioned as a 'peacemaker', since his main task was settle the case amicably, if necessary with the help of others from the immediate environment of the opponents. As an instrument of social control this procedure was probably as effective as the involvement of the deans of neighbourhood associations. Since the latter were much closer to the people than official functionaries, however, it can be assumed that they were more often consulted and that they had more success as conciliators.

Alas, we know nothing about the frequency with which urban neighbourhood communities exercised social control and the possible changes that took place therein. Thus we are in the dark as to the extent to which charivari occurred. This ritual sanction, which was directed against all sorts of deviant behaviour – in particular, in the areas of marriage and sexuality – was variously described. People spoke of making 'kettle-music', 'honking', 'pan-holes', holding a 'bell-market', 'hunting the beast', 'scragging', and so on. Charivaris continually altered in accordance with a fixed pattern, in which both the environment and period as well as subjects and things people did could be given a symbolic meaning. They might be regarded as purification-rituals: as public, collective and spontaneous demonstrations, whose purpose was to correct the person breaking the unwritten but generally accepted codes of behaviour or even to throw him out of the community, by which the latter was cleansed. People who had infringed the rules were usually subjected to all manner of ridicule, threats and humiliation at nightfall, to the accompaniment of a great deal of clamour, when those taking part often used violence against the victim and/or his possessions, both actual and symbolic. Although charivaris, which could last several days and even weeks, generally ended up in a great binge, they were not playful activities but intended to show disapproval and to punish. This was made clear in several ways: by publicly burning a dummy representing the person concerned, by doing humiliating things to him/her in public or demanding a ransom – which could be considered as a fine and thus as a symbol of guilt. There are indications that those who took the initiative sometimes played on social and political unrest among neighbourhood residents with regard to certain official regulations. Most cases of 'popular justice', however, involved infringements of marital and sexual *mores*: adultery, the pregnancy of an unmarried girl, the breaking of marriage vows and conflicts between married couples; in the last case it was a matter of severe ill-treatment, a wife's wearing the trousers in the relationship or the abandonment by one marriage partner of the other.[4]

A fine example of a 'domestic' charivari is provided by the events that took place in Deinze in the spring of 1788. On the evening of Saturday 19 April a large number of residents gathered before the house of the brandy-distiller Piet De Smet. They made an ear-splitting noise with all sorts of objects, which was interrupted now and then so they could scream in chorus: 'Let's scrag the whore! Ottevaere's bitch! Long live the air-balloon!' What led to all this was the fact that the wife, Catharina Baecke – nicknamed the 'Air-Balloon', which referred both to her corpulence and to her low stature – was having an extramarital affair with the brewer Ottevaere. The rowdy gathering grew into a riot in which several people fell wounded. When separation was granted on 7 June the displeasure of the community manifested itself for a second time. Although Pieter De Smet pleaded with the abusive crowd to cease their degrading actions for the sake of his children and paid a ransom to this end, a likeness of Ottevaere was dragged around and spat on for hours.

These charivaris did not just appear out of thin air. The residents of Deinze had been busy for some time with 'clapping and murmuring' about the scandalous behaviour of Baecke. The priest had intercepted the rumours and reminded the wife of her obligations, to no avail. He could do nothing else but show disapproval for the community's interference, as rough justice was forbidden by both the civil and

HAY – OPPA   SIGNOORKEN

*Hier ziet men dat ik niet en lieg;
't is zoo dat ik ten hemel vlieg!
die my bevryd van wedervat
bezit de grootste kunst van all'.*

Plate 8 J. Hunin, *Opsinjoorken*, 1825. In the seventeenth and eighteenth centuries the so-called *smijtpop* (dummy) 'Vuylen Bras' or 'Opsinjoorken' represented a hardened drinker or a wife-beater. Such men were subjected by their fellow citizens to all manner of ridicule and humiliation.

ecclesiastical authorities – though he was of the opinion that those who took the initiative and those taking part in this case did not deserve to be punished. After all,

> ... under certain circumstances, the actions of the rabble-rousers can often be excused to some extent, because they serve as the most powerful

admonitions and an encouragement to return to better ways for those to whom their attentions are directed; it has often been noted that some wife-beaters, adulterers and others have by this means been brought back from their erroneous ways and have thereafter never returned to such excesses.[5]

It was not always possible, however, to neutralize an objectionable person by means of popular justice or to throw him out, even when he lived in a small and relatively autonomous community. The noisiest charivari in the eighteenth century in the United Provinces – the famous incident with Jan van Es from Oss (a place with some 2,500 inhabitants in the Mayory of 's-Hertogenbosch) – shows that rough justice expeditions could go wrong, so that the family of the 'pariah' saw themselves obliged to make use of even more drastic means for exerting pressure.

It was a Saturday evening, 2 March 1765. A crowd of about a hundred people, mostly women and boys, set off with a great deal of 'kettle-music' for the house of Jan van Es, a trader by profession, who did no credit to the family nickname – the *Schaapmannekes* ('Little Shepherds'): he had for a long time been branded as a hardened drinker and brute, a wife-beater, for he very often ill-treated his wife; in addition he had sired an illegitimate child and was suspected of wanting to join the Reformed Church for the purpose of obtaining an official post. It did not remain simply a matter of noise, screaming and threats. The crowd smashed his windows and began to chop the door down. Van Es fled in panic to the attic, reached for his pistol and fired two shots, the second of which hit a deaf and mentally handicapped girl from next door. Fearing that there would be more victims, the retreat was sounded. On Sunday 17 March there was a new outburst. At about midday Van Es was publicly denounced as a 'rogue' and a 'Protestant' and challenged to a man-to-man fight. Once again he made it an unequal affair and shot the challenger in the leg. Van Es realized that things were getting totally out of hand and pleaded with the aldermen to protect him. The result was that he was placed in an isolation cell to await trial. It did not get that far, however. His relatives requested the magistrate to drop the prosecution with the argument that the prisoner had declared he was prepared to take up service with the East India Company. In their opinion this was the best solution, because everyone would then be relieved of a troublesome burden. The authorities agreed, but on condition that Van Es should never more set foot in the mayory. The events at Oss also made the Estates-General supervise more strictly such old interdictions regarding actions against wife-beaters as 'harnessing [them] to the plough', 'bear-hunting', *toffelen* ('giving a drubbing'), and so on. Local court officials were given the task of 'ensuring the strictest vigilance against all riotous assemblies, conspiracies or mob violence, whatever name might be given to them.'

The Jan van Es case did not end there. After seven years he turned up once again in Oss, to the consternation of the family, who had in the meantime appropriated a portion of his possessions. Both parties reacted vehemently. Van Es instigated a prosecution, which led to so much domestic squabbling (*huiskrakeel*) that his wife left with the children. The other members of the family did not sit idly by, either. Together with the neighbours, they overpowered him on 3 October 1772, dragged him outside by the hair, beat him about the head and legs with pickaxe-handles and clubs, threw him onto a cart and drove him to the Prussian border, where he was handed over to a press-gang working for the army. After a short time Van Es succeeded in obtaining a discharge and returned once more to the mayory. For caution's sake he installed himself not in Oss, but in nearby Oijen. When he tried to find witnesses to bring his case against members of his family, the latter lost no time in setting upon him a second time. His promise to go to the East Indies of his own accord this time fell on deaf ears. No, ran the verdict of the family, for 'there, you rogue, you can still write and bring charges against us. We shall give you a small four-walled room in a monastery and there, you scoundrel, you shall not be able to write and bring charges against us.' On 27 July 1773 Van Es was indeed locked up – not in a monastery, however, but in St Joris' Hospital at Liège, which functioned as a house of correction. Nine years later he managed to escape with a number of other detainees, once more returning to the mayory, where he led a wandering life. In May 1790 a warrant for his arrest was issued, because he was reputed to have murdered a poor man who had given him shelter. But Van Es seems to have disappeared into thin air, from the mayory and from our sight.[6]

This remarkable – and undoubtedly extreme – case shows that the local community played a crucial role in the punishment and ostracization of persons who tried to destabilize social and cultural order. It is possible that the family were the silent directors of the street theatre, but the question here is not who took the initiative on the ritual sanction. The point is that the inhabitants of Oss considered the 'Little Shepherd' as a pariah and that they supported all the actions directed towards the elimination of this 'pollution'. They were not only prepared to organize a charivari, but also to cooperate in kidnapping the trickster and to erect a wall of silence when he tried to find witnesses for his case against his relatives. The Jan van Es case also shows that collective forms of social control were not necessarily very efficient. For the person who was the butt of all their activities the year 1765 was a dramatic turning-point, but it was his uncontrolled behaviour and not rough justice as such that determined the course of events. Given that Jan van Es acted as a coward and that, moreover, he appealed to the law, the family had little choice but to intervene, whereby they did everything they could to avoid a court case. By first sending Jan van Es to the Cape of Good Hope and then having him signed up for the army, the family tried to keep matters in their own hands. The failure of all these attempts at an informal exercise of power finally led to the decision to enter a request for confinement, which was clearly granted by the Liège authorities without demur. In short, confinement was the ultimate means of discipline.

We have devoted a great deal of attention to this case because it supports the hypothesis that the growing inability of the neighbourhood residents to act effectively against infringers of the marital and sexual order drove increasing numbers of people in the large towns of Brabant and Flanders to the process of private confinement. It is true that the aldermen of Brussels, Antwerp, Ghent and Bruges issued interdictions that were probably directed against charivaris. Thus the magistrate at Ghent stipulated in 1704 and 1709 that thenceforth no one 'might play upon cymbals or drums, by which at night great unrest and trouble was caused . . ., either in houses or other places.' One order was a little less vague: in 1749 the people were forbidden to receive their fellow citizens who had been attending the Holy Blood Procession in Bruges 'with stabbing by baker's horns [*sic*], inciting people to hang out disparaging inscriptions and otherwise, their being extremely disrespectful and matters of evil consequence'.[7] After the middle of the century we find no further trace in the court archives of the aforementioned cities of anything which might allude to charivaris. It is difficult to ascribe the silence of these sources to the passive role of the aldermen, since in the numerous chronicles, travel commentaries and literary texts we have consulted there is equally little mention of such demonstrations – with the exception of the Antwerp 'Shrove Tuesday Uproar' of 1780, which shows all the characteristics of a political charivari, a subject to which we shall return.

Whatever the case may be, the fact that the number of confinement requests during the second half of the eighteenth century increased in number in all the cities in this study, regardless of the means of social control to which the neighbourhood residents had access, indicates that the power of informal social relationships was weaker rather than stronger, or at least that the intervention of neighbourhood residents produced results less often in cases of domestic conflicts. This is not surprising, since there were social changes taking place that deeply influenced reciprocal relationships.

Until about 1760 most smallholders and farm workers earned a relatively good living, but thereafter their material conditions gradually began to decline. Although only a small percentage of the rural poor abandoned their place of birth in the hope of finding means of subsistence elsewhere, such emigration was sufficiently significant to increase urban populations further. The number of inhabitants in Antwerp and Brussels increased respectively by 20 per cent and 29 per cent between 1755 and 1784 and that of Bruges and Ghent by respectively 13 and 17 per cent between 1760 and 1790. This demographic expansion led to a considerable rise in the cities' domestic rents: towards 1795 they were on average 35 per cent higher than at the beginning of the century. For those of modest means the consequences were all the more serious, because family incomes were dropping and a greater portion had to be set aside for the purchase of food. The only way out was to move to cheaper accommodation, by which certain neighbourhoods acquired a more pronounced proletarian character. The trend towards spatial segregation was further facilitated by the deliberate gentrification policy of the better-off, which underlined the growing socio-cultural differences by which the lower classes were also literally being distanced. Of course, there was at that time still no mention of forming ghettos; that process first appeared in the nineteenth century. At the end of the *ancien régime* rich and poor still often lived in close proximity in the large towns of Brabant and Flanders, though they were more unevenly spread over the town than previously. Between 1740 and 1780 the number of destitute people in three Ghent parishes remained at the same low level and in two others it rose only slightly, but in two other parishes it rose from 12 to 23 per cent and from 16 to 24 per cent. An investigation into the spatial distribution of wealth in Antwerp points in the same direction: around 1796, 31 per cent of privately owned buildings in two districts consisted of dwellings of the lowest quality, as against less than 16 per cent in the rest of the city.[8]

Studies of modern-day metropolises indicate that spatial segregation is often accompanied by social dislocation. It is not only poverty and unemployment that eat away at mutual helpfulness, but also the removal of social upper and middle classes from a neighbourhood. That departure causes the neighbourhood to lose its structure and its ability to solve problems itself, because the precarious living conditions of the least stable social group make it extremely difficult to maintain all kinds of reciprocal relationships.[9] This paradox – the growing need of the poor for solidarity and the diminishing possibilities of giving shape and expression to it themselves – was noted by a doctor from Leiden by the name of Johannes le Francq van Berkhey, who was attached to the university as lecturer in natural history. Around 1770 he wrote that neighbourhood life was being lost through the inclination of the better-off to distance themselves, which meant the end of 'that old and excellent brotherly companionableness and community of spirit, of that benign and civil intercourse'.[10] Given that social polarization and spatial segregation often went hand in hand in the large towns of Brabant and Flanders, it can be assumed that the changes in neighbourhood life were more or less paralleled by those in Leiden – particularly because the continuing immigration of impoverished country-dwellers was increasing the social problems even further.

It should be noted that we are in no way arguing that neighbours were no longer prepared to help one another. On the contrary, it was those selfsame social changes that were making it necessary to maintain relationships with others more closely. Without a network of reciprocal relationships it was very difficult to develop adequate survival strategies. The basis for the upkeep of such networks was becoming narrower, however, since on the one hand more and more proletarians were having to face problems which they could not solve themselves, and on the other they were able to count increasingly less often on the cooperation of better-off neighbours. Hence families who were shunned because of the reprehensible behaviour of one of their members could count on little by way of understanding: because of their material and emotional instability they were not in a position to enjoy reciprocity and in addition their continuous domestic squabbling caused a nuisance to the other residents of the neighbourhood. In other words, the processes of proletarianization and impoverishment led both to an increase in domestic conflicts and to a lowering of tolerance thresholds. As the socio-economic situation of wage-earners and the lower middle classes worsened and they felt themselves more vulnerable, they increasingly came to regard infringements of the unwritten rules of society as threats to social order – thus as forms of *quaed gedragh* – and their inclination grew to correct and throw out the perpetrators. Since utilizing informal repressive measures was becoming less effective, the burden of intervention also gradually shifted away from the community to the problem family itself, which meant that the housemates of the unwanted person were put under pressure to put an end to the scandal and to have him/her locked away if necessary. It was made clear to the family concerned in all ways possible that the nuisance could not be tolerated and that they threatened to isolate themselves if they refused to take drastic measures. Ultimately it was the regard of others that was the greatest worry, particularly for the poor, since the loss of reciprocal relationships confronted them with insuperable problems. Their dependence on other people was so great that they simply could not afford to ignore public opinion. This is why social pressure – namely, that of the neighbourhood community – in this context often played as great a role in the decision to enter a request for confinement as the domestic misery itself.

In many cases private confinement was thus not simply a family matter, but a collective action. By acting as witnesses for the prosecution the neighbouring residents let it be known that the limits of the permissible had been overstepped and that confinement was the only possibility of restoring peace and quiet, both within the family and in the community. By locking up the unwanted person, those who lived with him/her could absolve themselves of all blame and reconcile themselves with the community. Moreover, they were providing convincing proof that they subscribed to the norms and values of their social group, that they respected the interests and feelings of others, that they shared their attitudes towards *quaed gedragh* – and, last but not least that they themselves were innocent and, as a result, entitled to understanding and support.

The neighbours came in at every possible stage preceding the confinement. They intervened when a woman was continually mistreated by her husband, especially when the latter committed other outrages. This was the case, for example, for Carel Van Nieuwenhuyse of Bruges, who disturbed everyone's sleep because he 'daily and until one or two o'clock at night lived in scandalous fashion with his wife with much cursing and swearing.'[11] Mathias De Munter of Antwerp, nicknamed Slappen Tist ('Spineless Tist'), was also repudiated by his neighbours because he continually raised hell and behaved as a total beast to his wife, to everyone's 'scandal and disgust'; when he went for his wife with a knife, they did not hesitate to wrest the weapon out of his hand and give him a good beating.[12] Such interventions were, however, the exception. From the requests and the statements of witnesses it can be deduced that men seldom went to the aid of a woman if she were being thrashed by her husband, even when her screams roused the entire neighbourhood. It is striking, though, that seven out of ten witnesses for the prosecution in such cases were women from the neighbourhood. Given that the reverse is true of the opposite sex – thus that the complaints of male petitioners about the unruly life of their wife were almost always backed up by men – it might well be concluded that solidarity was limited to people of the same sex, at least as far as conflicts between married couples were concerned. In both cases, nuisance was the main reason for coming forward as witnesses. Thus was Egidius Peys of Antwerp forced by his neighbours to enter a petition for confinement, because his wife wandered blind drunk day and night creating mayhem instead of looking after the children, 'to the great scandal of the neighbours, who often have had to return her home and ensure that she stay there'; on the basis of their testimonies, Mrs Peys, nicknamed Lamoentje, ended up in a penal institution for a year.[13] The husband of Marie Joanne Portuart turned to the aldermen of Bruges for the same reasons: the neighbours were sick of continually having to pick her up out of the gutter, where 'she lay as drunk as a pig'.[14]

The unruly lives of youths also gave rise to interventions. The parents of 15-year-old Leonard Hooremans pleaded with the Antwerp magistrate to have their work-shy son put under lock and key because his behaviour as a thief was deeply disquieting to the neighbours; the latter indeed declared that they were so afraid 'of losing their possessions to such a malicious youth that they no longer dared to leave their houses unattended.'[15] Neighbouring residents did not hesitate to make their disapproval known or to take action if a young whore drew too much attention to herself or latched on to married men from her immediate environs, or if her activities led to rowdiness at night. When the mother of Anna Françoise De Rijk requested the aldermen of Antwerp to place her daughter in a reformatory because she 'sought out menfolk in public for the purpose of dishonourable conversation', she emphasized that the whoring of her daughter made good neighbourliness impossible: 'people' were sick and tired of all the comings and goings, all the bragging and quarrelling. She was not in any way exaggerating, since five witnesses testified that their sleep was continually disturbed by the soldiers tramping over the floor to get to Anna Françoise.[16]

It ought now to be clear that the neighbourhood community was playing an important role in confinement cases, either directly or by exerting pressure on the family to whom the unwanted person belonged. It determined in any case the limits of the acceptable and in consequence what people should understand by the term *quaed gedragh*. From that point of view confinement on request was a continuation of charivari. We should not blindly stare at the different *forms* of action. Both sanctions largely fulfilled the same functions. They occurred in times of socio-cultural tensions, which were closely bound up with socio-economic changes and which increased the chances of violence between members of the same household, between members of a family and between residents of the same neighbourhood. Because the traditional norms and values were no longer being respected, new patterns of behaviour were manifesting themselves and morals were becoming 'looser', people felt insecure and threatened – which gave rise to irritations and defensive reactions. Both charivari and confinement on request met the need to neutralize social anomalies, it being understood that the community in the first case cleansed itself by means of ritual violence while in the second use was made of an external instrument for social control – that is, an appeal was made to an official means of violence. Just as with charivaris, most of the confinement requests were also public, collective and unanimous demonstrations of displeasure, which were directed towards the ostracization of the infringer of the community's norms and which also strengthened the informal bonds between neighbourhood residents. The repairing of social order was as important to the petitioners as the restoration of domestic peace, since the antisocial behaviour of their relative undermined their own position within the neighbourhood community and called reciprocal relationships into question.

The parish priest as mediator

In the United Provinces it was not only the neighbourhood residents who exercised social control. The Reformed Church played an important role in the maintenance of standards of behaviour and the disciplining of those who infringed them. During the weekly meetings of the church council, which consisted of elders and deacons, attention was turned both to religious matters as such and to infringements of good morals, from drunkenness to adultery, whereby it was mainly the behaviour of the poorer members that was most closely examined. After information had been gathered from privileged witnesses – persons who led irreproachable lives and who were closely in touch with the comings and goings within the community – the sinner was invited to appear at the meeting to show contrition and to undergo the humiliation of disciplining. The admonishing sermon and the censure of the church – which meant exclusion from communion and the church's social welfare – had the purpose of setting the man or woman concerned on the right path once more. Anyone who was obdurate and, for example, persisted in committing adultery, could be exposed to prosecution. Although the church council continued to intervene in the daily lives of its members, whereby the poorer ones, as a result of the censure measure, could find themselves in material need, this form of exercising power was having less and less effect as the eighteenth century progressed. The growing inability of the church council to exercise social control is reflected in the spectacular rise in the number of separations and divorces, as the preachers themselves reported. When Johanna Teegers, who came from Amsterdam, complained in 1770 to the church council about the bestial manner in which her drunken and unfaithful husband treated her, she was advised to take the case to the aldermen and to separate from her husband.[17] Many similar examples can be given. In the large towns in particular, domestic conflicts were increasingly fought out in the civil courts, regardless of the church to which the contending parties belonged. In the Reformed Church the opinion came to be established that disputes between members of the same household or relatives were best settled by other courts.

In the Austrian Netherlands there were no other institutions to compare with the Reformed Church council. While the ecclesiastical officials were empowered to give judgement in matters concerning marital and sexual order, they could not put infringers under censure or throw them out of the church community. They were, moreover, too few in number and had too little contact with the faithful to exercise social control over them. It does not in any way follow from this that the Roman Catholic Church in the South lacked means to counter deviant behaviour and to act against 'immoral' persons. Pastoral guidance in the towns was very intense, at least until about 1770. There was no shortage of priests and most of them were well educated, conscientious and devoted. In some parishes it was probably impossible to follow closely people's religious practices and moral conduct because there were very many inhabitants and the priest had to minister to them alone, but in general the care of souls seems to have been efficient. The 1770s and 1780s seem in this respect to have been a turning-point, since the influx of uprooted country-dwellers caused urban populations quickly to swell and the number of priests could not be extended for financial reasons (and perhaps also because of a drop in the number of vocations).[18] As a result, many priests were no longer in a position to know all their parishioners personally and to come to them when 'something' went wrong. Anyone who stood at the head of a poor parish had the greatest difficulty in acting preventively or even in issuing admonitions, since the least well-off neighbourhoods were undergoing the strongest demographic growth and had the largest 'floating' population, both in absolute and relative terms.

Because there has still been no systematic investigation into the relationships between parish priests and their flocks in the towns of the Austrian Netherlands, it would be risky to make pronouncements on the cases the priests had to deal with, the extent to which this occurred and the effects their interventions had. The confinement requests do certainly show that they often stepped in as intermediaries in domestic conflicts. Almost one-third of the petitioners in Antwerp and Bruges declared that the priest had on more than one occasion tried to make the unwanted person see reason; in many cases he had not hesitated to admonish him/her in public. Some priests were so indignant about the objectionable behaviour of a parishioner that they went to the aldermen to plead for his confinement in person. Thus the priest of the parish of Our Lady in Bruges stated in 1787 that the wife of Jan Vandekerckhove was at her wits' end:

> not only did her husband refuse to contribute to the family income, but in addition he drank and swore from morning till night. Recently he had lain

Plate 9 J. J. Horemans II, *Saying Grace Before a Meal*, eighteenth century. An idealized image of family life in a period during which family relationships were coming under great pressure.

asleep in broad daylight in a drunken stupor in the gutter and the neighbours had to carry him home, to the utter scandal of the public. Since he ignores all admonition and continues to create mayhem both at home and in the street, I believe it necessary to have him placed in a house of improvement.

In the Peter De Roo case the priest also functioned as a witness for the prosecution. He not only confirmed the account of the wife, who was accusing her husband of severely ill-treating her, but he also laid emphasis on the numerous scandals the man caused. The priest was especially shocked by the disrespectful attitude of the wife-beater towards the Holy Sacraments: 'so far ... having been called to an adjacent house to that of the same Peter De Roo to hear the confession of a sick person, it was impossible to administer the Holy Sacrament because of his abominable cursing, swearing and beating of his wife.[19] Such cases, though, were exceptions to the rule of silence on the part of the parochial clergy in confinement cases. Once the request had been entered, most priests kept in the background. Generally speaking, they played a part in the procedure only if it was a question of a declaration of insanity or if the authorities wanted information about the financial situation of the petitioners. Did they refuse to act as witnesses against 'debauched' persons because they feared bringing themselves into discredit as intermediaries by openly choosing for one of the parties? Or did they consider it inadvisable to pronounce on the question of guilt before the aldermen had investigated the case? This cannot be excluded, either, since the latter refused to grant some requests for confinement, and then there was a risk that the parish priest might get the worst of it.

Of course, we do not know how often the clergy succeeded in patching things up, thus reconciling married couples and resolving parent–child conflicts. The requests for confinement throw light exclusively on the unsuccessful attempts at social control. Given that the number of petitions in the 1770s and 1780s increased considerably and that objectionable behaviour usually involved matters of morality which the Church considered important, it could be concluded that the influence of the clergy was waning. It does not necessarily follow from this that the standards of the time were deliberately being trampled on, but enlightened ideas were being accorded more recognition towards the end of the *ancien régime* and the ecclesiastical authorities were much disquieted by them. The Bishop of Antwerp was so alarmed that in 1777 he found it necessary to publish a pastoral letter in which he warned the faithful against the 'false prophets' who had arisen and who were claiming 'that the Gospel is a fable: that there is neither God nor hell: that people die like animals and that their happiness is to be found in satisfying their bodily desires.'[20] The 'pernicious' writings of Voltaire, Raynal and other enlightened authors did indeed enjoy a wide distribution, but their greatest success was among the better-off sections of the population. The growing rebelliousness of the *jeunesse dorée* was probably a side-effect of this tide of secularization. The sons of rich parents could easily come into contact with the new ideas and find in them a breeding ground for doubts about traditional attitudes to authority and Christian teaching and morality – and for developing other, more 'libertine' patterns of behaviour.

The ecclesiastical authorities were much more preoccupied about the waning of religious life among the lower classes. Quoting once more from the Bishop of Antwerp: 'When do we see their coming to church for instruction? for confession? to the table of the Lord? Their whole life is a string of sinful deeds: cursing and swearing, quarrelling, fighting, foul language, drunkenness, uncleanliness . . . In a word, they live not as men but as unthinking animals.'[21] Antwerp was not an exceptional case, because the Bishops of Bruges and Ghent speak in much the same tones. From the confinement requests, moreover, we can see that infringements of ecclesiastical rules were becoming more numerous. In our opinion the explanation has to be sought in a combination of two factors. On the one hand, the material and emotional lives of many proletarians and people with small businesses were being deeply disturbed by the socio-cultural changes taking place during the second half of the eighteenth century. The frustrations of adult men were further increased by the shifts in the balance of power within the family and those of adolescents by the postponement of marital age, which explains both the increase in *quaed gedragh* and the sharp rise in the percentage of prenuptial births. On the other hand, it seems reasonable to assume that the growing distance between the ideals that the clergy continued to extol to the less well-off sections of the community and the hard reality with which they were confronted was leading to a greater indifference on their part towards religion.

Is it any surprise, then, that it was the young who were most inclined to reject the church and to leave it of their own accord? Of course, there were men and women who accused their marriage partner of unchristian behaviour, but they were in a small minority. Uncontrollable sons, on the other hand, were very often depicted as utter heathens. That accusation was used in no fewer than 49 of the 87 cases involving proletarian youths who ended up in the Brussels house of correction during the decade 1770–9. Some of them had clearly only blasphemed ('cursing and swearing'), but most showed 'a disdain for all Christian devotion and life', as one of the petitioners put it. The parents involved made it clear what they understood by irreligiousness: the youth openly disparaged the clergy and hurled the roughest terms of abuse at the parish priest; he deliberately ate meat on fast days; he refused to go to confession and communion; he did not observe Easter; he was never to be found in church of a Sunday.[22] Similar accusations were made by 27 of the 55 Antwerp wage-earners (male and female) who had a son put under lock and key between 1770 and 1789. It is not easy to work out which was the deciding factor, but the fact that the majority of them were on the threshold of adulthood supports the assumption that sexual frustrations contributed. Young wage-earners in any case were adopting a much freer attitude towards the church than the previous generation; until about 1770 there was talk of only blasphemy in the confinement requests, and in a small number of cases at that. Emancipation and patronization went hand in hand, however: as the priest lost prestige and became less successful as intermediary in domestic conflicts, so the civil authorities gained more significance, and particularly because the social control exerted by neighbours was becoming weaker, or at least produced fewer lasting effects.

6

The Language of Authority

Why did the aldermen grant almost all of the confinement requests without much fuss? The fact that they did not put any spokes in the wheels of families of high standing is not surprising: but why were they just as accommodating to petitioners who could not pay for the cost of confinement themselves? Their flexible attitude is all the more remarkable because it was this very sector of society which was growing so rapidly in size. Humanitarian motives might have played some part, but it seems hardly probable that they were the deciding factor, because at the end of the 1760s the public institutions could no longer take the influx of unwanted people, which obliged urban administrations to extend existing provisions or to create new ones – and thus to incur heavy financial burdens. An explanation has to be sought in another direction: many types of objectionable behaviour went beyond the family framework not only because they led to the interventions of neighbours or the priest, but also and especially because the authorities saw and defined them as a problem. As we have remarked elsewhere: it is just to the extent that the social consequences of transformation processes are considered a threat by the elites (who take up a controlling position at economic, political and cultural/ideological levels) that they become a social problem. In situations where similar phenomena pose no risks to social order this happens to a much lesser extent. It should be mentioned here that different sections of society can make a problem of the same phenomenon in very different ways and, as a result, can develop widely differing and even conflicting socio-political strategies.[1]

In the following pages we shall be examining the reasons why both the urban elites and the central government towards the end of the *ancien régime* were increasingly inclined to perceive the 'orderlessness', 'idleness' and 'immorality' among broad sections of the population as core aspects of the 'social problem' and what effects their intervention produced, paying particular attention to the reactions of the most prominent target-group, the proletariat.

The maintenance of order and forced labour

The urban magistrates defined the social problem in the first place in terms of lawlessness. They noted that criminality was increasing hand over fist. The growing number of brawls between individuals did not worry them, since such conflicts were no threat to public order. It is not impossible that they even considered individual violence as a release for latent social tensions, since they punished the perpetrators increasingly less often: in Ghent the number of sentences dropped from 33 per cent in 1755 to 14 per cent between 1775 and 1784. The aldermen, however, were greatly alarmed by the increase in crimes involving property. In Antwerp and Bruges the average number of thefts, burglaries and similar felonies rose during the second half of the eighteenth century from 15 to 25 per year, and in Ghent it actually rose from 18 to 37 per year.[2] Most of the victims belonged to the lower middle classes and the objects stolen were generally of limited value, but that had nothing to do with it: private property was sacred. Anyone who misappropriated another man's possessions undermined one of the fundamentals of social order and could not, as a result, expect clemency. The order promulgated in 1767 put it very clearly: 'Among the crimes that most offend against the rights of a civilized society and those of natural law, theft has always been punished severely in our provinces of the Low Countries.' 'The maintenance of public order demands that thieves be severely punished', was the reasoning of the Empress Maria Theresa, 'particularly when it involves servant girls, since they cause their masters not only material damage, but they violate, moreover, the trust placed in them; the judges should therefore be implacable and impose the death sentence.'[3] The city sentencing records show that thieves were indeed given heavy sentences, even when they had stolen only small sums or objects of limited value; both men and women were punished by public floggings and lengthy periods of banishment.

The problem, however, was that the gangs that went shoplifting consisted mainly of children. Youth was certainly not in principle a mitigating circumstance. When the draft law concerning the punishment of theft was being discussed in 1767, one member of the Privy Council asked whether it would not be advisable to stipulate that the life of a minor should be spared; he was thinking of the sons of well-to-do parents who were apprenticed to a merchant. The proposal was rejected, because the majority were of the opinion that leniency would encourage criminality among the young; the parents had simply to put in a plea for mercy.[4] Yet the city magistrates never sentenced a minor to death for theft or burglary. They knew that broad sections of the population took account of both the nature of the crime and the age of the delinquent and that the execution of young people provoked a great deal of resistance. Even a public flogging could lead to riots, as the Antwerp aldermen discovered in December 1767 when they sent a 17-year-old serving-maid to the whipping-post.

The fight against youth crime was not a simple task therefore. 'How are we to teach a lesson to "scoundrels" of 13, 14 or 15 years old and set them once more upon the right path,' asked the aldermen in desperation, 'if we cannot impose corporal punishment without having public opinion thrown at our heads? How are we to discipline them without being accused of excessive severity and bringing our fatherly authority into disrepute?' The absence of an extensive and professional police force indeed implied that the petition of discipline was highly dependent on the degree to which the ruling classes were able to count on the approval and cooperation of the other social groups.

The 'paternalism' of the aldermen was to be further put to the test by another form of objectionable behaviour, namely the increasing destructiveness of young people, for which there was clearly no remedy. More and more urban youths tried to vent their frustrations during the 1770s and 1780s by inflicting damage on private and public property. There was a flood of complaints about vandalism, in spite of all the interdictions and punitive measures. In 1770 the magistrate of Antwerp offered a reward of one hundred guilders for any information that led to the arrest of the 'rogues' who had destroyed some street lanterns. In 1774 he forbade, on pain of a heavy fine and imprisonment, 'the throwing of stones, festoons, balls or other materials, the casting out or breaking of window panes . . . including those of the lanterns, and writing, damaging or daubing the walls, doors or windows of buildings'; parents were held responsible for their children and guardians for their wards. In 1777 he stipulated that youths who dared 'to throw stones, sods or other dirt from the ramparts and other places at each other or at passers-by' would thenceforth be considered as disturbers of the peace. In 1781 he announced that youths who were 'so audacious as to remove the wooden barrels which collected the water that ran down from the roof guttering' would be clapped into jail without mercy; anyone who caught such a vandal in the act and denounced him to the court officials would receive a reward of fifty guilders, and anonymity would be respected – and so on, and so on.

The city fathers of Brussels, Bruges and Ghent also had their hands full with the fight against vandalism. During the course of the 1770s they continually repeated that anyone causing an affray, or who damaged houses or churches, destroyed cultivated flowers and plants or committed other acts of vandalism would not only have to make good the damage but also pay a heavy fine: if he was caught again he would be put in the pillory. It was a waste of time, as the aldermen declared in 1785: vandalism among the young rose to proportions previously unheard of. In the large towns of the county of Flanders things were no different. Year after year it was forbidden to daub the walls of houses 'with coal, red or black earth, chalk or similar materials' or to inscribe 'indecent' drawings upon them, to rattle doorbells, to shove in windows, to break the glass panes of the street lamps, to smash the coping stones on quay-walls and bridges, to break open the drain-hole covers, to work loose the iron chains hanging at the corners of market squares, to chop the trees on the city embankments, and so on. The patrols did their best. They arrested numerous street violators who were punished – but it achieved nothing. There was no stopping the youths.

The continual appearance of new groups of criminal or vandalistic young men worried the city magistrates to such an extent that they tried to put a brake on any kind of public amusement that might lead to the formation of gangs. Everywhere children were forbidden to play 'wild' games on the street, which in concrete terms meant that they could not 'bounce balls, play with spinning tops, stroke or flick them with whips, fly kites, shoot with bow and arrow' – all on pain of a fine, which had to be paid by their parents or guardians. Youths who dared to parade around in the evening or at night making a noise with drums, or in some other way, were threatened with a stay in prison on bread and water. The same applied to those who processed through the city in costume after 6 o'clock in the evening.[5]

Increasing 'orderlessness' was just one aspect of the social problem. The impoverishment of the urban proletariat was accompanied by increasing beggary, since on the one hand the competition on the labour market was growing stiffer – as a result of progressive proletarianization and population growth – and on the other the charitable institutions had insufficient funds to support all those in need. Initially the authorities limited themselves to regulating begging more strictly. They specified that only people who, because of old age, invalidity or other factors, were unfit for work and who had lived in the town for many years were eligible for a licence to beg; those concerned also had to give proof of good behaviour and morals and they had to carry a registration number. The court officials were given the task of arresting unemployed newcomers and removing them from the town. Anyone who did not have a

Plate 10 J. Buys, *The Old Beggar*, late eighteenth century. At the end of the *ancien régime* begging was forbidden in the large towns. However, despite all the interdictions, the phenomenon could not be eradicated.

licence and still continued to ask for alms was considered as a vagrant and prosecuted as such.

During the 1770s urban entrepreneurs gradually began to plead for an economic approach to pauperism. The fight against beggary was in their opinion not simply a question of enforcement. It came down to compelling idlers to work for the lowest possible wages. The new system of general charity as sketched out by François-Joseph Taintenier, a textile entrepreneur and alderman of the town of Ath, offered the possibility of increasing the supply of cheap labour, since it was based on a combination of four elements: a strict interdiction on begging, centralization of charitable funds, accurate registration of those in need and strict selection of those to receive charity. A social policy that was essentially towards regulating the labour market could of course be realized only in centres where industry provided a lot of employment. For instance, the aldermen of Brussels did not think it opportune to mobilize the 'scum' of society, because lace-making was the only branch of the capital's textile industry which employed large numbers of women and children. In important textile centres such as Bruges, Ghent and Antwerp, on the other hand, a reorganization of the poor relief along Taintenier's lines enabled part of the 'reserve army' to be integrated into the labour market.

It is possible that the aldermen of Bruges used the Council for the Eradication of Beggary mainly as an instrument for controlling and disciplining paupers with a view to social and political stability, but with other city magistrates it was generally economic motives that were uppermost. In Ghent, Taintenier's programme was put into practice on 17 May 1777. Begging was forbidden and stringent criteria were laid down for the granting of charitable relief. All those who were fit and able to work had to report within 14 days; if they did not, they would be classed as vagrants. This also applied to children who had reached the age of eight. Anyone who then continued to beg or live the life of a vagabond spent six days in prison – and if the offence was repeated it meant three years in the provincial penitentiary. Anyone who gave alms had to pay a fine of six guilders. Unemployed outsiders under the age of six who lived in Ghent and who had no means of subsistence had to leave within three days. The court officials did their duty: the number of beggars arrested rose from two in 1776 to 31 in 1777 and even to 54 in 1781. In Antwerp a similar policy was put into force on 29 July 1779, where economic considerations were also the deciding factors. Barely two weeks after the establishment of the *Nieuwe Bestiering van den Algemeynen Armen* ('New Administration for the General Poor'), 18 textile manufacturers requested the directors to send them four hundred able-bodied persons in need. Four years later the aldermen declared proudly that the new system had enabled several entrepreneurs to cut the wages of their employees drastically, 'because they were persuaded to take on more than before, since the individuals receiving charitable benefit are obliged to work without interruption throughout the entire week instead of working but a few days and begging the rest of the time.'[6]

In both cities the authorities conducted a vigorous campaign against all forms of popular entertainment that brought with it 'time-wasting'. On 19 February 1778 the Ghent magistrate forbade dancing parties in hostelries unless official permission had been obtained first, which cost so much money that it was only the better-off customers who could permit themselves the luxury of a ball. A year later, popular celebrations themselves were attacked. The directors of the new charitable relief institution argued that 'many overseers from every business found themselves almost without workers during the fairs' and that in consequence it was necessary to replace the eight parish fairs, which lasted all of nine days, by one single festival for the purpose of 'making the general public forget about such frivolities and turn their minds to work.' On 1 December 1779 – thus more than six years before Joseph II promulgated his notorious edict on public fairs – the city fathers stipulated that thenceforth only the fair of St Baaf could be celebrated. In 1780 they did away with the right of orphans to hold an annual jay shoot (which was just a pursuit 'to indulge their playfulness') and they gave the court officials an order to note closely on what days and at what times schoolchildren had free time.[7] These measures not only carried the approval of the entrepreneurs, they were also applauded by the clergy, because they closely connected idleness with immorality. In a pastoral letter the Bishop of Ghent emphasized the beneficial effects of the new social policy:

> Not only do we see that there are far fewer men and women staggering about under the influence of drink and that the number of brawls, blasphemies and 'acts of lechery' have decreased to a considerable extent but we see, moreover, that those who once spent their lives in disgraceful idleness are now usefully employing their able-bodied limbs and are laudably spending their time doing profitable work.[8]

The aldermen of Antwerp lost no time in issuing a whole series of orders to put a brake on popular entertainments and to discipline youths on the street. It was forbidden to mount theatrical entertainments in hostelries or private residences without the prior consent of the city administration, to make music in public, to organize masked balls and to play on the streets during working hours. Workers could no longer even parade through the town on 'Lost Monday' (1st after Epiphany) to offer New Year's greetings, since the money they pulled in would be used only for 'drinking and otherwise uselessly squandered'.[9] But the city administration went too far when, on 24 January 1780, they proscribed all carnival celebrations. The populace reacted with indignation to the argument that the 'excesses of Shrove Tuesday were old relics of paganism, intolerable in a well-policed town and even in conflict with good citizenship.' The Lenten letter that Bishop Wellens published the day after, in which he applauded the proscription, aroused more bad blood. Everywhere in the town acts of 'great malice' were committed, which reached a high point on Monday 27 January, when the law enforcers were attacked by a crowd of young 'scoundrels' and put to flight. A detachment of 130 soldiers and three cannons were not enough to quell the rebellious youths. They paraded through the streets with a life-sized caricature, the inscription beneath which left little to the imagination: 'Wellens what a nose is that!' Next day, things really got lively. Hundreds of masked youths and girls turned up with drums at the Market Square, where they pelted the town hall with mud, stones, excrement and dead cats. A high court official, who tried to calm them down, was beaten with sticks and chased all the way to the cathedral. Since both the civil and military authorities shrank from opening fire on young people, they decided to withdraw the interdiction, after which peace was restored. They had learned their lesson from the 'Shrove Tuesday Uproar'. Only five youths were arrested and four of them were later pardoned; the fifth had to spend three months in jail. In the Shrove Tuesday letters of the following years Wellens said not another word about 'heathen' carnival celebrations, and the city administration made no further attempt to forbid them.[10]

The city magistrates also turned their attentions to visiting the tavern. In common with the employers, they found that the 'Jenever Plague' was causing great damage to the economy. The demand for cheap manufactured goods was dropping because of it and discipline at work was being undermined by it; according to numerous (bourgeois) eye-witnesses, more and more proletarians were turning up in a drink-befuddled condition for work on Monday mornings or did not turn up at all. Moreover, they subscribed to the complaints of the clergy, who considered the increasing alcoholism as a threat to spiritual and moral order. Two factors in particular made the 'gin palace' the antithesis of everything the church stood for: it enticed many people away from religious services and promoted both alcohol abuse and relaxation in mixed company, a combination that led to adultery and premarital sex and in consequence contributed to the break-up of the family. The clergy had since the end of the seventeenth century conducted a vigorous campaign against the so-called *conventicula* – the meeting of boys and girls in taverns for the purpose of dancing, drinking, having a laugh and other 'frivolous' reasons – but the evil seemed to be ineradicable. In 1779, the year in which the *Nieuwe Bestiering* (as the new regulations were called) came into being, Bishop Wellens noted to his horror that it was taking an ever greater hold. In sharp words he warned the poor about

all that public intercourse in which many of you, through your lechery, drunkenness, quarrelling, cursing and swearing, do so bitterly offend against God; intercourse which is all too common among your sort, and which is the source of your downfall and of all that misery into which you are plunged, both body and soul.[11]

However, the aldermen were not at all inclined to restrict the number of taverns or to hit out at their customers. Since the community chest was filled principally with the excise duties on alcoholic drinks, they had an interest in the high consumption of beer and jenever. While they did oblige the innkeepers to close earlier than previously, and placed all manner of restrictions on them, it was just a matter of paying lip service to the employers and the clergy, because they seldom prosecuted anyone. The few sentences that were passed involved persons who had a lot more on their records than being drunk.

The same applied to gambling. Of course the urban administrations made all the possible gambling games a matter for prosecution, because 'many children are so misled by the seductive appearance of winnings that they not only waste their time and money, but even steal from their parents and others', as the city fathers of Antwerp explained.[12] However, they did not prosecute a single gambler unless he caused scandal or was receiving charitable benefit. Those on relief had otherwise to watch their step: they were not allowed to visit any drinking house on pain of being struck from the poor list – and a close check was kept on them.

It fell to the almoners of the *Armenkamer* to separate the 'worthy' paupers from the 'unworthy' ones, which in concrete terms meant that, in addition to formal standards, they employed moral selection criteria. Anyone who did not act according to the book – thus did not conform to the accepted norms and values – forfeited his 'right' to benefit and could even be put under lock and key. From the Antwerp sources it seems that the almoners, shortly after the setting up of the *Nieuwe Bestiering*, embarked on a real moral crusade. They visited the families in need, interrogated the neighbours, consulted with the parish priest and drew up a written report whenever they came across 'deviations': a beggar, a profiteer, a work-shy son, an objectionable or scandalous wife, a rowdy troublemaker . . .

The confinement requests of the almoners were always granted. After he had been abused in the street by the wife of Zacharias Kittevilder because he had refused to give her charitable benefit, an almoner by the name of Tassart went to the magistrate with a request to place the woman in an institution, on which occasion he mentioned that Zacharias had also complained about her misbehaviour; the aldermen made no further enquiries and sent the woman for a year to Vilvoorde. Frans Erckels was more severely punished. When his request for benefit came to nothing and he shouted out in public that 'the money for the poor was not being given to us citizens but to outsiders', the almoners reacted vigorously: they interrogated the neighbours, noted from them that Erckels was separated from his wife, spent his days in the tavern and went begging; the aldermen then made an order for him to be placed for two years in the house of correction, which was promptly enacted. The almoner who was insulted by Franciscus Van Campen was also able to count on the cooperation of the neighbours: they damned him for a brutal rogue and an incorrigible drunkard; he even sold the shirt off his back so he could drink. 'Recently he tricked me out of a loaf of bread under the pretext that it was for the poor relief administrators', the baker revealed. The verdict: two years behind bars. Woe betide those of the poor who did not pay the necessary respect to the clergy, as 57-year-old weaver Joannes Zaeyers found out: two years' hard labour was not too much 'to enforce and strengthen the authority of the Reverend Fathers', argued the almoners; the aldermen agreed.

Those on benefit who received goods in kind from the almoners and later sold them off or brought them to the *Berg van Barmhartigheid*, the public pawnshop, ran great risks. The almoners took such 'thieves' to court, which automatically meant a prison sentence: two weeks for the cotton-spinner Maria Catharina Fleger, who had taken a new dress to the pawnbroker; six weeks for Maria Barbara Vanopbergen, although she was able to prove that she earned too little from cotton-spinning to support both herself and her young daughter; two months for the 19-year-old Helena Okkaert, who had pawned a new shirt and a new apron; three months for the widow Anna De Clopper, who had sold a pair of stockings and the bedding.

The directors of the *Nieuwe Bestiering* sometimes considered confinement as a means of preventing worse happening. For example, Catharina Cornelis who, according to Canon Beeckmans, led a 'godless, abominable and debauched life', was sent to Vilvoorde because it was feared that during her 'excesses' she might cause injury. In the case of Adriana Jennes the motives were somewhat less pure: drinking and immorality had, according to the almoners, ravaged her body to such an extent that 'her constitution had totally deteriorated' (a euphemism for venereal disease). 'Shut her away', ran their advice, 'otherwise we shall have to look after her at the cost of the poor-relief fund'; the magistrate complied.[13]

We know that it was not only the almoners who used confinement as a means of discipline; individuals did the same and much more often. If we add to this the growing numbers who were put under lock and key for theft, we can quite well understand that the magistrates of the large towns in Brabant and Flanders during the 1780s counted themselves fortunate that there were provincial penitentiaries. The urban houses of correction could no longer absorb the growing tide of thieves, beggars and 'debauched' proletarians. The initiative nonetheless did not come from the local administrations but from central government. Why?

New ideas on punishment

In the eyes of most government officials the social problem was synonymous with beggary and vagrancy, two plagues that, according to them, formed a breeding-ground for street vandalism and thieving. Their growing disquiet was expressed in intense activity with regard to legislation. The orders were largely not put into effect, however. How could it be otherwise? The legal authorities were extraordinarily fragmented. The policing apparatus was insufficient. The lower court officials did not spend much time on a prosecution for fear of increasing the costs thereof; many of them were otherwise unqualified and some even corrupt. Now and then *traques*, or round-ups, were organized – but their success depended on the extent to which the local population was willing to cooperate, and there was not much enthusiasm to be expected from that quarter; some villagers feared reprisals and others found that the sentences handed out, from long-term banishment to hanging, were out of proportion to the crimes.[14] In 1771 Goswin de Fierlant, a leading jurist and member of the Privy Council, brought things out into the open. The policy had utterly failed: 'For three centuries now, people have been trying to eradicate mendicancy in this country and to purge it of idlers, disreputable persons and vagabonds, almost all of whom commit crime, and for this entire period such work has been utterly in vain.'[15]

Jean-Jacques Philippe Vilain XIIII had already realized much earlier that the classic 'remedies' had been useless. As the Mayor of Aalst and chairman of the administrative council of the 'Land of Aalst', he had been confronted in the years 1745–8 with all sorts of banditry, and he had noted that round-ups and punitive measures were not sufficient to enforce existing laws, let alone prevent the formation of new gangs. For this reason he pleaded in 1751 not only for the setting up of a professional police force, but also for the building of a provincial penitentiary, where loafers and idlers could be re-educated.

> Obviously we must deal with beggars and vagabonds severely, since they steal from the state and the citizenry, but corporal punishment and banishment do not make them better people. We must put idlers and loafers under lock and key, teach them a trade and put them to work. The new institution must on the other hand be so fearful in character that they will accept any sort of work from fear of being confined therein.[16]

This was a new approach to the social problem, because beggars and vagabonds were up to this time simply flogged and banished. There were certainly prisons, but these did not function as penal institutions; they served mainly as remand centres for people awaiting or undergoing trial for crimes of which they were either suspected or accused. Vilain XIIII took a step forward by making the training and improvement of the detainees a central issue. Indeed, during the first half of the seventeenth century several town councils had set up shredding and spinning houses for the purpose of bringing idlers and loafers back to an orderly life. At that time, however, the emphasis lay both on forced labour as a means of discipline and on the gainful employment of the detainees. With Vilain XIIII on the other hand, re-education and integration were the most important issues. Despite this he could not shake himself completely free of traditional attitudes. Poor relief and repression went hand in hand, according to him, since both the 'work-shy' paupers and criminals alike had to be put under lock and key. The provincial penitentiary thus had to function as an institution for improvement *and* as a penal establishment. Although the project was not realized during the 1750s for completely different reasons, its incoherent character mortgaged future developments. Fierlant was especially vehement in his opposition to the creation of dual-purpose institutions.

As far as the reform of penal law was concerned, Fierlant and Vilain XIIII were still largely on the same side. Both considered the removal of a person's liberty as being preferable to corporal punishment as a means of controlling beggary and vagrancy. Most local notables and magistrates, however, did not wish to do away with the traditional punitive measures because they considered them to be a necessary backup for their positions of power. All attempts at softening trial practices fizzled out during the 1750s. Yet the government proved to be tenacious. In September 1764 Chancellor Kaunitz began a new offensive, this time in relation to the discussions on the abolition of the rack and branding. Plenipotentiary minister Karl von Cobenzl, who had been strongly influenced by the publications of Voltaire and Cesare Beccaria (whose book caused a considerable stir when it appeared in 1764), immediately got to work and sent a communiqué to the Provincial Councils, which first decided to consult the Estates (thus the political representatives of their province). The reactions were very negative. Most of the deputies declared that they had no objection to the confinement of beggars and vagabonds, but only on condition that they were made subject to a regime of hard labour and above all that corporal punishment remained.[17] There need be no argument that such a standpoint was in direct conflict with enlightened ideas about re-education and integration.

The government decided to drop the matter for the time being and wait for a more favourable opportunity.

Around 1770 the time was ripe for reopening the debate. The draft law of 1765 on poor relief had produced few results, if any at all. The number of vagrant paupers remained on the increase. More and more crimes against property were being committed in both town and country. It was clear that things could go no further. Fierlant was charged by the Privy Council with convincing the magistracy that 'something' had to be done urgently, in particular with regard to trial practices. In 1771 he drew up two memoranda, one entitled *Observations on torture* and the other *Observations on the insufficiencies and inconveniences of corporal punishment and on the advantages there would be by replacing it with houses of correction.*[18] In the same year, Vilain XIIII brought out a report which he had drawn up at the request of the Estates of Flanders (of which he had in the meantime become president). Whereas with Fierlant criminal arguments were of central importance, with Vilain XIIII the emphasis lay on the corrective aspect of the removal of liberty, as can clearly be seen from the title of his treatise *Memorandum on the means of correcting malefactors and idlers to their own advantage and of making them useful to the state*. He was above all stuck on the able-bodied beggars who tramped from one village to the next, damaged woods and new plantations and misappropriated food and fuel. These 'good-for-nothings', whom he dubbed professional vagabonds, swindlers who passed on their trade from one generation to the next, caused damage to the state not only through their refusal to work but also by pestering people for alms. Removal of their liberty and forced labour were the most suitable strategies to deal with all this – to put a check on vagrancy, to call a halt to criminality and to stimulate the economy. Discipline and re-education had to go hand in hand as well. All detainees had to receive training which would put them in a position to be integrated into society at some later stage. In this way employers would finally have enough workers at their disposal and could then exert pressure on wages. Did people realize that there were 64,681 rural persons in need in the county of Flanders and that more than half of them were fit and able for work? Experience had taught that corporal punishment and banishment were ineffective. It came down to making idlers into useful workers and that was possible only in houses of correction. 'Mobilize this reserve army', went his conclusion, 'and a host of new workers, coming from the centre for mendicancy and idleness, will contribute by competition to reducing the cost of labour.'[19]

Although he was a supporter of confinement, Fierlant did not approve the approach of Vilain XIIII. He not only rejected the latter's suggestion to grant wide powers to the directors of the new penitentiaries (and in

Plate 11   J. Van Dulken, *The Vagabond*, 1774 (after P. Van Neck, 1698). According to
the elite the social problem was synonymous with beggary and vagrancy, two plagues that
in their eyes constituted a breeding-ground for street vandalism and theft.

consequence the provincial Estates that appointed them) in regard to
punishment and removal of liberty, which he considered an impermissible infringement of the prerogative of the Crown, but he was also
opposed to his plan to put the most diverse groups of people under lock
and key. No one, he argued, could be put into a house of correction
unless they had been tried in the proper manner:

> In justice, one cannot confine any inhabitant of the province as an idler, at
> least until he has been recognized and declared as such by a judge with
> authority to do so. Many of the poor ask for alms not because they do not
> wish to work, but because no one will employ them. It would be a matter
> of excessive severity, even of injustice, to lock up such people.

A watertight dividing-line had to be drawn between those in need on the
one hand and criminals on the other. A mixing of both groups led to
legal uncertainty and was pernicious from a social point of view. Poor
relief was one thing, enforcement another. Every suspect had the right to
a proper trial, with the exception of the notorious vagabonds, who
could, without close investigation, be locked up after a short procedure
– even if no specific misdeed could be laid to their charge.[20]

There was thus no consensus as to the target groups. That people
without any means of subsistence and without fixed abode belonged in
a house of correction was not under discussion – but what was to be
done with destitute people who were fit for work, who belonged to an
urban or rural community and who asked for alms? Certainly, the law
of 1765 stipulated that men and women who were of sound body and
mind might under no circumstances go begging. Most local administrations had, however, made no attempt to put the social provisions into
practice, so that those in need often had no other choice than to ask for
alms. Was it possible to round them up and put them to work in a house
of correction? Yes, according to Vilain XIIII, for it was being done in
their best interests; they would after all be receiving training in a house
of correction. No, as maintained by Fierlant, for incarceration implies
that there has been an infringement of the law *and* a condemnatory
sentence, by which the punitive measure must be in proportion to the
crime. Public workplaces must be brought into being in the new
institutions where men and women who have no income can turn up
every day to do paid labour. Since they are volunteers who have
committed no wrong, they must be kept separate from the detainees and
must under no circumstances be locked up. It should not be forgotten
that

> unjust incarceration is the most revolting thing in the world; it is a violent
> assault upon the liberty of the citizen, it plunges the honest man into an
> abyss of horror and brings upon him and his family a plague which the
> most detailed justification would never be able to cure completely.

This was why he paid so much attention to preventive custody, by which
he made a distinction between a civil judgement and a criminal decree.
In the former case it was a question of persons who were suspected or
accused of small infringements of the law; they had either to be placed

under house arrest or in a 'suitable' institution. The criminal decree was applicable only if the person arrested was a vagabond or if the judge strongly suspected or was certain that a serious crime had been committed; such delinquents/suspects had to be confined in prison.[21]

As to confinement on request, Fierlant and Vilain XIIII showed little interest. This is not surprising, since both reformers were preoccupied mainly with the social consequences of the dislocation processes taking place in the countryside, in particular the increase in vagrancy. However much they differed in opinion with each other, their target groups had nothing to do with the men and women who were locked up at the request of their relatives. The latter formed a very heterogeneous category of people, as regards both social background and the behaviour being objected to. Many of them, it is true, came from the less well-off sections of the population and had overstepped the norms to which the authorities attached so much importance, but they did not come from families of drifters, they were not destitute and they had committed no crime punishable under the law. Since they were not perceived and defined as problem cases at national or provincial level, the discourses of the higher administrative councils contained no elements to which the families who wanted to enter a petition for confinement could relate.

The new attitudes to the disciplinary functions of houses of correction nonetheless came up to the needs and expectations of numerous individuals. With both Fierlant and Vilain XIIII expulsion or punishment were no longer of central importance, but the moral improvement of the detainees was: they had to be moulded body and soul by means of forced labour and continual supervision with an eye to changing their behaviour. Correction was also the precise aim of most petitioners who requested the aldermen to lock up a relative. The problem was that neither initiators nor central government had the intention of opening the new institutions for this category of unwanted person. The aldermen of the large towns saw things quite differently of course. They were after all confronted with a growing number of confinement petitions, and these were coming more and more from persons of very limited means, which meant on the one hand that they were being hounded to pay the costs thereof and on the other that the capacity of the urban correction houses was being squeezed. Their representatives did not neglect to bring the attention of central government to this question.

After much tussling between all the parties involved, the central government gave in: article 68 of the rule approved on 18 February 1773 by the Empress Maria Theresa gave permission to the directors of the provincial penitentiary in Ghent 'to take in children from families who led evil and debauched lives, with the authorization of their competent judge and subject to payment, on which they shall come to an agreement with the parents or guardians.'[22] In the Duchy of Brabant things were no different. The central government had tried in 1776 to persuade the Estates of this province to set up a house of correction, but the cities of Antwerp, Brussels and Louvain, which together formed its third member, were reluctant to burden themselves with the costs of doing it. In 1772 Charles of Lorraine urged them once more. He pointed out that the Estates of Flanders had in the meantime accepted the proposal of their president, Vilain XIIII, and that as a result the duchy (of Brabant) would be flooded with vagabonds if something were not done about it in time. The Estates of Brabant put up all kinds of opposition, but in June 1772 they finally declared themselves willing to foot the cost of building a new house of correction in Vilvoorde, near Brussels. They did make two conditions, however: there could be no products made in the new institution which might damage the trade of private enterprise, and it would be permitted to send men and women there who had committed no offence against the law. The magistrate at Antwerp made this last a *sine qua non*. 'The matter shall progress no further', he declared, 'unless we be able to send to Vilvoorde unruly or debauched persons, from whose behaviour there is danger or severe difficulty to be feared, even though they have not been proven to be guilty of a crime nor to have been begging on the streets.'[23] The central government agreed, provided the confinement took place after thorough investigation by authorized judges, who had to draw up a written order for confinement if they considered the family's complaint to be justified.

It should be made clear that the populations of the provincial penitentiaries were by definition an amalgam of heterogeneous elements. Regardless of the differences in age and sex, they consisted of three groups: criminals, 'unworthy' poor (thus vagabonds) and people who had been a nuisance to their housemates or relatives. Only the first two groups were imprisoned on the grounds of a court sentence passed upon them, even though in the case of vagrants it was without proper trial. What was the proportion of convicts to the number of people confined on request? In other words – what functions did the provincial penitentiaries fulfil in practice? Was the central government able to realize its primary purpose – namely, the reduction of beggary and vagrancy – through these institutions? Did the urban magistrates use them as instruments for backing up their social policy? To what extent did individuals make use of them for resolving their own problems? The one does not, of course, exclude the other. The social and political interventions of central government supported the interests of the urban magistrates insofar as they could be used as means of exerting pressure in disciplining the lower classes and in integrating them into the labour market. On the other hand the confinement requests put the aldermen in a position to act preventively; it was, after all, a question of *quaed gedragh* which was not formally a matter for prosecution, but about which they felt strongly because public order and/or the morality of work were being undermined by it. There was no question of a complete convergence of interests, however. Thus the question remains: who were the detainees?

Public and private: a contradiction?

Let us come straight to the point: the provincial penitentiaries fulfilled the purposes that Vilain XIIII and the representatives of central government had in mind only to a limited degree. Since their inception they housed large numbers of adults and minors who were confined there at the request of housemates or relatives. From February 1779 to the end of December 1784 – thus a period of about six years – 623 people were sent to Vilvoorde. No fewer than 211 – or almost 34 per cent – had committed no wrong; their relatives had asked for a deed of private confinement and been granted it. Most of them – 174, or 82.5 per cent – were city-dwellers. Brussels and Antwerp sent the largest contingents: respectively, 92 and 54, which gives us a total of 146. Confinement on request was thus a big-city phenomenon. This can also be seen from the fact that the aldermen of Brussels and Antwerp sent more people to the provincial penitentiary at the request of their relatives than they did convicts: 146 as against 136, or 52 against 48 per cent.

If we consider those who were imprisoned *ex officio* – those who were locked up by the courts – then we see, moreover, that the provincial house of correction served the interests of the local administrations much more than those of central government. Of the 412 convicts only 73 were vagabonds and *baanstropers* ('highwaymen') – i.e., barely 18 per cent. The largest group – 133 people, or 32 per cent of the total – had actually committed crimes against property, but in no way were they drifters. All of them were born or had lived many years in the community where they had committed the theft – and it is worthy of note that those from Brussels and Antwerp together formed the majority. The same applied to the 124 men and women (30 per cent of the total) who were sentenced because of immorality, begging or profligacy: all of them had a fixed abode and most came from the 'capitals' of the duchy, of which once more Brussels and Antwerp had the lion's share.[24]

It can therefore hardly be surprising that the magistrates of the large towns soon came to consider the new instrument of social control as indispensable. When the representatives of the nobility and the clergy voiced their doubts in 1785 as to the use of an institution that took in few vagrants and which cost the Estates a great deal of money, the third member indignantly rejected the criticism out of hand. It was true that expenses were higher than expected, but the provincial penitentiary had to stay at all costs, argued the Antwerp aldermen, since 'we have observed that many persons of this town, after having completed their sentence therein, have led irreproachable lives and have renounced their former unruliness.' This applied not only to criminals in the actual sense of the word, but also to the numerous 'libertines' who were put under lock and key by their relatives. A love of work was instilled into them in the institution, which caused them to behave as useful citizens when they were released, making a contribution to the family income and in consequence to the economy of the town.

> What should we do with young people who commit small misdeeds or who, according to their parents, lead unruly lives if they can no longer be sent to the provincial penitentiary? Has experience not taught us that things can go from bad to worse if people are whipped or banished? Re-education in a house of improvement is the only means to bring youths and girls back to the right path – those whose only crime was to have followed too inconsiderately their first impulses where the effervescence of their age led them to libertinous ways and to the excesses of whose consequences they were ignorant. This is why more than half the people we send to Vilvoorde have not yet attained their majority. Only the provincial house of correction affords an opportunity for disciplining and improving unrestrained youths.

Thus concluded the city fathers of Antwerp. Since the representatives of Brussels and Louvain spoke in similar vein, the nobility and clergy resigned themselves to the status quo.[25]

From the arguments of the Antwerp aldermen it can be deduced that they considered private confinement as an important aid in their fight against lawlessness in general and against criminality among the young in particular. The explanation is to be found partly in the social policy they had been carrying out since 1779. The main purpose of the *Nieuwe Bestiering* was the regulation of the labour market, which necessitated both a dogged fight against beggary and a strict selection of families to be supported on charitable relief. Anyone begging for alms or who did other things that were forbidden was automatically put under lock and key. The same applied to those on relief who led an unruly life. The problem was, however, that the almoners from the *Armenkamer* had a grip only on the destitute who were receiving benefit or who were hoping to be put on the list for it. In other words: only a minority of the urban proletariat could be controlled through poor relief. While most of the men, women and children who ended up in the provincial penitentiary belonged to the less well-off sections of the population, they did not

come from families on relief or even from destitute ones. Their housemates were active wage-earners or small shopkeepers, who on the one
hand earned too much to receive charitable or public relief, and on the
other too little to be able to pay the costs of confinement. They were
indirectly playing the card of the upper classes by denouncing forms of
behaviour that undermined the work ethic and yet were not indictable.
For example, work-shyness was not of itself an infringement of the law.
Since the aldermen were of the opinion that idleness was the devil's
plaything and attacked the very foundations of social order, they had an
interest in granting requests in which individuals complained about the
unwillingness of relatives to put their idle hands to work. The initiatives
of the petitioners allowed them not only to act in a preventive capacity,
but also afforded them the opportunity to emphasize that work was the
essential condition for improving one's personal lot in life. After 1779
the aldermen were even more amenable to such accusations than
previously, because the reorganization of poor relief had among other
things the purpose of increasing the supply of cheap labour.

The new social policy explains why during the 1780s the almoners
entered or supported in increasing numbers requests for confinement in
which unruly living that was not formally subject to prosecution was
the central issue. They often acted on their own authority or exerted
pressure on the family of the 'immoral' person to request his confinement. This was not always the case, however. Some petitioners declared
themselves grateful to the almoners because they would never have
dared take the initiative themselves. It is not easy to find out whether
they were speaking the truth or not. Was the mother of Antonius
Janssens, a 17-year-old weaver's journeyman, really happy to be rid of
her son? Her description of his objectionable behaviour gives rise to
doubts: Antonius was not only bone idle and a frequenter of taverns,
but he had also taken the weaving shuttle he had received from the
Nieuwe Bestiering to the public pawnshop. Did his mother really think
this offensive or did she play up to the almoners for fear that she would
lose her benefit (10.5 *stuiver* per week)? In contrast to such dubious
cases there are others which support the assumption that the intervention of the almoners was approved of, even applauded, by the family of
the person to be locked away. The thieving activities of 20-year-old
Jacob Van Linthout had brought his mother, a widow, into such
disrepute that not a single merchant-entrepreneur would entrust her
with silk for her to work, which meant she was not able to earn any
money; according to the almoners she did not dare make a formal
complaint because Jacob was terrorizing her. The wife of Joannes
Baptist Caffa, a shoemaker's assistant, would also probably have been
relieved when the almoners went to plead for his confinement: her

husband brutalized the whole family and was the cause of 'great troubles, difficulty and gossip in the neighbourhood'.

There were in addition proletarians who turned to the almoners of their own accord. The hat-maker's journeyman Benoit Poncet, for example, pleaded with them to put in a good word for him with the aldermen: although his wife was blind, she ought to be sent to Vilvoorde because she attacked him with anything she could lay her hands on and caused havoc in the home; the almoners made enquiries of the neighbours, who confirmed that Poncet had suffered for many years, and thereupon drew up a request for her confinement which was promptly granted. The wife of the previously mentioned Joannes Baptist Van Evenbroeck also called in their help: 'During his stay in the provincial penitentiary I never had cause to make appeal to you', she wrote, 'but since his release I have been living in misery, since he drinks his way through my wages and those of the children. Therefore I pray you: lock him away once more . . .' The almoners informed the magistrate, who immediately gave permission for the man's confinement.[26]

In short, the attitude of the almoners cannot be interpreted in a straightforward manner. It is true that they often acted repressively. This could hardly be otherwise, since it was part of their task to report beggars, to curb 'abuses' of the benefit system and to ensure that those on relief behaved in a 'civilized' fashion. However, they did not use confinement exclusively as a means of social control or always for the purpose of disciplining paupers. Sometimes they turned to the aldermen at the express request of families who wanted to be rid of a troublesome burden, where socio-political considerations played no part, as the Poncet case shows. How are these interventions to be explained? It is possible and even probable that the magistrate granted these petitions because they had been entered by the almoners: but why did the aldermen also appear well disposed towards individuals who took the initiative themselves and made objection to patterns of behaviour which fell outside the framework of the social policy? They were certainly not keen on granting such requests, since in most cases it was the city that had to foot the bill for the costs of confinement. Why did the petitioners involved seldom, if ever, receive a negative answer to their requests?

The relationship of public and private was of crucial importance in private confinement cases. The authorities had to be convinced that the objectionable behaviour was no longer merely a private matter and that, as a result, confinement served the public interest. Complaints about theft or idleness were taken seriously, of course. If, however, the accusations involved patterns of behaviour to which the authorities did not take serious exception, because they took place within the domestic circle, then the petitioners had to make them out be 'problematical' – in other words, to show that the unwanted person not only made their lives a living hell, but that he/she also caused scandal, threatened to cause accidents or constituted a danger to society in some other way. People had to try and make it clear that it was not simply a question of a family affair and that, by putting an end to such domestic misery, the aldermen were acting as city fathers, as the guardians of standards and values on which a *policed* society, a well-ordered society, was based.

Sight should not be lost of the fact that there was a great, great deal at stake for the petitioners. If the case fizzled out, then they could expect acts of revenge from the unwanted person, which would entirely poison the atmosphere within the family. This is why they had to build up as convincing an argument as possible and embroider those points to which they knew or assumed that the magistrate was particularly susceptible, which meant that they had the greatest interest in their petitions in subscribing to the standards and values which the authorities themselves employed and in laying emphasis on patterns of behaviour that bordered on the criminal or which at least were branded as serious infractions of Christian morality. Well-to-do families knew how to crack the whip, of course. They could appeal to specialists, moreover: advocates, notaries or, in the case of insanity, doctors. It does not follow from this that members of the lower middle classes and wage-earners entered requests which were less well founded. They employed the services of a public scribe and he was seldom lost for words. Differences have been noted between requests signed with a cross and the others. The former generally contain more concrete details and have been written with sharper wording than the latter. In both cases, however, the emphasis is on the public scandal that the unwanted person was causing, and it is argued that the petitioners are acting in accordance with society's rules of behaviour and patterns of expectation. The public scribes thus knew just as well as the jurists to what arguments the magistrate would be inclined to attach importance.

Since those who were drawing up the request had to use the language of authority to have a chance of succeeding, they usually tried to criminalize the behaviour of the person to be locked up. 'Though our son is no scoundrel in the real sense of the word, he is treading the wrong path', argued most proletarians. Their pronouncements can seldom be verified, but it is not a question here of whether the youth really had something to answer for. The point is that the aldermen were deeply preoccupied with increasing criminality among the young and that they were in consequence inclined to take such complaints and insinuations seriously. Even when the neighbours made no mention of thieving activities, the aldermen granted requests for confinement. It in any case involved a rebellious youth, as the witnesses testified, and it was preferable to act in a preventive capacity. Parents furthermore had a traditional right to punish disobedient children.

The amenable disposition of the authorities must also be ascribed partly to the fact that parent–child conflicts were becoming much more numerous in their own environment. They could hardly put members of the *jeunesse dorée* under lock and key for profligacy or a deliberate *mésalliance* and then refuse to grant the requests of parents from the less well-off sections of society. If they wanted to maintain the ideal of an 'organic society' or at least keep up the appearance of paternalism, then they had to be consistent.

Now we have come to an important aspect of confinement on request. The socio-political interventions of the urban magistrates had unforeseen consequences. As the authorities used increasingly broader definitions of 'unsociable behaviour', so individuals found it easier to include their problem cases under this heading, particularly since all sorts of aspects were grouped together in the official discourses: both forms of unruly living that might pose risks for social and political order and infractions of morality that constituted no real threat, but which were given a place for ideological reasons – namely, to move the clergy to support the disciplinary offensive of the civil authorities. Such arguments were an invitation to families who were having problems with one of their members to intervene. Arguments that justified the confinement of the unwanted person were being handed to them on a plate. The aldermen could not refuse requests in which deviations were the central issue and which they themselves denounced without denying their own principles. For example, they were not so keen on prosecuting gamblers in court, but they could hardly refuse to put them under lock and key when individuals asked them to: it was indeed an infringement of the law.

From the substantive descriptions of objectionable behaviour it can be deduced that many petitioners deliberately used the language of authority to rid themselves of an unwanted person. It is not purely by chance that so many men branded their wives as public whores: they knew that prostitution was punishable by law and they did not neglect to remind the aldermen of this fact, at which point they invariably laid emphasis on the scandal that their partner was causing. This last point was of the utmost importance, since the city magistrates usually let prostitutes go on their way so long as they did not give offence or commit serious crime. Some petitioners explained that the parish priest could testify that they were speaking the truth, which was enough to win them their case in advance. The clergy after all had been fulminating in every way possible against 'moral corruption', which according to them was becoming ever more widespread, and the civil authorities could not permit themselves to deny this viewpoint. In other cases the aldermen felt themselves obliged to grant a request because neighbouring residents openly let it be known that they would not tolerate a public whore in their midst. The impression is inescapable that married prostitutes had less to fear from court officials than from their husbands and the neighbours. If they caused a nuisance in any way, they could not expect much tolerance in their own social environment.[27]

It should be clear now that petitioners often took advantage of official discourses and that they succeeded in getting the authorities tangled up in their own ideological nets. It does not necessarily follow from this that the person to be locked up was accused falsely. It does mean, however, that the accusations that were most emphasized in the requests were not always the ones that weighed most heavily with the petitioners; for strategic reasons it might have been preferable to present their real motives as additional elements. Was the husband of Catharina Koets, a lace worker, speaking the truth when he petitioned the magistrate at Antwerp to put her under lock and key because she was an 'incorrigible whore'? Or was it her infidelity, of which mention was made only as a subsidiary item, that was the deciding factor? The statements of the witnesses – all of them relatives – do not enable us to get to the real heart of the matter. What are we to think in the case of another resident of Antwerp who accused his wife of a whole series of misdeeds, including shoplifting, after which he mentioned 'in passing' that she had 'also' had an extramarital affair?[28] Where does the husband's jealousy begin and the wife's virtue end?

The city magistrates were aware of the fact that some of the petitioners were using improper or even false pretexts to achieve their aim, as can be seen from several case refusals. They were, however, able to see that the complaints were baseless, or at least dubious, only if the various parties involved (in particular, the witnesses) made conflicting statements, which seldom happened, or if the insanity of the unwanted person was not backed up by a medical attestation; in this last case the director of the city's mental institution had to make an examination of the patient. It is therefore not surprising that abuses arose. People were taken for mad and locked away who had nothing wrong with them at all, but such cases appear to have been the exception to the rule. Most of the requests and statements by witnesses contain so many salient details which were so easy to verify that there could be little doubt as to the seriousness of the case.

This does not lessen the fact that the interests of the petitioners and those of the authorities often converged, at least up to a point. On the one hand, the processes of proletarianization and impoverishment were lowering the tolerance thresholds of broad sections of the community with regard to all sorts of 'unruly living' and were undermining the efficiency of infra-judicial practices, whereby interventions from higher authority were considered to be increasingly more necessary. On the other hand, the families concerned legitimized and strengthened the authority of the aldermen by voluntarily – that is to say, in the absence of alternatives – appealing to them to resolve their conflicts. Given the fact that the members of the lower middle classes and wage-earners usually took exception to behaviour that was considered a threat to public order or the morality of work, their actions fitted in with the social policy of the elites. Furthermore, confinement on request offered the last-mentioned the opportunity not only to put a check on 'deviations', but also to ascribe these to individual shortcomings: the people to be locked up were cancerous growths that affected the healthy parts of the social body and which therefore had to be removed. The causal relationship was being reversed: people with morally reprehensible behaviour were bringing about social tensions. Yet the rising number of requests for confinement in no way indicated an increasing readiness on the part of the lower classes to accept without demur the norms and values propagated by the authorities. From numerous requests it does seem that the official arguments were interpreted and used in a very selective manner: people played down some elements and emphasized others that suited their purposes nicely and to which they hoped the aldermen would be favourably disposed.

There can be no doubt that all the parties involved considered private confinement mainly as a means of disciplining and correcting the unwanted person, where the emphasis lay on moral improvement. It is possible that with some petitioners thoughts of vengeance were of primary importance – in other words, that they wanted to fight back, to repay pain with pain, to punish. That could seldom have been the only motive, however. People after all knew that it was only a temporary solution, that the unwanted person would be released after a time and take up his/her place in the family and in the community once more. Their pattern of expectation was much broader: the nuisance had to be brought to repentance by being disciplined or at least (re)moulded in such a way that the family could live in peace when they were reunited. As far as wage-earners were concerned, the aldermen also had an interest in ensuring that after their release they behaved in a civilized manner and that they would make themselves useful members of society. If we add to this that re-education and integration were the essential aims of Vilain XIIII in the creation of the provincial penitentiary at Ghent, then we are inclined to think that all the conditions had been fulfilled for hard but decent treatment of human beings. The gap between hope and reality, between theory and practice, can also be very great, however. Let us have a look at the daily conduct of affairs in the various institutions.

7

Sledge-Hammers and Treadmills

And what of the voices of the accused? The sources say nothing about the reactions of the unwanted. They could seldom, if ever, offer an explanation for their unusual or reprehensible way of life, and if they were given the chance then no one bothered to record their words. This applied both to those who were 'insane' and to those who were 'debauched'. In the first case the doctor who was consulted drew up a report in such brief and vague terms that it is impossible to gain any insight into the thoughts, feelings and emotions of the patient. In the second case there is scarcely more to be learned, since the aldermen limited themselves to an examination of the members of the family and a number of privileged witnesses. It is true that people in Bruges whose behaviour was challenged by housemates or relatives were given the opportunity to defend themselves, but their explanations were never written down.

It is, moreover, difficult to find out how the unwanted persons reacted to their confinement in a mental or penal institution. Once they found themselves in a 'house of improvement', they no longer had a right to be heard. They were gagged, at least in the sense that contacts with the outside world were made impossible or could take place only under strict supervision. The directors of the institutions generally forbade detainees to write letters and, if they did make an exception to the rule, then they were invariably censored. Visits from housemates and close relatives were sometimes allowed, but they by definition left no written traces. We have never come across any memoirs from people who had been confined. This is not surprising, since most of them had the greatest interest in keeping quiet about this dark period in their lives. Did their confinement not prove that they had acted in an anti-social manner?

While in the case of insanity moral disapproval was less outspoken and perhaps even absent, who would wish to rake over the coals after being released from the institution and risk being taken for a madman once more?

In any case, there can be no doubt that confinement was a painful and, frequently, even a traumatic experience. Most unwanted people ended up in a world that seemed like a foretaste of hell, even though there were many gradations to be found there. This was true both of the religious and of the public institutions, as can be seen from the letters that some detainees were able to smuggle out despite the strict surveillance, the testimonies presented to official investigation committees and the reports drawn up by priests and officials regarding the conditions in the reformatories. It could be assumed that the experiences of those confined varied according to their sex, age, financial situation and position. Thus people who were better off could most likely expect better treatment than proletarians, since both the choice of place and the care within that institution were dependent on the financial resources of the family. These differences, however real and important they might have been, nonetheless do not detract from the fact that an enforced sojourn in a mental or penal institution was an extraordinarily severe 'school' in which to learn to better one's ways. Before going on to give substantive details, we shall first say something about the duration of confinement.

Duration of confinement

In the Austrian Netherlands it was not possible for someone to be put under lock and key at the request of relatives for an unspecified time. The aldermen had to note down the duration of the confinement in their judgements and had scrupulously to ensure that that period was not exceeded. The law and reality often concurred, but not always. From 1710 up to and including 1769 the aldermen of Antwerp neglected to mention in 10 per cent of cases how many months or years the unwanted person had to serve in a reformatory. As far as the objectionable behaviour was concerned it involved a very heterogeneous group, including both the 'insane' and the 'debauched', but all of them were from the upper stratum of society, since the men were placed in a monastery run by the *Cellebroeders* and the women in a hospital run by the *Zwartzusters* (Black Sisters). Undoubtedly they ran the risk of being completely forgotten about. So long as their relatives acted in unison and continued to pay maintenance there was little chance that the head of the institution concerned would let them go or even just permit them contact with outsiders. The 'oubliettes' seemed to be bursting at the seams. In the early 1770s the central government was flooded with complaints about the abuses resulting from the readiness of the courts to allow the duration of confinement to depend on the judgement of the families as to the degree of the detainee's improvement, which ultimately meant the families took the law into their own hands. On 10 October 1774 the governor-general, Charles of Lorraine, ordered the provincial councils to make an end to such practices, which violated all principles of justice. The authorizing body had thenceforth to ensure that the period of detention in a reformatory had a limit, and they alone could give permission for an extension to the period of confinement they also had to investigate whether the behaviour of the detainee really did warrant it.[1] It is doubtful whether this last stipulation had any effect, since the requests for extensions were dealt with just as flexibly as before, but after 1774 the courts did mention an explicit period of detention much more often; in Antwerp this happened in 98 per cent of cases.

Some petitioners wrote expressly that they were leaving the decision on the duration of confinement up to the 'discretion' of the aldermen, but most of them – about 60 per cent in Bruges and almost 70 per cent in Antwerp – named a period themselves, running from three months to six years. It is difficult to decide what factors played a role in this, since no explanation is given in the requests. Well-to-do families were more inclined to plead for a lengthy confinement than the families of labourers, which might have been connected with the financial means of the former and the survival strategies of the latter. The reverse appeared too often, however, to consider the social background of the petitioners as being decisive. The individual's objectionable behaviour provides even less of an adequate explanation, since the periods of confinement varied just as greatly for the 'insane' as for the 'debauched' – it being understood that they were usually the longest for persons who had committed acts of violence, regardless of their social background, although the exceptions here again are also too numerous to speak of more than just a tendency. The same applies to age: a short period was requested for children or adolescents more often than for adults, but there was no hard and fast rule. The fact that tendencies can be seen proves in any case that the petitioners were not blinded by feelings of vengeance and hate, insofar as such emotions played a role in the decision to have a relative put under lock and key. It is clear that they took account of several factors to arrive at an explicit period of detention. However, we are lacking too much information to be able to reconstruct their deliberations.

In general, the aldermen of Antwerp agreed to the period of detention requested by the petitioners. In a third of the cases each of the parties had different opinions – and here it should be noted that until about 1770 the courts appeared to be more reticent than the families, thus awarding a shorter sentence than that requested.[2] What motives did the aldermen have? Nothing can be deduced from their sentences and the requests of the families concerned do not differ at first sight from those which were granted straight away. The explanation is not to be found in the fact that petitioners pleaded for an exceptionally long period of confinement. It might be thought that the courts were more reticent if the city administration had to foot the bill. This reasoning does not work either, since most differences of opinion as to the duration of confinement involve precisely those cases in which the families were prepared to pay such costs. Did the aldermen get the impression during the examination of the petitioners that the case was less serious than the latter were trying to make it appear? We can only make a guess at the reason.

In the 1770s and 1780s the magistracy was on the contrary inclined to put the unwanted person under lock and key for longer than the family had asked, especially when this involved the sons of wage-earners. This more repressive attitude was no doubt connected with the increasing incidence of youth crime, which was expressed not only in the spread of vandalism and all manner of aggressive begging, but in the new formation of more and more gangs of thieves. The 'Shrove Tuesday Uproar' of 1780 strengthened the view of the aldermen in Antwerp that youth had to be dealt with more severely. During the decade 1780–9 they gave confinement sentences which were longer in almost 60 per cent of cases than those requested by the parents – that is, twice as much as in the preceding decade.

In any discussion about the actual duration of confinement we should bear in mind that an extension was always possible, and that anyone who had served his time could later be locked up again. If we discount these cases (for now) and calculate the number of months spent in a mental or penal institution by persons who had been prosecuted only once, then we can see that age was often taken into consideration as a mitigating circumstance. In the period 1710–69, the average confinement period came to 12 months for adults and six months for those under age – boys as well as girls. Of course extreme cases can be cited, but they are few in number.

After 1770 two striking shifts took place: unwanted people were usually confined for longer and youths could expect much less sympathy. At the end of the *ancien régime* the average duration of confinement came to 25 months for adults and 19 months for minors. However, this last figure gives a distorted picture: most children and adolescents (62 out of a total of 86) had to spend 12 months in a reformatory in all, but of the 24 remaining there were no fewer than 19 who were imprisoned for far longer. The 'front-runners' were all youths whose ages varied from 18 to 24. The severest case was that of Joannes Latter: he had completely destroyed his mother's little shop, attacked her with a knife and smashed in the neighbours' windows into the bargain, because they had been meddling in the business; on 3 March 1781 the aldermen sent him to Vilvoorde for six years.[3] The exceptional character of this case can be seen from the fact that only one adult had been given a sentence of this length: the aforementioned Anna Catharina Masseau, who according to her husband had been living a very lecherous life and had regularly had 'criminal conversation' with a married man. Although the petitioner had not asked for a specific period of confinement himself, on 9 June 1780 the magistrate decided that his wife could under no circumstances be released from the provincial penitentiary before the summer of 1786. The fact that the *Armmeesters* (administrators of poor relief) had pleaded for a lengthy confinement no doubt influenced the passing of this sentence.[4] The aldermen of Antwerp did hand down an even longer sentence on one occasion, but the person concerned was released before time. On 1 March 1780 the wife and only son of Petrus De Paep wrote that things could go no further: Petrus refused to contribute to the family income, squeezed their meagre earnings out of them, had sold their beds and all the other household effects so he could go drinking, caused havoc everywhere, got into fights with everyone – in short, he had made their life and that of the neighbours into a living hell. Twelve years' imprisonment was the decision of the aldermen – clearly to the consternation of the petitioners, because in April 1785 they were arguing that Petrus had behaved himself very well in Vilvoorde and that they would very much like to give him another chance; their request was granted, so that his detention was limited to five years and a few weeks.[5]

These exceptional cases are, from yet another point of view, not representative: wage-earners usually did less time in an institution than members of the upper classes, and this applied to both adults and minors. The fact that the city administration had to foot the bill when the financial resources of the petitioners were insufficient could have played a role in this. However, most proletarian families themselves asked the aldermen for a confinement of short duration: the longer their relative spent behind bars, the longer the family had to go without his income. The great weight of financial considerations can thus be seen not only from the type of behaviour objected to, but also from the sentences. It is no accident that all requests for the release of a detainee by proletarians were granted. As Isabella Van Heurck wrote on 11 May 1785 to the aldermen of Antwerp: 'If my husband – a silk-weaver – must spend yet another year in the provincial penitentiary, then I shall no

Table 7.1 *'Recidivists' as a percentage of the total number of detainees, Antwerp and Bruges*

Age/sex	Antwerp		Bruges	
	1710–69	1770–89	1740–64	1765–89
Adults				
Men	33.7	23.6	13.3	9.3
Women	23.9	15.1	14.0	9.1
Minors				
Youths	29.0	18.2	5.1	8.5
Girls	19.2	7.4		

longer be able to sustain our two small children, for I earn too little to feed so many mouths.'[6] In the other requests for early release material motives are cited just as explicitly. As we have noted before: proletarians were aiming not only to punish their housemates, but also to correct them and to get them to contribute to the family income.

If in the opinion of the family the detainee showed no signs of improvement, then they could ask for an extension of sentence. The requests show that this happened only when the wardens of the institution supplied an attestation stating that the detainee had been behaving badly. There were also detainees who, after they had served their sentence and left the institution, were put under lock and key once more because, according to the family, their improvement had been only transitory. Although the term 'recidivists' is in fact applicable only to this last group, we shall use it for the sake of convenience to refer to anyone whose confinement was simply lengthened (see table 7.1).

The limited percentage of 'recidivists' in Bruges must be ascribed to the fact that far fewer detainees came from well-off families than in Antwerp. Few wage-earners put in requests for an extension of sentence. In both cities they represented barely one fifth of the petitioners concerned. This explains why the proportion of 'recidivists' in Antwerp dropped considerably towards the end of the *ancien régime*: as time went on, more and more unwanted people were coming from the proletariat or the lower middle classes. Is it any wonder that many insane persons were to be found among the 'recidivists'? Some of them never emerged from the monastery in which they had been placed by their relatives. This was the case, for example, with Franciscus Laurijssens and Gerard Van Sons, who spent respectively 15 and 17 years in the monastery of the Antwerp *Cellebroeders* – the first at the request of his guardian (a member of the well-known Van Hencxthoven family), the second at the request of his sisters. They were certainly not the record-holders. We do not know how old Michael Brants was when ended up with the *Cellebroeders* in 1767, but he must have been fairly young because his father accused him of neglecting his studies. Michael had a great deal to answer for: misuse of alcohol, squandering money and above all a whole series of fights; according to the neighbours, he had on more than one occasion beaten his father up. Two years later the latter put in a request for an extension of sentence, which was supported by the *Cellebroeders*: Michael was under no circumstances to be sent home; he had 'lost his reason'. During the years that followed his situation got worse. With every extension of sentence he became even more violent and aggressive. After the death of his father, J. F. van der Straelen, the Sheriff of Kiel, stood in as his guardian. For the last time he asked the aldermen in 1783 for an extension of confinement; Michael died three years later in the monastery. He had spent 19 years behind bars. The absolute record, however, goes to Hyacinthus Mellerio, who had been depicted as a dangerously insane person by his mother in 1769: he had been behaving 'as an utter fool, making mad and furious threats'. He remained uninterruptedly with the *Cellebroeders* until 1795. We can find no trace of him after that time. Was he transferred to a public institution when the Austrian Netherlands were annexed to France or did he die? Whatever it was, he had been detained for 26 years up till then.

People did not have to be insane to spend many years behind bars. For example, Jacob Sira was collocated four times by his guardians: in 1748 because he refused to study and ran up gambling debts; in 1749 because he showed no signs of remorse; in 1751 because he had run away from the monastery, which persuaded the aldermen to increase his sentence by three years; and finally in 1754 because he had behaved so badly that the Antwerp *Cellebroeders* no longer wanted to keep him, for which he had to serve an additional two years – this time in a Brussels monastery. When he was finally released he had reached the age of 30. Such cases were quite rare, though. Eight out of ten 'recidivists' who, according to the requests, were still in possession of their faculties ended up in an institution three times at most. If we make a calculation of the actual time spent in confinement, then we see that this doubled during the 1770s and 1780s; minors at this time were confined on average for 33 months and adults almost four years – in other words, twice as long as detainees locked up only once.

The most important conclusion to be drawn in any case is that the overwhelming majority of petitioners never asked for an extension of sentence or entered a new request for confinement. Are we to deduce from this that confinement and re-education were synonymous – that most of the unwanted people during their detention came to repentance, realized and regretted their wrongdoings, learned to put into practice the accepted standards and values: in short, that they became 'new' men? We shall never know if there were improvements in the real sense of the word. All we can know for certain is that the behaviour of the people concerned did not give cause for further complaint, which does not necessarily mean that they thought differently about their housemates, relatives and neighbours, or that they had developed a different outlook on life and morality. What was going on in their hearts and minds is hidden from us. However, it could be argued that they had learned to control themselves better. From that point of view confinement was extraordinarily effective. Even those who had spent only a few months behind bars were prepared to go to great lengths to avoid being locked up again, in any kind of institution.

Religious institutions

It seems clear that the detainees who came from well-off families had less reason to complain than did their proletarian counterparts. After all, their housemates or relatives were paying for their upkeep, the costs of which could be very high. They could therefore expect to be looked after in a more than adequate manner, as regards both food and clothing and hygiene. Their individuality was respected, moreover, at least in the sense that they did not have all their hair shaved off and have to wear a uniform, which was usually the case in houses of correction. However, we should entertain no illusions about their treatment. Anyone who reads the pathetic letters that some of these 'privileged' prisoners were able to smuggle out will be dismayed. Not only does it seem that the religious treated their 'patients' in a very hard-hearted manner, but, moreover, that they considered them as milch-cows – in other words they tried to keep them as long as possible in the institution and to spend as little as possible on looking after them so as to make the maximum profit. The detainees will in all probability have been inclined to bemoan their lot and to portray their living conditions in the darkest colours. Their pronouncements on the pitiable circumstances in which they were living in the monasteries concerned are nonetheless confirmed by impartial contemporaries.

Wealthy families preferred to place an uncontrollable son or adult man in a monastery run by the *Cellebroeders*. This religious order was set up in the fourteenth century and was initially concerned with caring for the sick, particularly plague-victims, the transportation of whom was one of their tasks. In addition, the brothers (who were also called the Alexians) took it upon themselves to comfort the dying and attend to their burial; they washed the body and wrapped it in linen, held a wake by the coffin and, as the case may be, arranged for the funeral, at which they often took part as 'mourners'. From the sixteenth century onwards (or even earlier) they also began to care for the mentally ill; if the latter could not be treated at home, then the brothers were prepared to nurse them in the monastery.[7] During the course of the seventeenth and especially the eighteenth century this activity acquired significant proportions because the number of declarations of insanity was rising considerably and existing provisions were very limited. The upper classes were, moreover, not inclined to place their uncontrollable relatives in public madhouses; they had need of discretion and in consequence gave preference to religious institutions that were so expensive that they were exclusive by definition. The order of Alexian Brothers fulfilled their requirements. They only took patients from wealthy families or those who, through great merit, received a considerable contribution from the public purse. They did not protest when the detainee appeared to be completely healthy in mind. On the contrary, they were increasingly turning their monasteries into reformatories, in which youths and adult men were confined who had given themselves over to drink, gambling or other 'devilish' practices. From the Antwerp *Requestboeken* it seems that six out of ten unwanted persons incarcerated with the Alexian Brothers belonged to this category. In their house at Bruges the proportion of 'insane' persons during the second half of the eighteenth century was much smaller: 24 out of a total of 79 detainees – less than 30 per cent.[8]

The *Cellebroeders* did well out of these particular works of charity. Private confinement brought much, much more money into the kitty. On 12 February 1718 the director of the Ghent house informed a desperate father that they could not take his son in because of lack of space, unless he paid three thousand guilders towards a new altar.[9] Between 1764 and 1777 the family of Jozef Carette paid out no less than 1,296 guilders per year for his 'provisions' in the monastery of the Bruges *Cellebroeders*.[10] Exceptional cases? Perhaps. In any case we find only rarely payments of less than 240 guilders a year. It will not have been purely coincidental that the Alexian Brothers embarked upon an intense programme of building works in the second half of the eighteenth century, nor that their assets were estimated by the French in 1796 to have been very substantial – in Antwerp at about 138,000 guilders, which meant that they were among the four richest religious institutions.[11]

The housemates and relatives of the detainees clearly asked few questions about what was going on behind the monastery walls. They

Plate 12 Anonymous, *The Alexian Brothers at their Works of Charity*, late eighteenth
century. Wealthy families preferably placed an 'uncontrollable' youth or adult man in a
cloister run by the Alexians. In the foreground two of the brothers are seen carrying an
insane person.

went only to the director to discuss the financial side of the case or to
find out how the unwanted person was behaving. The fact they were
informed in writing as to his condition gives rise to suspicions that the
detainee seldom if ever received a visit. Some families nonetheless knew
that things were going wrong, as we shall presently see. Did they keep
quiet because they had no alternative? This is possible, since there were
very few 'civilized' institutions and they could each take in only a limited
number of patients. As a matter of fact, this is why Joseph II classified
them among the useful monasteries, ones which could not be dissolved.
Or were the families concerned of the opinion that their troublesome
burden deserved to be taught a lesson and that a hard-handed approach
would therefore do no harm? If this was the case, then they certainly got
value for their money.

   In October 1690 Jan-Baptist Cotengys, the priest of a place called
Potterie, wrote to the aldermen of Bruges that his protégé, Lieven Praet,
had been imprisoned with the *Cellebroeders* unjustly, since he had done

nothing amiss and had shown not a single sign of insanity. 'Moreover, I must protest at his inhumane treatment', the priest added:

> Inhuman . . . to see him suffering at the mere sight of the cells; first Brother Philip called out 'Seize him!' and pulled off his wig as he himself confessed and he . . . heard Lieven van Praet call out 'Oh ye buggers, tear me limb from limb – I shall not enter that hole!' The one taking his head and others his arms and legs, they hurled him into it . . .[12]

Louis Marotte of Ghent could count himself fortunate that his wife, who had placed him with the *Cellebroeders*, died in 1703. Before settling the current account, his brother-in-law first wanted to find out what provisions were being made for him. He made an unexpected visit to their house and found to his horror that Louis

> had been locked in a cell day and night, summer and winter, for eight full years, only receiving the sunlight therein through a chink and being able to do nothing more than stand and lie down . . . as if he had been the greatest evil-doer in the world.

Moreover, the brothers had not offered him the opportunity to have confession, to attend mass or to receive the Holy Sacrament.[13] This was clearly the normal run of things, because eight years later the young Joannes Servaes Adrians, also from Ghent, was able to smuggle out a note in which he informed his mother that he was not permitted to hear mass on Sundays. The brothers kept him permanently under lock and key 'in a pen where he could scarcely see, with four madmen for company . . . who day and night disturbed his rest'. The worst thing, he continued, was that they had to empty the chamber pot themselves and that, because of the faulty construction of the floor, the urine could not flow out, which left an indescribable stink hanging in the air. 'I have been here five months, but it seems five years. I beg you, dearest Mother, have pity on me and deliver me from this slavery.' In 1713 another detainee used even stronger terms to describe the abominable living conditions in the monastery of the Ghent Alexian Brothers:

> . . . one of the brothers has brought me pen and paper in secret, that I might tell you, my uncle Pastor, that I fear I shall go quite mad in this living coffin. I have been imprisoned here for three years and five months and have never once been allowed a visit. I am being treated as a vagabond: my clothes are utterly in shreds and my linen stinks to high heaven . . .[14]

So far as we can ascertain, only once was an official investigation ever made into the conditions in a *Cellebroeders* monastery. It is not clear what precipitated it, but from the available documents it seems in any case that the aldermen of Bruges were receiving more and more reports during the 1770s and 1780s about the scandalous conduct of the Alexian Brothers and their lack of dedication regarding the care of their patients. The director of the house caused scandal not only through his drinking habits, but also through his continuous chasing after women, which gave rise to a great deal of gossip. Add to this that the court officials had repeatedly to intervene and put an end to fights between the brothers and their patients, during which some were severely wounded and even killed, and it will be quite understandable that the city fathers of Bruges were becoming very disturbed. In 1777 a commission was appointed with the task of making a thorough examination of everyone who had been confined with the *Cellebroeders* at the request of their families and who was still in possession of their faculties. The aforementioned Jozef Carette and three other detainees provided such damaging testimony that the magistrate decided to lay a formal complaint before the central government. The procurator-general of the Council of Flanders was entrusted with the task of making a thorough investigation. He made several visits to the monastery, heard all the parties involved and set down his conclusions in a detailed report, which was discussed by the Privy Council on 12 September 1777.

The procurator-general's judgement was devastating. While he did not support all the viewpoints of the aldermen of Bruges (who in his opinion gave an all too one-sided view of things), and he thought some of the detainees' accusations were completely unfounded, he found so many faults and shortcomings in so many areas that he considered radical reforms to be absolutely essential. 'Management and supervision left a great deal to be desired', he argued.

> The director, Stevens, is an incorrigible drunkard who spends the greater part of his time outside the monastery, mostly in dubious company, and he is of such a narrow mind that everything is bound to be at sixes and sevens. Most of the brothers suffer from the same weaknesses, [these] being alcoholism and narrow-mindedness, against which they set no example. I can name but two, Joseph Lemmens and Jacob Vander Haeghen, who lead irreproachable lives and who have a sense of responsibility; under the present circumstances there is not a lot they can do. The atmosphere is so poisoned that the slightest remark can lead to a row and even to fisticuffs. As for the persons detained therein: they have simply resigned themselves to their fate. Some complaints must undoubtedly be taken with a pinch of salt. The food, for example, is not so bad. Indeed, all those who complain of the food are persons detained for bad behaviour who are therefore not in a position to make such a song and dance about it. However, they do justly complain about the utter lack of hygiene: the lack of cleanliness and the filth which reigns in this house, and in several others of similar type, is repugnant and induces a feeling of nausea ... the more so as it renders the air one breathes quite insupportable. I have obtained information from the

magistrates of other towns and from their reports it alas appears the house at Bruges is no exception: everywhere there reigns a sort of lethargy and dissolution which gives rise to such scandal that the entire public is desirous of reform. The Father Provincial of the Alexian Brothers does not deny that the misuse of alcohol, indolence and immorality are frequent phenomena. The problem is that he does not wish or dare to take measures to counter these evils. For this reason I propose that the government put matters in order and make all the monasteries involved subject to a single rule, which on the one hand offers an opportunity for intelligent and conscientious brothers to be put in charge of the institution, and on the other contains precise instructions on how the persons detained are to be treated. The latter not only have a right to adequate food of a reasonable quality, but also to hygienic care, which among other things means that the director must personally see to it that the kitchens, the refectory, the corridors and the cells are regularly cleansed and ventilated. Moreover, he must encourage the brothers to moderation and goodness, in particular when a detained person has committed some misdeed; his 'penance' may not in any case last longer than two weeks and may consist solely of solitary confinement and a diet of bread and water. It is for the civil authorities to ordain more severe punishments as the case may be.[15]

The regulation was endowed with the force of law, but did the *Cellebroeders* put it into practice or at least make some attempt to improve the living conditions of their patients? The available sources do not enable us to give a definitive answer. Fragmentary information suggests in any case that a period of enforced confinement in a house run by the Alexians remained a fearful prospect. A single example will suffice. When Hyacinthus Stanislas van Waesberghe was given leave to attend the funeral of his brother-in-law in 1783, he took advantage of the occasion to write to the aldermen that after so many years in solitary confinement with the Ghent Alexians he was a broken man and that any further extension of sentence 'would strike him so hard that it would be the death of him'. He had experienced in the monastery nothing but 'unspeakable miseries and woes', which weighed on him all the more heavily, since he had always behaved well. Kindliness was evidently something of which the brothers knew nothing: they held him 'locked in a cell and cut him off from all access with living human beings, apparently to ensure that the suppliant did not bring their wrongful treatment of him to the light of day.' On what did his sister and brother-in-law base themselves when they were asking for further extensions of sentence? Exclusively on the declarations of the brothers, who 'had had the adroitness continually to make out bad reports'. Was Van Waesberghe trying to blacken the *Cellebroeders* so that he could be released? Whatever the case may be, both his relatives and the aldermen believed him and not the Alexian Brothers.[16]

Wealthy families could also have insane or debauched men – minors as well as adults – confined in the *Maison forte* at Froidmont, near Tournai. This large religious house was originally run by the Frères de la Charité de Saint Charles-Borromée, a new community founded by Gaspar De-vleeschouwer, the parish priest of Froidmont, at the end of the seventeenth century with the primary aim of 'providing accommodation for persons of weak mind, those who had lost their reason and the debauched'. Shortly after official recognition had been granted the congregation by Charles VI there arose a flood of complaints about the bad treatment of the inmates. The Bishop of Tournai instigated an enquiry and found himself obliged to agree with the accusations: the brothers were not in a position to provide proper care; no one worried themselves about the moral education of the inmates; the director was completely lacking in anything regarding pastoral guidance. The bishop made a formal complaint to the governor-general, Maria Elisabeth, who in 1728 granted him not only authority to visit, but also permission to replace the director and to take disciplinary measures against any brothers who neglected their duties. The congregation rebelled tooth and nail. It was not until 1736 that matters were put in order, which meant among other things that the director was given fewer powers. It was of no avail. The brothers could not or would not manage the finances properly and, which was much worse, they neglected the detainees, so that they were living in thoroughly degrading conditions. In 1766 the ecclesiastical authorities finally turned to Maria Theresa with a request to disband the order, which was promptly done. The foundation was placed under the guardianship of the government which gave to the chief bailiff of Tournai and the archdeacon of the cathedral the task of appointing two priests to run it.[17] It is doubtful whether things improved after this, because at the end of the *ancien régime* two residents of Bruges testified that the patients in Froidmont were still being treated very badly; the hygiene and the quality of the food were in their opinion immeasurably low.[18]

Although we have not come across any letters written by girls or adult women from well-off families who were locked up for deviant behaviour, it can be assumed that they were better off than their male counterparts. Not only were they far fewer in number, but there were plenty of places for them, which meant that it was greatly in the interest of the people running the institutions concerned to ensure that they were well cared for. During the seventeenth and especially the eighteenth century a growing number of monastic and religious orders were busying themselves with the care of insane and/or debauched women: the Beguine nuns of the Convent of Bethlehem in Duffel (near Antwerp), the Benedictine nuns at Menen, the *Cellezusters* at Diest, the Spiritual Daughters of St Lucy at Sint-Niklaas, the Grey Sisters-Penitent at Antwerp, Diksmuide, Nieuwpoort, Poperinge and Velzeke (in the district of Aalst) and the Black Sisters of Louvain and Lier, to mention but a few. Wealthy families could also put women with psychological disturbances into one of the many *gasthuizen* ('guest-houses' – hospitals, in effect) run by religious orders. Antwerp women from the better-off circles were preferably sent to Geel or Turnhout, two small communities in the Campine, a rural and very sparsely populated area. The first-mentioned community, where St Dimpna had been revered since the Middle Ages, eventually became the most important place of pilgrimage and a reception centre for insane people in the Southern Netherlands. The influx was so great that it became the usual practice to billet patients in private homes, which received payment or could set their 'guest' to work. This example was followed at Sint-Niklaas, where at the end of the *ancien régime* two new institutions were founded, known as Groot Geel and Klein Geel, for which their directors appealed to local farmers' families to take patients in and look after them. Several witnesses at the beginning of the nineteenth century speak of many kinds of abuses. There was a great temptation to regard this 'home nursing' only as a source of supplementary income and therefore to spend as little money as possible on the food and clothing of their house-guests; but then on the other hand the latter were free to come and go as they pleased. The 'insane' daughters and wives of rich Antwerpians will probably have been extremely envious of this freedom, since they had been locked up in the 'sick-room' or *gasthuis* at Geel.[19]

There was only one religious institution in the Austrian Netherlands that functioned as a reformatory for women who had been guilty of morally reprehensible behaviour: the *Maison de Sainte Croix* (House of the Holy Cross) in Brussels. It was founded in 1647 by a Dominican friar, Ambroise Druve, whose mission was to restore 'fallen' daughters to the paths of righteousness by means of prayer, work and discipline. Although complaints flooded in right from the beginning about the abuses in the institution, it was not until 1731 that the civil authorities intervened. The central government's representatives found so many of them, with regard both to the duration of confinement and the living conditions, that the governor-general, Maria Elisabeth, entrusted the magistrate of Brussels with running the House of the Holy Cross, which led in 1734 to an expansion of the institution. Too few archives have been preserved to make far-reaching conclusions, but it is beyond dispute that it was mainly the middle classes that made use of the reformatory and that most of the detainees were girls who had not attained their majority and who, according to their parents or guardians, had been living immoral lives. They certainly could not have been happy in the institution, because in 1784 Joseph II closed the house down with the argument that the abuses were unspeakable; his decision aroused not a word of protest.[20]

Madhouses

The public mental institutions and reformatories were not populated exclusively by the poor. Unwanted people were also to be found there who were wholly or partly maintained by their families and who in consequence might expect somewhat better treatment. As with the proletarians, the members of the lower middle classes could only 'choose' between one of the city's madhouses on the one hand and a city or provincial penal institution on the other. Bruges was the only city in the Southern Netherlands where there was a third possibility: to place harmless insane persons in private institutions, the owners of which charged lower maintenance costs than the regular orders. Nothing is known about the social background of the owners, except that not a single doctor was to be found among them. They were always small entrepreneurs. The widow of Frans De Meyere was the head of the largest private institution: in 1771 she had 44 patients in her care. Her successors did not succeed in expanding the business, and the number of patients actually fell to 31 in 1780 and even to 23 in 1785. A year later the institution was closed down, which also signified the end of private mental care in the Austrian Netherlands.[21]

There is not a word about medical treatment in the urban madhouses. In both Antwerp and Bruges several doctors and surgeons visited the institutions, but they were summoned only to cure physical ills or to shave the patients. Anyone who was unjustly declared insane and ended up in a madhouse was therefore not able to prove that there had been a wrong diagnosis in his case and/or that he had been put there as a result of malicious intent. Protesting vigorously often made matters worse, since there was a risk that the confinement would be extended on grounds of misbehaviour. It was best to keep quiet in the hope that the director of the madhouse would make out a favourable report at the end of sentence. Nonetheless, this seems to have been a forlorn hope. We have already mentioned that in 1791 the Brussels *Simpelhuys* housed no fewer than 44 persons who showed no (further) sign of insanity. It seems hardly probable that the director had no knowledge of these cases. He had definitely had no medical training, but that was also true of the commissioners who came to inspect the institution at the time. Financial considerations will most probably have been the deciding factors, since he received from the magistrate a fixed payment per patient and per day, so that it was to his advantage to have as many 'insane' patients under his care as possible.

It is not easy to work out how many people had been unjustly confined in a madhouse or remained confined after they had been cured, but there can be no doubt that institutions everywhere were prepared to take in men and women who had not lost their reason. In some cases humanitarian considerations played a part. Thus, in June 1771 the poor-relief administrators of Antwerp decided to place Anna-Maria Daems in the madhouse because she was 'frequently given to the falling sickness, in such manner that on different occasions she had been in danger of burning herself in her mother's house, where she must spend most of her time alone while her mother goes out to do the washing in other burghers' houses; thus clearly to prevent some accident and because her mother cannot support her.' In other cases the motives were less pure. Whenever a person's family was prepared to pay for his upkeep the directors of the Antwerp madhouse would not oppose the confinement of a patient who appeared to be healthy in mind and body, and they made no attempt to return him to liberty. When Joannes Cornelissen, who had been confined at the instigation of his parents, escaped from the institution on 4 April 1772, the board of management reported that in fact there was nothing amiss with the young man, at least that he 'had shown no sign of mindless actions'; the Cornelissens couple had been paying a great deal of maintenance money.[22]

However, whether it was now a question of insanity or morally reprehensible behaviour the detainees were left largely to their fate. Just as in most other European countries, the madhouses in the Austrian Netherlands served a purely custodial purpose. They were prisons as well as houses of correction. No one cared about the psychiatric condition of the patients. Anyone who was not amenable to reason and caused trouble was beaten and had to spend several days and nights in a dark cell. Anyone who remained 'agitated' was put in chains. From the accounting documents of St Julian's Hospital in Bruges – a public institution – it seems that a wide range of instruments was available to hand: ordinary hand and foot bindings in leather or iron, as well as wider ones for binding arms and legs together, hoops or bands placed about the loins, *pyenkerels* or strait-jackets, iron masks for biters, and so on.[23]

In the absence of detailed studies it is impossible to make general statements about the hygiene and diet in public institutions. According to the Englishman John Howard, the patients in Sint-Jan-ten-Dullen in Ghent – probably the oldest separate institution in Western Europe – had nothing to complain about. However, he did not know that most insane people in Ghent were sent to other institutions; the men found themselves in the *Rasphuis*, which had an evil reputation. From several reports it seems that the Antwerp madhouse around 1765 was in a pitiable state and that the care of the patients at the time left a great deal to be desired. The building of a new foundation, offering places for

Plate 13 Instruments of restraint used in the Antwerp *Zinnelooshuis* or mental institution in the eighteenth century.

about two hundred people, probably led to an improvement in living conditions, but there is no certainty about that. The *Simpelhuys* in Brussels is the only institution about which we are well informed. We can only hope that this was an isolated case! The cells and dormitories were so badly ventilated that the inmates – about 134 in 1764 and almost 200 in 1794 – were permanently breathing in a suffocating smoke; because of the excessive dampness a candle would gutter out after only a short time. Since the parish priest was not able to administer the last rites to dying patients because he could not get any air, an infirmary was built in 1768; this was also so badly constructed that after a report in 1794 it was dubbed the 'Tomb of the Mad'. In the same report we read that most of the cells (or rather, holes) had no windows; they could only be 'ventilated' through a tiny hatch in the door. '. . . And that is not the worst thing by any means'; wrote one contemporary: the nerves in the knees of some detainees were so withered through being forced to live enclosed in their dungeons they could only go about upon their hands and feet, like animals. Add to this that the patients maintained at the expense of the city were fed on the same 'pig-swill' day in and day out and that their clothes were never changed, except for other rags, and it is quite understandable why the French revolutionaries considered that radical reform was due.[24]

The *Simpelhuys* in Brussels is probably an extreme example of the care of the mentally ill. It should not therefore be considered as representative of the Austrian Netherlands as a whole without comment.

The abuses regarding the declaration of insanity, the absence of any medical treatment, the frequent use of instruments of restraint and the silencing of the 'patients' are also structural features to be found elsewhere in Europe during the age of Enlightenment. The madhouses of the Austrian Netherlands differ from those of England and the United Provinces in only one respect: they were not open to the public. However, given that the *concierges* had to be reminded many times that it was strictly forbidden 'to allow the house to be seen by anyone, whether kinfolk, friends, acquaintances or strangers', it can be assumed that the curious were being allowed to visit. In any case, real 'madhouse fairs', in which the insane were literally put on exhibition, never took place in the cities of Brabant and Flanders. In the London Bedlam, on the other hand, the public could until 1770 just come along and look at the inmates as they pleased, and this was quite usual in the mad-houses of the United Provinces until the beginning of the nineteenth century.

Urban houses of correction

Given the fact that their families seldom pressed for a declaration of insanity, the overwhelming majority of unwanted people from the less well-off sections of the population ended up in a 'house of improvement'. These were in principle not prisons, but houses of correction and workhouses, which were designed to get the detainees used to an orderly and disciplined life through forced labour. Until 1773 in the County of Flanders and until 1779 in the Duchy of Brabant there were 'houses of improvement' only in the towns. Thereafter, both men and women guilty of morally reprehensible behaviour were sent in increasing numbers to the provincial penitentiaries.

Michel Foucault has argued that confinement in the seventeenth and eighteenth centuries was the principal strategy with regard to people from the lower classes who were considered to be socially deviant. The *Grand Renfermement* started, according to him, in 1656 with the foundation of the *Hôpital Général* in Paris. However, the magistrate of Amsterdam had set up a house of correction as early as 1596 and this example was quickly followed, both in the United Provinces and in neighbouring countries. Although the statutes of the Antwerp *dwinghuys* ('house of coercion'), opened in 1613, stipulated that individuals could make use of the institution to discipline housemates or relatives who were 'of unruly life and disposition, in particular for the castigation of rebellious and disobedient children', the main aim initially was to lock up beggars and vagabonds and to make useful workers out of them.

'Thus', thought the aldermen, 'we can kill two birds with one stone: on the one hand we protect our citizens, thus maintaining public order, and on the other we exert pressure on wages . . .' The latter aim had to be realized through the fearful reputation that forced labour would have among the loafers and idlers who were not (yet) in the house of coercion, which would make them accept working for entrepreneurs for the lowest possible wages. For the same reasons the magistrates of Brussels, Ghent and Bruges set up similar institutions in the 1620s. It soon became clear, however, that this social policy did not produce the effects being sought, so that one house of correction after another was being closed or used for other purposes.

Shortly after the establishment of Austrian rule, the theme was taken up again. The initiative did not come from central government, although it urged local authorities to set up *rasphuizen*, especially in the capital, built by the municipalities themselves. In 1717 the magistrate of Bruges founded a 'spinning-house' for women. Twenty years later the institution was considerably extended and the *rasphuys* for men was also reopened and enlarged. In the meantime the houses of correction in Antwerp, Brussels and Ghent were functioning once more essentially as reformatory institutions. Just as in the seventeenth century, they housed beggars and vagabonds as well as prostitutes, but the largest contingent now consisted of men and women who were confined at the request of their families. The continual growth of this category, both in absolute and relative figures, compelled the aldermen of Antwerp, Brussels and Bruges at the end of the 1760s to build new cells, dormitories and/or workplaces. The transformation of the urban houses of correction in the eighteenth century was thus brought about by the need of ever increasing numbers of families to discipline their uncontrollable members. The local administrations handed them 'just' the instruments required for this.

What was expected from the inmates? The rules of the Bruges *rasphuis* put it as follows: 'Since this house is a house of correction and sorrow, for the conversion and improvement of lives, so shall the persons detained therein accordingly try at all times to set themselves to work and, through offering prayers, attending the Holy Service of Mass and hearing sermons, they shall be exhorted to conduct themselves in a respectful manner.' The so-called institutions of improvement were indeed houses of sorrow. The programme of setting norms showed some variations, but the same principles applied everywhere: discipline, discipline, discipline.

On his arrival it was made clear to the newcomer that he had no business but to keep silent, take what was coming to him and obey. He was thrown into a dark hole or, if he gave the impression of being a

Plate 14 M. De Visch, *The Prison at Bruges*, 1746. It was mainly people who could not pay off their debts who found themselves in the city prisons. Many women from the upper classes mentioned profligacy as their main motive for confinement, arguing that their husbands would otherwise end up in prison.

'difficult case', barefooted into the *penitentiekot* (penitential cell), the floor of which was covered with sharp wooden ribbing so that every movement was torture. After 24 hours or even several days of 'medita-tion' the detainee had his head shaved completely and he was put into a uniform, the house rules were read out to him and he was informed what sort of work he was to do. The men were usually set to weaving and the women to cotton-spinning, where they had to keep up a daily quota. The timetable was rigorous. Depending on the season, the day began at five or six o'clock in the morning and ended at eight or nine o'clock in the evening with prayers and sleep. The intervening time was precisely divided up into dressing and undressing, cleaning the cells, prayers, hearing Mass and attending catechism classes on Sunday – and, for the rest, the greater part of the day (12 to 14 hours) was spent in forced labour.

The system of reward and punishment varied from one institution to another. Just as in the *tuchthuizen* ('bridewells') of the United Provinces, the positive sanctions disappeared under the welter of punitive measures which were hardly subtle or corrective; fear was uppermost, not the exercise of positive faculties and abilities. Every deviation from the house rules was punishable; getting up too late, making mistakes at work, producing too little, complaints about the food, swearing, using foul language, making rude gestures, singing, insulting the warders, speaking after the evening bell had sounded, and so on. For even the slightest infractions a person would have to spend 24 hours in a *cachot* (dungeon), which in some bridewells automatically meant an extra day added to sentence. Anyone who repeated an offence or committed a major transgression ended up in the penitential cell for several weeks, depend-ing on the case; to make the punishment more severe, their arms and legs could be bound and they could be collared to a wall, thus making it impossible to sleep. This method reduced even the most uncontrollable persons to 'bitter lamentation and promises of absolute improvement in their behaviour', the wardens of the Bruges *rasphuis* assured. They forced the 'convert', moreover, barefooted and in the presence of the other inmates, to 'go and kneel on the steps of the chapel to ask the forgiveness of God ... and to beg pardon in a loud voice first from the father [director], then his assistant and thereafter from all the other inmates for the bad example he had set them.' Floggings in the presence of fellow-prisoners also took place. If all of this had no effect, then there were always the thumbscrews to weaken resistance.

The fundamental feature of the discipline was continuous supervision. It was not only the official wardens who had to keep a close eye on the prisoners. Some of the inmates were also given supervisory powers and thus functioned as *kapos* ('bosses'). To prevent attempts at rebellions and escapes, the directorate also made use of spies who were chosen from among the criminals and who received reductions in sentence as a reward for their 'squealing'. If there was any suspicion that plotting was under way, then the disciplinary council stepped into action: the staff members and the *kapos* jointly conducted a hearing of the suspects, sentenced them and determined their punishment.

The regulation food rations were very meagre everywhere. In the Antwerp house of correction the inmates had to content themselves with two slices of rye bread in the morning and the evening. Their midday meal consisted of a mash of bread and vegetables, to which boiled meat was added on Sundays and feast-days. Finally, every week they were given a pound of butter and fruit to the value of half a *stuiver*. In principle, only water was given to drink. In the canteen, however, it was possible to buy *klein bier* ('small beer') or tea, which immediately indicated social differentiation. The poor inmates, who were in the majority, had only two ways in which to obtain money: by performing major services for the personnel or fellow-prisoners or by doing more work than was officially required of them. Anyone who had his own income or was confined at the expense of his family belonged to another, privileged category of prisoner who had the right to more and better food and who would be permitted other little extras.

However, whether people behaved well or badly, had possessions or not, a sojourn in a house of correction was very unpleasant. No one was in any doubt about that. Most contemporaries thought that that was the way it should be. It was *the* symbol of disciplinary power. People with deviant social behaviour had to realize 'that in these houses the certainty of death was all they had a right to', as a high-ranking functionary put it in 1761. The fact that a growing number of proletarians and members of the lower middle classes were confined in such institutions at the request of housemates or relatives shows that it was not only the authorities who were the advocates of the hard-hearted approach. The strictness of the disciplinary regime depended on the institution's director. In theory, the aldermen had the last word, but in practice they gave a free hand to the 'father' or *concierge* of the house of correction. They seldom visited the institution and their inspections were so hurried and so superficial that it was not possible for such abuses as there were to come to light. If they did do their duty properly and wanted to release an inmate, then they were tactful enough to examine him in the presence of the director. So long as financial matters were in order the last-named was free to lay down the law in the institution and no questions were asked about the methods of discipline he employed.[25] There is no question that the dividing line between punishment and mistreatment, between maintaining discipline and terror, was easily crossed. That risk was greatest in the houses of correction leased out to merchant-entrepreneurs, as the Brussels prisoners found out.

Since its inception in 1625 the house of correction at Brussels was run by manufacturers who covered most of the expenses in exchange for the profits to be made from forced labour and the maintenance costs paid by private individuals for an unwanted person; in addition, they enjoyed tax advantages and could sell fabrics to the city administration. Some of them treated the inmates humanely, but others made use of brutal violence, gratuitous or otherwise. For example, Antoine Dambremé, who ran the institution from October 1741 up to and including September 1750, was depicted as a savage by his successor Barthélémy 't Kint. He not only made frequent use of the whip and birch, but he also ensured that the cane lashed down upon the backs of all inmates who did not turn out enough work or who were at fault in some other way. It must have been a relief for the prisoners when the aldermen handed over the reins at the end of 1750 for 12 years to 't Kint. He also ruled with an iron hand, but he showed it only when it was necessary, as several ex-prisoners declared during the investigation into the financial malpractices of his successor, Charles Joseph Frison. We have a great deal of information about him and the sources leave us in no doubt that he exercised a reign of terror.

Frison was 25 years old when the aldermen leased the house of correction to him on 1 October 1762. Although he had little professional experience and knew nothing of prison life, he was firmly convinced that he was going to make his fortune from the employment of convicts. 'I shall transform this institution into a veritable manufactory, wherein shall be produced woollen fabrics and mixed weaves, and I shall turn part of the prison into a "'spinning-school", where both the female inmates and the daughters of free wage-earners can receive an education', he wrote to the magistrate. He kept his word. By September 1764 he had installed as many as 34 weaving-looms and three spinning workshops. Annual production at that time came to no fewer than 2,750 items, with a total value of 84,650 guilders, which made his 'textile factory' the third largest in the Duchy of Brabant. We do not have production figures for the following years, but it can be assumed that manufacture continued to flourish, which was praised by the city administration and the Council of Finances alike. Indeed, on 1 October 1771 Frison was granted an extension of the leasing contract, and that for a period of no less than 15 years. But during the spring of 1772 his kingdom collapsed. He was accused in anonymous letters of financial malpractices, which came to the authorities as a bolt out of the blue. The Fiscal Office of the Council of Brabant instigated an inquiry, found out that the complaints were justified and had Frison arrested on 24

December; for fear of revenge attacks by the inmates he was not locked up in his own institution, but the Treurenberg prison, where he was grilled for months. Frison defended himself vigorously, but the procurator-general demonstrated incontrovertibly that he had been guilty of misconduct and dismissed him from his post.

The prisoners could count themselves lucky that Frison had committed financial malpractices, because his other misdeeds would never have brought him into conflict with the law. The aldermen and their representatives were not concerned with the fate of the prisoners, and their 'inspections' were a mockery of all the obligations they should have fulfilled. Even the procurator-general considered the accusations of ill-treatment only as aggravating elements, thus as points of secondary importance. Did he believe that the testimonies of (ex-)detainees lacked conclusive force or did he not object too much to the excesses which they had had to suffer? Whatever the case may be, there can be no doubt that hell itself could hardly have been worse than life in the Brussels house of correction during Frison's reign. Obviously not all the accusations should be accepted without question. There were troublemakers no doubt among the detainees, as Frison argued. Guillielmus Janssens from Antwerp, for example, who was continually being thrown into the penitential cell and who many times had to endure an avalanche of blows from the cane, had been depicted by his mother and sisters as a real villain who 'continually went abroad in brutalities and other intolerable excesses'. From the inquiry it appears, however, that Frison used the presence of troublemakers to legitimize his terror. He ruled by fear, which was all the more unbearable because he interpreted and changed the house rules capriciously. No one felt safe because a 'wrong' word or gesture could lead to the most extreme punitive measures, which could be applied to both the individual 'culprit' and the prisoners as a whole. This permanent uncertainty was in fact the worst torture, as many witnesses testified: 'We were unable to predict how the director would react. There was no question of an ordered system in the administration of punishments. For the same infraction one person would receive ten strokes and another person fifty. Anything was possible . . . '

When the procurator-general called him to account for himself, Frison defended himself with the argument that anyone 'having deserved to be confined to a house of correction has put himself there, beneath all other persons of the same nature, and has degraded himself in some fashion from the level of a human creature, to be reduced to the condition of brute animals, which are subject to the empire of Man.' We can see that those confined under such a man had the worst to fear, the more so because he flew into an attack of rage at the least provocation. The merchant-entrepreneur Jean Baesten, who had been his trading partner from 1765 to 1770 and who was to follow him in 1773 as director of the house of correction, testified that 'he is as a rule strongly subject to fits of excessive choleric temperament which then cause him to utter a great number of oaths and he appears to take leave of his senses, to the point where there is no reason to be had from him, and where his fits of anger are of such violence that on occasion he does not even spare his own wife.' The detainees also commiserated with Frison's wife because of the numerous brutalities and humiliations she had to undergo. It is possible and even probable that Frison was showing signs of sadistic tendencies. According to some witnesses he wielded the whip or cane himself and took pleasure in the victim's suffering; it was advisable to bite one's tongue, because begging for mercy and crying out only excited him further.

Yet the terror was quite intentional. Frison wanted in the first instance to make the house of correction into a profitable business. To this end all means were permissible according to him, which automatically led to exploitation and ill-treatment. The milch-cows par excellence were of course the people who were there at the expense of their families. He divided them into two groups. Those who paid a hundred guilders or more per year had the right to wheat bread, vegetables, a piece of meat and a pint of beer. The other 'guests' had to be content with ordinary rations, and these were not only extremely meagre but of dubious quality. Numerous prisoners testified to the inquiry that the food was almost always tainted; even the stockfish, which was sometimes kept for weeks, was full of worms. While the detainees could obtain beer, jenever, tea and tobacco in the canteen, they had to dig deep in their pockets for it, because Frison was charging twice the normal price. This also applied to the uniform, which then cost 31.5 guilders, although the fabric was of the poorest quality. The detainee's family also had a whole series of other expenses: a 'servant's due' of 12.6 guilders, a payment of four to seven guilders for the use of eating and drinking utensils, the purchase of bedding, the cleaning of clothing and medical attention. Anyone who could not pay had to sleep on straw, to walk about in befouled clothes and above all to stay in good health, since Frison called in the surgeon only when the person concerned was half-dead.

The social differences among the inmates played no role at all, however, as far as work and punishment were concerned. Here everyone was equal before the law – which meant before Frison himself. Whether people were paying or not, high or low maintenance costs counted for nothing: everyone had to produce. When Charles Joseph du Seuwoir, a 31-year-old advocate, arrived in the institution on 9 May 1770 and was told that he would have to do forced labour, he protested vigorously: his family had made a contract to pay 150 guilders a year on condition that he would not have to do any jobs. Frison did not bother to reply. The advocate was put in chains and thrown into the penitential cell, where he was left for the rest of the day and the whole night. In the morning he was given a little piece of black bread and water, after which he was offered a choice: either stay in the penitential cell or work in the manufactory. Fortunately for him, Frison had a weak spot: the garden. When a warder heard by chance that the advocate knew a lot about flowers and plants, he hastened to inform the director who immediately gave him the job of gardener; during the winter months, however, du Seuwoir had to work in the wool workshop and undertake the same labour as the other inmates.

Indeed, Frison considered the obligation to work not as an element of correction but as a source of profit. According to the detainees the established quotas were so high that no one succeeded in keeping to them all the time, let alone doing more. Their declarations cannot be verified, but Frison in any case did not make use of a reward system. Payment for good behaviour was otherwise out of the question, unless someone was working as a *kapo* or a squealer. People were given only negative sanctions because punishment, or rather the fear of it, was according to Frison the most suitable stimulant. Whippings and canings were the order of the day. They were given mostly to the 'idlers' and those 'unwilling to work', but diligent labour was no guarantee of avoiding chastisement. When a certain Kempenaer, a resident of Louvain, complained about the quality of the food, he was regaled with fifty strokes of the cane. When the young Van Gansen, the son of a butcher from Borgerhout, refused to wear shoes which were much too small for him, Frison had him given eighty strokes of the cane and thereafter the victim had for three days to wear foot-irons which were so tight that they ripped the flesh from the bones with the slightest movement. Women were not spared. Anna Maria Hertochs, a 28-year-old woman from Mechelen confined at the request of her mother, was given so many stripes with the cane that she was left with scars and internal bruising; one year after her chastisement she was still coughing up blood. It is not surprising therefore that the inmates did everything they could to escape. In the period 1760–72 there were no fewer than 13 break-outs. Woe betide anyone who was recaptured: he would have to run the gauntlet of a double row of inmates wielding sticks upon his bare back until the blood dripped to the ground; anyone who did not hit hard enough was himself given a flogging.

Frison and his assistants would stop at nothing. A single example will suffice. After Anthoon Rousseau, a 51-year-old wigmaker confined at the request of his family, had been beaten with whips and canes for hours he died in the dungeon. The director was not in the least perturbed about the rumours of manslaughter and even murder going the rounds of the inmates. He should have called in the surgeon to establish the cause of death, but there was no need: a rope was tied around Rousseau's neck and the matter was settled. Frison did not even bother to inform the widow, although she only visited the place once a year. She first learned of her husband's death many months later, through an ex-detainee who advised her to make a formal complaint and declared himself ready to act as a witness for the prosecution. The woman refused 'for fear of the cost': 'money wasted', she said, 'for who would believe the word of a prisoner?' Rousseau was not forgotten, however. During the inquiry into Frison's financial malpractices many inmates informed the procurator-general that Rousseau was not a man to commit suicide and that the director and his assistants had either murdered him or that he was so severely punished that he had succumbed as a result of his wounds. They provided so many substantive details that the procurator-general summoned to court the surgeon who wrote the death certificate. The testimony of Jacques Chinay ran as follows: 'Yes, the deceased did have a noose about his neck and the rope was attached to a nail in the wall. I found the affair quite bizarre, because the ceiling of the cell in which he was found was so low that a man could not stand upright in it ... Why did I not carry out an autopsy? On a convict? That is not at all customary.'[26]

Provincial penitentiaries

During the second half of the eighteenth century more and more enlightened minds in Western Europe were directing their criticisms to the existing penal institutions. They censured the mixing of all categories of prisoners, the capriciousness of the directors, the brutal methods of discipline, the inhumane conditions under which people lived and worked – in short, the absence of any proper system, order and gradation which meant that the essential purpose of the confinement, namely moral improvement, could not be fulfilled. They pleaded for the establishment of new, modern institutions which, they argued, should be designed as houses of reform in the real sense of the word: places where a change in behaviour would be of central importance – which would mean, among other things, that positive effects would have to be produced. To this end, attention would have to be paid both to the structure of the building and to the internal regulations, to the standard sanctions and the training, to the control of the body and that of the mind. In other words, the new houses of improvement had to function as 'machines for grinding rogues honest', to quote the expression of the English moral philosopher Jeremy Bentham.

At the heart of the new approach, which was being propagated and concretized in a growing number of writings, lay a belief in the perfectibility of human beings. Both criminals and people with morally reprehensible behaviour had to be treated as children under tutelage: they could not subdue their tempers and passions because they had not received any education directed towards learning to control their bodies and minds, towards learning self-discipline. The penitential institution had to correct this fault by offering a re-education programme leading to moral, spiritual and social improvement. In order to realize these aims a person's anti-social tendencies had to be kept under iron discipline. The key to changing behaviour was not the power of persuasion, but coercion. However, absolute authority was not synonymous with arbitrariness, and violence could not simply be the result of cruelty or be used by the supervisors at will; it had to be made clear that the punishment was just. Treat those confined as human beings, so John Howard's argument ran, show that you are humane, that your only concern is to make them into useful members of society and that all the activities in the institution are for that purpose; read them out the house rules so that they shall know their duties and rights and have the certainty that they will not be deceived by the warders. Corruption, favouritism and cruelty must be done away with. Firmness of principle, justice, clarity of structure, orderliness, regularity: these are the foundations of the penitentiary system. The reformatory must become transparent, impersonal *and* humane. Indeed, what is rational is impersonal and it is precisely here that the humane is to be found. For this reason it is necessary to supervise the staff closely; they must observe the regulations as much as the detainees. It is also necessary to look for 'scientific' techniques of discipline so that the use of physical violence can be kept to a minimum. When corporal punishment is administered the emotions of the person administering it can have no part in it. Chastisement must remain impersonal. Bentham thought of a 'whipping-machine', which would make it possible to make the strokes land with regularity and the same intensity upon the back of the transgressor. In short, the prison had to be a crystallization-point of 'scientific humanity', compatible with philanthropy.

Solitary confinement became the new panacea. The reformers realized that total isolation is an extraordinarily painful experience, but the cellular system was in their view the cornerstone of the re-education programme: it confronted the prisoner with himself, which made repentance possible. Is it any wonder that the roots of the system can be traced back to the world of the Church? The prison of San Michele in Rome, set up by Pope Clement XI in 1703 with a view to disciplining disobedient children, showed the way. The building contained sixty little rooms grouped around a central courtyard, which meant that each pupil could be both isolated and controlled. The motto was 'Little is achieved by punishment unless discipline instils goodness'. This idea was supported by Howard and many other enlightened spirits. They considered solitary confinement not as a punishment, as was the case in the existing houses of correction, where the dungeon and the penitential cells in fact served as torture chambers, but as a therapeutic instrument that induced introspection and thus brought about repentance. This is the reason why all prisoners, regardless of whether they behaved well or badly, would be put into separate cells.

The moulding of a person's character was, according to the reformers, indissolubly linked with the remodelling of his body, which implied that the external forms of disorder had to be set right. Their plea for cleanliness and care of the body, in particular for regular washing, was part of their battle against moral decline and indiscipline. For the same reasons they laid great emphasis on the duty to work: idleness was the mother of all vices. Through unrelenting, disciplined work the convict would learn to conform to the requirements of morality. A person who learned to control his body was in a position to tame his mind as well, so the theory went. This view of things fitted in with the medical theory of the time according to which disturbances to bodily functions gave rise to mental ones, just as psychological disorders affected the body. In the latter case the view was that immorality could manifest itself as an illness, which 'explained' why so many poor people suffered from physical complaints; with the same reasoning, criminality was the external manifestation of internal chaos. This infernal interaction could be interrupted only by correcting body and mind together, and no technique was better suited to the purpose than hard and regular work. The reformers in no way considered obligatory work as a means of instilling fear, as a form of terror, much less a source of profit. They utterly rejected notions like these, which were the norm in many of the existing houses of correction. Their essential concern was to make the prisoners into different, that is, better, people. Forced labour was in their eyes indispensable, because self-control could not be exercised and optimized in any other way. For this reason the tasks had to be accurately described and carried out in accordance with a rigorous timetable. When Pinel freed the prisoners of Bicêtre in Paris from their chains in 1792, he was not so much carrying out an act of fellow humanity as one of a therapeutic-disciplinary nature: the chains had to be replaced by more subtle forms of control, based on useful employment and constant supervision, whose purpose was to 'normalize' both body and mind.[27]

Matters did not remain just a stream of words. The new ideas were put into practice, and in this the Austrian Netherlands played a pioneering role. Indeed, it was not Howard who was the father of modern prison life, but Vilain XIIII, and not Bentham who created the panopticon, but the same Vilain XIIII. Like the British reformers, he pleaded for a radical reorganization of prison life, because he had an unshakeable faith in the perfectibility of men. Place people guilty of morally reprehensible behaviour in the right environment, use the right techniques, and 'one should not be the least embarrassed nor perturbed by the possibility of bringing them to order, to a spirit of work, and of rendering the majority of them, upon their release, useful to the state and to themselves'; by isolating them, setting them to work and subjecting them to an all-encompassing series of norms, 'it would be possible to make them better men and subsequently to put them back into society.' This conviction was fundamental to his design for the building and organization of the provincial penitentiary in Ghent, the purpose of whose external form and internal regulations was to discipline body and mind. The complex consists of an external and internal octagon, whose corners are linked together by connecting buildings; this results in the formation of eight trapezoid courtyards concentrated around the central octagon and courtyard from which all the other parts can be overlooked.[28] Although when he visited the penitentiary for the first time in 1778 only half the complex had been completed, Howard immediately saw the innovative character of this structural form, which on the one hand guaranteed total control and on the other offered the opportunity of putting each category of inmate into separate buildings, thus dividing the men from the women and the criminals from beggars and petty offenders; he also reproduced the ground plan in his book *The State of the Prisons*.[29]

We do not know where Vilain XIIII got his inspiration from. With the exception of the stables at Versailles there had been no other example of a panoptic construction in Europe before the erection of the reformatory at Ghent. For the cell-system he might have based his ideas on the San Michele prison in Rome, but there is no certainty about that. He was in any case the first to apply the principle of solitary confinement consistently. In the urban correction- and workhouses there were actually one-man cells, but they were few in number and most of them served as punishment cells. On the other hand, in the Ghent *Maison de Force* each male detainee had to spend the night in an individual cell which was 1.9 metres long, 1.5 metres wide and 2.2 metres high and was furnished with a bed, a chamber-pot, a small bench for sitting, a folding shelf and a small built-in cupboard. Only the female section contained larger sleeping rooms, which could take two to four detainees.

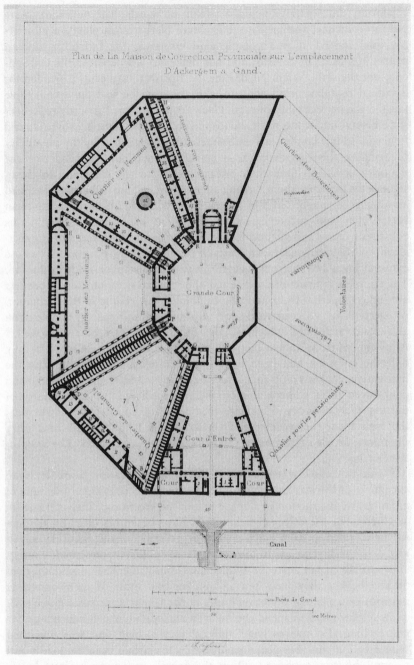

Plate 15 Ground plan of the provincial penitentiary at Ghent, 1775. The new architectural design conceived by Vilain XIIII guaranteed total control of the inmates.

The architect of the provincial penitentiary at Vilvoorde did not follow the example of Ghent as regards panoptic vision. He kept to tradition and designed a rectangular complex. By grouping the buildings around inner courtyards, however, the various sections could easily be controlled. Just as in Ghent, each section was also reserved for a specific category of detainee and each category had its own workplace and refectory, and it should be mentioned that both men and women were locked in individual cells.

Given that the new disciplinary project was not directed towards exclusion or punishment, but to moral improvement and reintegration, a great deal of attention was paid to the duration of confinement. The period doubtless had to be in proportion to the misdeed or misbehaviour, but it could not be too long or too short. As Goswin de Fierlant remarked: 'when the guilty party is kept apart from society it will be a matter of consistency to make him useful to that society by imposing upon him a penalty capable of correcting him.' On the one hand it was not desirable to drive the detainee to despair, because in that case confinement would achieve nothing. On the other hand the view was that the salutary effects would be felt only after a certain time had elapsed, which in concrete terms meant that the detainee had to remain at least a year in the institution. It is possible that these ideas were echoed by the city magistrates and persuaded them to lock up unwanted people for longer than the family had asked. Whatever the case may be, the average duration of confinement amounted to 31 months in Vilvoorde for adults and 18 months for minors. These periods clearly sufficed to bring about a change in behaviour, since the number of recidivists was negligible. We cannot know whether the detainees really were brought to repentance – in other words, whether they went home as 'better' people. However, there can be no doubt that they had learned 'something', even if it was only that hard labour outside the penitentiary was preferable to the disciplinary treadmill within the institution.

In comparison to the urban houses of correction the provincial penitentiaries were the epitome of disciplinary power, which had both positive and negative consequences for the detainees. Terror and capriciousness were practically done away with, since the governors, the subordinate officials, the overseers in the places of work and the guards had to make written reports on every intervention, every expense paid and above all every deviation from the rules. In addition, the deputies from the Provincial Estates saw to it that all members of staff adhered to the regulations. Not only did they regularly check the dossiers of the detainees and the registers containing the names of the sick, those who had died and those who had been punished, as well as book-keeping documents, but they also made frequent visits to the institution, where

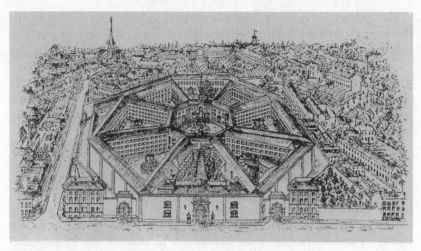

Plate 16   View of the provincial penitentiary in Ghent after completion in 1827

they set to work in a thorough manner, as can be seen from numerous letters. Although those who took the initiative were hoping that the penitentiaries would have some economic use, they certainly considered the obligation to work above all as a means of discipline and re-education. This is why the standard was established in such a way that industrious detainees could do more work in the day and be rewarded; they first received the total amount of money when they were released from the institution. Reward was also possible for good behaviour, namely a reduction of punishment or, for persons who had been confined at the request of their family, early release. Anyone who produced too little, made mistakes in his work or infringed a house rule knew in advance what sanction awaited him (or her): the rules summed up all the infractions imaginable and the punishments to be applied. Initially these were mainly corrective, thus directed towards the exercise of positive talents. The 'director of police' ought preferably to impose heavy jobs, provide a scantier diet, hold back a certain percentage of the pocket money, and so on. As extreme punishment there was the bread and water diet in a punishment cell and flogging, but in the first case the maximum period was two days and in the second 25 or 30 lashes (in Ghent and Vilvoorde respectively); for a flogging, permission had to be given by the relevant authorities, who first held a hearing. The frequent disturbances and escape attempts eventually led to a harder approach in both institutions, which meant that all the old punishments were brought back and the 'director of police' was granted permission to put recalci-trant prisoners in the dungeon for longer periods or to have them given the maximum number of strokes of the cane for several consecutive days; in the case of a recidivist he could also lengthen their sentence. He was not given carte blanche, however: for every chastisement he had to make out a report for the council of administrators, who held an inquiry on each occasion, and he could under no circumstances increase a prisoner's sentence by more than six months.

As for clothing and hygiene, the prisoners had nothing to complain about. They were certainly not dressed in rags. They were uniformly given summer and winter clothing of a decent quality, which was regularly washed and replaced as necessary; the Ghent prisoners in principle had the right to a clean nightshirt every week and a pair of clean bed-sheets every month. In Vilvoorde the newcomers were even given a comb and two brushes, one for his clothes and one for his shoes. In both institutions it was seen to it that the detainees washed themselves every morning and tidied up their cells. If we can believe contemporaries, the battle against uncleanliness was not just part of disciplinary procedure but was of real significance because, according to them, the buildings were being well maintained. Diet was also regulated in detail. The council of administrators gave the governors precise guidelines on the type and quantity of food that had to be provided. Calculations show that the detainees never suffered from hunger. Initially, rations were even fairly well balanced: in addition to bread, everyone was given some butter in the morning and evening, and, at midday, vegetable soup with a portion of salted meat or fish. Over the years, however, the quantities of protein and fats were drastically reduced in both institutions, despite the opposition of the governors, who advised the authorities that the detainees had to carry out heavy work and that, moreover, the meals were the only bright points in their daily existence.

The certainty of justice did not make daily life in the provincial reformatory any more pleasant, however. Against the absence of arbitrariness there was the routine of activities carried out to a rigorous timetable in absolute silence, broken only by the ringing of the bell, the treadmill of regulations, which covered every single aspect of behaviour, and the inspections that took place from morning till evening, and even at night. Of course, the norms were just as strict in the urban houses of correction, where every deviation was equally punishable in principle. The application of the rules and the determination of punishment also depended on the director, however – which could lead to excesses, as the Frison case shows, but which also made it possible to turn a blind eye to certain 'deviations'. In the provincial penitentiaries relations between detainees and members of staff were much more impersonal. The former carried a number and were treated as such. The warders were not inclined to turn a blind eye to infringements of the rules, since they themselves ran the risk of being punished if they let the matter go: and that risk was very real, since anyone who caught a colleague not doing his duty was given a reward, and there were many warders – on average one for every five prisoners, not including the work supervisors. The punishment registers at Vilvoorde furthermore show that the rules were applied to the letter: almost 40 per cent of the men and about a third of the women were 'corrected' at least once because of negligence, inattentiveness, impoliteness, speaking when not allowed, or an 'incorrect attitude' In other words, the reformatory functioned as a drill-school, with the understanding that much stiffer demands were made of the prisoners than of soldiers, since they were never allowed to lose their self-control.

The purpose of the strict discipline was not only to get prisoners used to an orderly life. The governors were scared to death of plots, escape attempts and all forms of collective violence. Their fear is quite understandable, since on the one hand the provincial reformatories housed more prisoners than all the urban penal institutions put together, and on the other they realized all too well that their 'pupils' were under such great physical pressure that eruptions were far from imaginary. This is why they continually hammered home the necessity of keeping a close eye on the inmates and promptly reporting every infringement. It is also why prisoners were only allowed to write and receive one letter a year, everything being censored that had nothing to do with family matters. This is why prisoners had to keep silent for most of the day and the whole night and why the wardens had to be in sufficient numbers during 'recreation' in order to be able to listen to what the prisoners were talking about. The warders did their duty: at Vilvoorde they intercepted 11 of the 13 escape attempts that were made between 1780 and 1794 and they were able to nip in the bud the six protest movements that arose during the same period. It is not surprising therefore that the atmosphere of tension within the institution could be cut with a knife, as the warders themselves reported.[30] The words of the prisoners are alas not available to us. Which term would they have used: sledge-hammer or treadmill?

Epilogue: Power and Powerlessness

We have taken a long walk through the social and mental landscape of a number of eighteenth-century cities. The purpose of this quest was to find an explanation for a phenomenon that moves the hearts and minds of today just as it did a hundred or two hundred years ago: confinement on request. During the *ancien régime*, legal and medical considerations seldom played a part in a compulsory admission to an institution. Families could make someone who was a 'nuisance' to them disappear from sight for varying periods without any form of trial and in most cases even without the help of a doctor; it was enough to enter a request for confinement because of misconduct to the local authorities, and they were generally inclined to accept the arguments of the petitioners without question. If, during the seventeenth century, relatively few families made use of this simple procedure, during the Age of Enlightenment their numbers grew continually, especially after 1770, when it was the less well-off population groups who were at the forefront of this disciplinary action.

It was not only in the major cities of Brabant and Flanders that private confinement functioned as an instrument for bringing an errant house-mate or relative back to a more orderly life. This was also the case in eighteenth-century France, at least up to the end of the *ancien régime*, as can be seen from the data collected by Claude Quétel and other French historians; they show that the *lettre de cachet de famille* was used ever more frequently in all the towns and regions studied, especially after 1750, when the annual average fluctuated between 2.9 and 3.6 per 10,000 inhabitants.[1] In the United Provinces, too, the number of initial requests for confinement presented by private individuals increased steadily during the eighteenth century: in Leiden from two per 10,000 inhabitants annually around 1710 to about three around 1790 – and in Dordrecht the annual average was even higher, rising to 13 per 10,000 inhabitants around 1800.[2] Unfortunately, there is little information on the social background of the petitioners and prisoners in these two countries, and the available evidence is far from being unequivocal. It would seem that from half to two-thirds of the Parisian petitioners were *gens de petite condition* (lower-class people),[3] but the occupations mentioned in the requests presented to the *intendant* of Provence suggest a greater involvement of middle-class families in private confinement[4] – though bare occupational data can be very misleading. Pieter Spierenburg claims that the middle and upper classes are over-represented in his Leiden sample.[5] In Dordrecht, on the other hand, the growing numbers of unwanted persons and those seeking to confine them came in the overwhelming majority from the lower classes,[6] and the patients in the Maastricht and 's-Hertogenbosch madhouses also came in increasing numbers from the poorer sections of the urban population; pauper lunatics represented more than half of the inmates by the end of the eighteenth century.[7]

In any case, the Austrian Netherlands, the United Provinces and eighteenth-century France were similar in many respects as far as private confinement is concerned. With the possible exception of Paris, the number of petitions everywhere shows a persistently rising trend. In all the towns and regions studied, the conflicts arose mainly within the nuclear family, and most committal dramas were being played out either between parents and children or between spouses. The overwhelming majority of requests for confinement presented to the authorities by private persons involved young people and adults who were declared to be of sound mind by their housemates as well as by the witnesses. The available evidence suggests, moreover, that the unwanted persons committed to prison workhouses or public asylums originated from the larger cities rather than from the smaller towns and rural areas.

In sum then, it would seem that during the second half of the eighteenth century increasing numbers of urban families in Western Europe were having to cope with 'troublesome' or even 'impossible' members, that they were finding it increasingly difficult to solve these problems themselves, and that it was for this reason that they were resorting in growing numbers to an external authority. There is no doubt that abuses occurred: 'disorderly conduct' was an extremely loose category, which could include nearly all kinds of behaviour considered counter to accepted standards or family interests, and this applied with even greater force to 'insanity'. The archival evidence proves that the fear of wrongful confinement was by no means illusory. There were petitioners who tried to obtain the imprisonment of a housemate or relative under false pretexts, and their machinations could indeed be successful on occasion.[8] Yet the rising numbers of confinement petitions cannot be explained in terms of growing abuse or arbitrariness. They do not reflect ever more despotic familial power, but rather a desperate response to practical problems on a novel scale. What were these problems and why did they increase to such alarming proportions towards the end of the *ancien régime*? This is precisely what we have tried to investigate, at least with regard to the major cities in the Austrian Netherlands, particularly Antwerp and Bruges.

Of course, a monograph will not suffice as an 'explanatory model' which could be applied to other Western European cities. The wide variations in the social background of the petitioners and prisoners indicate that, as we mentioned in the introduction, differing economic, demographic, political and cultural developments can bring about other kinds of social tensions and domestic troubles. However, our analysis of the social dynamics of confinement in eighteenth-century Brabant and Flanders yields some conclusions that might stimulate further comparative research.

The number of confinement petitions rose continually towards the end of the *ancien régime* because urban society was coming increasingly under pressure. The growing social problems had repercussions on its smallest units, namely families, which were being torn apart by internal conflicts increasingly more often while the usual channels for resolving them were being progressively blocked. What the historian with hindsight would define as a structural transformation or transition phase was experienced by contemporaries of the day as dislocation. This was translated into feelings of uncertainty and fear, which increased the inclination to cling on to certain standards and values, especially when people felt powerless to deal with difficulty – thus when there seemed to be no way out of their predicament.

The dismantling of the craft guilds, which in the past had offered some protection, the growing dependence on wages and the drastic fall in purchasing power confronted broad sections of the population with material problems that put the reproduction of the family into jeopardy. As a result, it was expected that individual members should provide as big a contribution to the family income as possible. Given that proletarianization and impoverishment formed a constant threat, everything, but *everything*, had to be subordinated to a strategy for survival. Everyone had to make an effort to keep the family from dropping down the social ladder or actually sliding into the dreadful depths of destitution. This led to the establishment of high demands, both of the individual and others. More than ever it was imperative that the husband-breadwinner should not fail in his duties, while at the same time it was becoming increasingly

difficult for him to fulfil his function as a good father to his family. It is
not surprising that the results from all this were frustrations released
through all sorts of acts of violence, of which the spouse and children
were the primary victims. More and more lower-class women were in a
position to fight back, however, because industrial restructuring offered
them the opportunity to make a cash contribution to the family income,
enabling them to be more independent of their husbands. Young people,
particularly males, also came under a great deal of pressure, since on the
one hand they had to get a job at a very early stage in their lives, and on
the other they were having to wait longer and longer before they could
build their own independent lives. In other words, many adolescents
found themselves in a 'threshold' situation: they could not function
completely within or completely outside the parental home. Considering
that frustrated youths comprised an ever greater proportion of urban
populations, a generation conflict was inevitable. Their dissatisfactions
were directed against not only their own parents but also relationships
of authority in general. Wantonness, vandalism and crime against
property were the expressions of rebellious youth, who considered the
present day as meaningless because they had no perspective on the
future.[9]

It did not escape the attention of the authorities that cracks in the
political and social order were beginning to show. The fight against
disorder became a real obsession. Every form of deviant behaviour,
insofar as it manifested itself in public, was regarded as a threat. The
movement towards control, regulation and discipline could be seen not
only in all manner of pleas for a more efficient prosecution policy but
also in the introduction of a new social policy, which relied to a large
extent on forced labour. More than ever before the urban magistrates
kept a watchful eye on the destitute in general and those receiving
charitable relief in particular. Anyone who stepped out of line ended up
behind the walls of a house of correction. It in no way follows from this
that the disciplinary argument and disciplinary actions remained limited
to the ruling classes and even less that their definitions of the social
problem were accepted as authoritative. The less well-off population
groups employed criteria of respectability and tolerance thresholds that
corresponded with their own standards and expectations – which were
not necessarily contrary to nor congruent with those propounded by the
elites. The lower middle classes and wage-earners set down demarcation-
lines between the tolerable and the intolerable, the permissible and the
impermissible, in accordance with their own needs – and they acted
appropriately, which in concrete terms meant that patterns of behaviour
which would affect the reproduction of the family were not tolerated. As
the material basis crumbled and the reciprocal relationships between

housemates became more difficult, so the inclination grew to label a husband or wife, son or daughter, as uncontrollable and throw that person out; misdeeds in the emotional sphere were often the straw that broke the camel's back.

Tolerance thresholds were certainly not laid down individually but collectively. Families from the less well-off sections of society had to conform to the norms and values currently in force in the neighbourhood community. They simply could not permit themselves to ignore the views of others, since participation in sociability networks was for them a *sine qua non* for guaranteeing the continued existence of the family. If reciprocal relationships with neighbours were called into question because a family member was causing a scandal, then they had to intervene in order to secure their own position.

The lowering of tolerance thresholds reflects the changing sensitivity towards patterns of behaviour that for structural reasons could be accepted neither by the family concerned nor by the neighbouring residents. What might be labelled as a change of mentality was in fact just one component in a global adaptation process, whereby people were trying to keep functioning in new and difficult circumstances, both material and emotional. There does not seem much point in speaking of a 'civilizing offensive'.[10] The less well-off population groups certainly did not alter their tolerance thresholds because they had been won over to the rules of behaviour which the elites wanted to lay down, but because they had to adapt their survival strategies to the altered social reality.

The request for confinement was generally the last stage in a long series of attempts to restore peace to the family and the neighbouring community. From this point of view the contribution made by some anthropologically oriented historians and jurists is extremely important. John Bossy and other researchers have pointed out that disputes could be settled in widely differing ways and that the range of strategies and the choice made from among them not only vary from society to society, but are also dependent on the place that the contesting parties occupy in the network of social relationships.[11] Indeed, it is not at all obvious that a large number of families in the eighteenth century who wanted to correct one of their members called in the assistance of a third party, one who did not belong to their own social stratum, nor that this third party seldom took matters into their own hands, usually limiting themselves to ratifying and legitimizing the decisions taken by those directly involved.

The neighbouring residents and the parish priest often played an intermediary role in conflicts between housemates or relatives. Their attempts to restore peace met with ever diminishing success, however.

They were usually powerless when faced with problems arising from shifts in the balance of power within the family, particularly because the changes in the relationship patterns between married couples and between parents and children were determined by social developments and in consequence had a structural character. The processes of proletarianization and impoverishment undermined the power of informal social ties, which meant that families being dislocated by the reprehensible lifestyle of one of their members could expect little in the way of understanding: as the less well-off experienced the breaching of social norms and values increasingly as threats to reciprocity and thus as a form of unacceptable behaviour, they were more inclined to rebuke those who failed to observe those social standards. At the same time, the growing distance between the moralizing discourses of the elites and the hard reality with which broad sections of the population were confronted tainted the ideal image of an organic community, which made it difficult to get people to accept the traditional relationships of authority, especially the young. Given that the horizontal sociability networks and the vertical bonds of paternalism were being called into question, problem families were being increasingly thrown back on themselves. There were still 'fellow-men' around and they were even more exacting than ever before, but they shifted the burden of intervention onto the family of the unwanted person. In this sense confinement on request was a symptom of collective powerlessness: it reflected the growing inability of the neighbourhood communities to solve their problems themselves.[12]

It is quite understandable that most families elected for private confinement instead of prosecution. Not only was a court case expensive and its outcome unpredictable, but it was regarded as something shameful, especially when the parties involved were housemates or relatives. This is why domestic disputes during the *ancien régime* were generally settled without the intervention of the courts and the injured party tried to obtain satisfaction and/or restore his honour through all manner of infrajudicial means, which in practice usually came to a compensation settlement.[13] Private confinement differed from informal methods of resolving conflicts in that the responsibility for the problem was laid on the shoulders of only one of the parties, whose character was blackened as much as possible. The paradox of confinement on request was that the question of guilt was the central issue and was 'resolved', although there had been no trial in the real sense of the word and the accused could not defend themselves.

We should not lose sight of the fact that the behaviour objected to in the petitions for confinement was seldom a matter for formal prosecution. Marital violence, for example, became a criminal offence only in exceptional cases. There was little or nothing to be expected from the authorities on this question. So long as the conflicts took place within the domestic circle, they did not intervene. Family problems were increasingly coming to be considered as private affairs. Just as in neighbouring countries,[14] the elites in the Austrian Netherlands were attaching increasing importance to the intimacy of the family, whom they wanted to screen from the all too obtrusive eyes of outsiders. One of the consequences of this revaluation of privacy was that adultery and prostitution were *de facto* decriminalized, unless public order was endangered.[15] This also applies to alcoholism and the addiction to gambling: so long as other people were not injured, the family had to deal with the problem themselves. In short, the authorities were no longer interested in 'sin', but in 'disorder'. Some members of the social upper stratum themselves fell victim to this shift in perception and appreciation, as can be seen from their requests, but for the less well-off the consequences were particularly serious, since on the one hand privacy was for them socially unthinkable and economically impossible, and on the other hand, because of the growing number of domestic conflicts, protection by the law was the very thing of which they needed to be certain.

It is within this complex field of tension that confinement on request must be situated. As regards the resolving of domestic conflicts, broad sections of the population at the end of the *ancien régime* ended up in a vacuum, both because the informal means of social control employed by the neighbourhood community were becoming less and less effective and because the authorities for their own reasons were not inclined to prosecute infringements of morality that posed no threats to what they perceived as the fundamentals of social and political order. Their battle against all forms of public 'disorder' did, however, provide a point of contact. Anyone who could demonstrate that private interests affected the general interest – thus that the disturbance of domestic order was accompanied by a disturbance of public order – was given a hearing. It is from this perspective that the 'meeting' between the interests of the families and those of the authorities must be viewed. Because the former presented their problem as a socio-political one, the latter were given the opportunity to discipline people who had committed no formally prosecutable offence and who in consequence were 'untouchable'. However, it was a double-edged sword: the petitioners were able to use the language of authority in order to rid themselves of a burden and thus to tie the authorities up in their own contradictions. The role assigned to the aldermen was as limited as it was unusual: they sanctioned the actions of the burghers. They did not punish; they only made the carrying out of punishment possible. They held the keys of the house of correction in their hands, but they could only open the doors when the families asked them to.

The fact that with time more and more proletarian families were requesting the confinement of one of their own members and that the urban magistrates were granting their requests is no proof of consensus: it shows only that the immediate interests of both groups were more or less parallel. It is true that numerous wage-earners objected to behaviour which the aldermen viewed with severity, such as work-shyness and theft, but it does not follow from this that their purposes were identical. The former were trying first and foremost to maximize their chances of survival, while the latter considered private confinement to be essential as an aid in their fight against orderlessness and indolence.

In enlightened government circles the more frequent use of private confinement was certainly not welcomed, as can be seen from the discussion about the functions of the provincial penitentiaries, where conservative viewpoints did battle with more enlightened ideas. The central government did its very best to convince everyone that deprivation of liberty was no light punishment and that only persons who had contravened the law and who had been sentenced in court should be imprisoned. It was to no avail. The champions of judicial reforms constituted only a tiny minority. Most members of the elites were against the abolition of corporal punishment and against more humane treatment for the detainees; the new institutions, according to them, had to have just as fearful an atmosphere as the urban houses of correction. Moreover, the magistrates of the large cities were of the opinion that the provincial penitentiaries had to serve as reformatories for persons (particularly those who had not yet come of age) who had been confined at the request of their families, because many forms of disorderly conduct that were not formally indictable undermined the work ethic and, as a result, social order.

It may be assumed that the lower classes were as much declared supporters of a hard approach as most members of the elites. From the fact that it was mainly proletarian petitioners who asked for a longer period of detention than the authorities considered desirable, it can be inferred that they wanted to 'fight back'. However, the wage-earners did not have punishment alone in mind. They simply could not permit themselves to throw out the unwanted person for ever or even just put them under lock and key for a lengthy period. Married female wage-earners in particular had an interest in ensuring that their uncontrollable husbands came home as soon as possible and started contributing to the family income again; for the same reasons they generally chose confinement in preference to separation *a mensa et thoro*. From this standpoint the provincial reformatories answered the expectations of the lower classes: correction and changing behaviour went hand in hand.

The history of the private confinement system in the Austrian Netherlands demonstrates that the functions of discipline-wielding institutions could be transformed by the active involvement of proletarian families, who were able to pursue their own interests through them. In that respect the passing of the *ancien régime* brought with it no fundamental changes. New laws were enacted, stipulating that only a person who was mentally ill and constituted a danger to public order could still be put into an institution. The protection of the family against the destructive actions of an individual member gave way to the protection of the individual against the attacks of housemates or relatives against his or her integrity.[16] By concentrating exclusively on the rights of the citizen and the psychological condition of the patient, however, sight was lost of the problems and needs of many low-income families, with the result that they desperately looked for loopholes in the law and procedures. If a declaration of insanity would do the trick, then they did not hesitate to take that step.

Andrew Scull claims that it was the 'expansion of the asylum system which created the increased demand for its services', and that 'the asylum inevitably operated to reduce family and community tolerance.'[17] That might be true, but the question remains: how are the class-linked differentials in tolerance-levels to be explained? Indeed, as he acknowledges, the number of private patients per 10,000 inhabitants increased only slightly in Victorian England, whereas the number of pauper lunatics per 10,000 inhabitants more than doubled.[18] Even more importantly, John Walton has shown that the peculiar pattern of admissions to Lancaster asylum reflected the differential ability to cope with the problem: the families in the textile-producing districts were better able and more willing to provide a supportive environment for people who might otherwise have been drawn into the asylum (or the workhouse) than the families in the county's two largest cities, Liverpool and Manchester. His analysis provides support for the contention that it was 'the poverty of low wages, large families, crowded accommodation and overwork' which played a crucial role in the casting out of pauper lunatics.[19] Much thorough research will be needed to assess the motives of the petitioners and the doctors' diagnoses. In any case, fragmentary data in the Antwerp records suggests that the overwhelming majority of mentally disturbed paupers were committed on their families' initiative and that alcoholic addiction, coupled with domestic violence, was the most common charge.[20]

It could be argued that the problem no longer arises today, in view of the fact that more and more psychiatric institutions (and hostels for the homeless) are closing down and the former inmates, as 'free' citizens, can now wander where they please. If we share the view of Thomas Szasz that mental alienation is merely a social construct, so that the existence of the asylum itself is an abuse and has no discernible purpose except to enforce confinement and control deviance,[21] then the process of deinstitutionalization is to be welcomed. However, we should also ask why most of the 'liberated' patients still have no abode, living permanently on the streets of the large cities together with the rest of the homeless. Anyone who does not understand that reciprocity and solidarity are not naturally spontaneous factors in human relations, and that the financial and emotional capacities of families and neighbourhood communities have limits, can only stand back and react with moral indignation – but this will not solve the problem.

Notes

ANP   *Archives Nationales*, Paris
ARAB   *Algemeen Rijksarchief*, Brussels
GRO   *Geheime Raad* (Privy Council), Austrian Regime
KK   *Kerken en Kloosters* (Churches and Monasteries)
MA   Modern Archive
OA   Old Archive
OCMWA   *Openbaar Centrum voor Maatschappelijk Welzijn*, Antwerp
PK   *Privilege Kamer*
RB   *Raad van Brabant* (Council of Brabant)
ROPBA   *Recueil des Ordonnances des Pays-Bas autrichiens*, 15 vols (Brussels, 1860–1942)
SAA   *Stadsarchief* (City Archives), Antwerp
SABg   *Stadsarchief*, Bruges
SABs   *Stadsarchief*, Brussels
SAG   *Stadsarchief*, Ghent
V   *Vierschaar*

Introduction

1 After the publication by Elisabeth Marain in 1988 of a semi-fictional novel entitled *Rosalie Niemand* (Rosalie Nobody), the tragic life-story of Liliane Rosalie Stynen aroused a storm of indignation in Belgium: she was placed in a private psychiatric institution by her mother at the age of 14, where she remained incarcerated for 38 years, until 1981, although she had shown not the slightest sign of psychological disturbance. See J. Vanhaelen and L. Stynen, *Rosalie Niemand vertelt* (Berchem, 1993).

2 After having been rebuked by the European Court of Human Rights in Strasbourg, because compulsory admission under the Insanity Law of 1850 required only a medical certificate and the mayor's approval, the Belgian legislators enacted a new law 'for protecting the mentally ill' in 1990, granting the power of decision to a Justice of the Peace. The Flemish General Practitioners' Forum, however, does not expect much reassurance from time-consuming legal procedures. According to the physicians, too little attention is paid to the fact that in most cases medical emergency is the basis of compulsory admission. Moreover, they are of the opinion that the legislators incorrectly based themselves on a model of conflict, taking for granted that the interests of the family and their doctor were at odds with those of the patient. *De Standaard*, 14 February 1990 and 14–15 July 1990; *De Morgen*, 16 February 1990.

3 C. Quétel, *'De Par Le Roy': essai sur les lettres de cachet* (Toulouse, 1981), pp. 25–6.

4 See especially B. E. Strayer, *'Lettres de cachet' and Social Control in the Ancien Régime, 1659–1789* (New York, 1992), pp. 146–50.

5 This explains why many historians assume that the well-to-do used this instrument of family discipline to a much greater extent than the less well-off. See, for example, P. Stead, *The Police of Paris* (London, 1957), p. 52, who concludes that 'the *lettre de cachet* was generally used for no darker purpose than the paternal disciplining of the upper classes.'

6 See P. Sagnac, *La législation civile de la Révolution française, 1789–1804* (Paris, 1898), and J. F. Traer, *Marriage and the Family in Eighteenth-Century France* (Ithaca, 1980); also S. Gutwirth, *Waarheidsaanspraken in recht en wetenschap* (Brussels, 1993), pp. 261–7.

7 W. L. Parry-Jones, *The Trade in Lunacy: A Study of Private Madhouses in England in the Eighteenth and Nineteenth Centuries* (London and Toronto, 1972), pp. 6–28; M. Byrd, *Visits to Bedlam: Madness and Literature in the Eighteenth Century* (Columbia, 1974), pp. 36–46.

8 P. McCandless, 'Liberty and Lunacy: The Victorians and Wrongful Confinement', in A. Scull (ed.), *Madhouses, Mad-Doctors and Madmen* (Philadelphia and London, 1981), pp. 341–62 (on p. 357).

9 A. Scull, *The Most Solitary of Afflictions: Madness and Society in Britain, 1700–1900* (New Haven and London, 1993), pp. 361–3.

10 McCandless, 'Liberty and Lunacy', p. 343.

11 N. Tomes, 'The Anglo-American Asylum in Historical Perspective', in C. J. Smith and J. A. Giggs (eds), *Location and Stigma: Contemporary Perspectives on Mental Health and Mental Health Care* (Boston, 1988), p. 3.

12 M. Foucault, 'La vie des hommes infâmes', *Les cahiers du chemin* (1977), pp. 12–29 (on pp. 23 and 26–7).

13 A. Farge and M. Foucault, *Le désordre des familles: lettres de cachet des Archives de la Bastille* (Paris, 1982), p. 9.

14 Scull, *The Most Solitary of Afflictions*, p. 7. See also R. Porter, *Mind-Forg'd Manacles: A History of Madness in England from the Restoration to the Regency* (London, 1987).

15 M. Ignatieff, 'Total Institutions and Working Classes', *History Workshop*, 15 (1983), p. 172.

16 J. K. Walton, 'Casting Out and Bringing Back in Victorian England: Pauper Lunatics, 1840–1870', in W. F. Bynum, R. Porter and M. Shepherd (eds), *The Anatomy of Madness*, vol. 2 (London, 1985), pp. 131–46 (on p. 139).

See also his 'Lunacy in the Industrial Revolution: A Study of Asylum Admissions in Lancashire, 1848–50', *Journal of Social History*, 13 (1979), pp. 1–22.

17 *Collocatie* is the official term in Belgium for enforced confinement in a psychiatric institution. In the Austrian Netherlands, families petitioned the local magistrates to confine their uncontrollable/insane relatives: *colloqueren*. We shall use the terms 'private confinement' and 'confinement on request'.

Chapter 1 Confinement Requested

1 ANP, BB 16/216.
2 SAA, PK 879, f° 221.
3 SAA, PK 861, f° 13.
4 SAA, PK 819, f° 86v°.
5 SAA, PK 873, f° 7v°.
6 *Placcaet-Boek van Vlaenderen*, vol. V, 1 (Ghent, 1763), p. 118.
7 C. Verlinden (ed.), *Dokumenten voor de geschiedenis van prijzen en lonen in Vlaanderen en Brabant*, 4 vols (Bruges, 1959–73); C. Lis, *Social Change and the Labouring Poor: Antwerp, 1770–1860* (New Haven and London, 1986), pp. 14–15, 175–6.
8 See C. Vandenbroeke's calculations in *Agriculture et alimentation dans les Pays-Bas autrichiens* (Ghent and Louvain, 1975), pp. 606–7.

Chapter 2 Unruly Living

1 SAA, PK 867, f° 43.
2 SAA, PK 870, f° 111.
3 See particularly R. Porter, *Mind-Forg'd Manacles* (London, 1987).
4 SABs, file 431 (31 October 1770).
5 Unless otherwise mentioned, all the subsequent examples concern people who were sent to the Brussels *Simpelhuys* during the 1740s or 1780s at the request of members of their families: SABs, files 427–8 and 431–2.
6 L. Van Damme, *Misdadigheid te Antwerpen, 1765–1794*, unpublished Licentiate thesis, Ghent, 1973, pp. 66–7. See also L. Vandekerckhove, *Van straffen gesproken: de bestraffing van zelfdoding in het oude Europa* (Tielt, 1985), pp. 119–33. A similar development took place in England: see M. MacDonald, 'The Secularisation of Suicide in England, 1660–1800', *Past and Present*, 111 (1986), pp. 50–97, and his book *Sleepless Souls: Suicide in Early Modern England* (Oxford, 1990).
7 J. Geldhof, *Pelgrims, dulle lieden en vondelingen te Brugge, 1275–1975* (Bruges, 1975), pp. 136–7, 192–3.
8 P. Bonenfant, 'L'ancienne Maison des Insensés (*Simpelhuys*) de Bruxelles', *Annales de la Société royale d'Archéologie de Bruxelles*, 45 (1941), pp. 136–7.
9 J. C. G. M. Jansen, 'Waanzin en repressie: de zinnelozen en hun behandeling in Maastricht in de 18e eeuw', *Studies over de Sociaal-Economische Geschiedenis van Limburg*, 23 (1978), pp. 63–97.

10 SAA, PK 866, f° 156v°.

11 SAA, PK 867, f° 61v°, and PK 870, f° 137v°.

12 C. Laenens and L. Leemans, *De geschiedenis van het Antwerps gerecht* (Antwerp, 1953), p. 280.

13 R. Van der Made, 'La prostitution dans l'ancien droit belge', *Revue de droit pénal et de criminologie*, 29 (1949), pp. 763–73.

14 F. Vanhemelryck, *De criminaliteit in de ammanie van Brussel van de late middeleeuwen tot het einde van het Ancien Régime, 1404–1789* (Brussels, 1981), p. 136.

15 SAA, V 1822.

16 A.-M. Roets, *'Rudessen, dieften ende andere crimen'. Misdadigheid te Gent in de zeventiende en achttiende eeuw: een kwantitatieve en kwalitatieve analyse*, unpublished doctoral thesis, Ghent, 1987, pp. 269–76, and appendices 102–3, 128–30; Van Damme, *Misdadigheid*, pp. 29, 54, 61, 68–75. We have not included women who were prosecuted for having abandoned their children.

17 P. Godding, *Le droit privé dans les Pays-Bas méridionaux du 12e au 18e siècle* (Brussels, 1987), p. 111.

18 H. Soly, 'Kroeglopen in Brabant en Vlaanderen, 16e–18e eeuw', *Spiegel Historiael*, 18 (1983), pp. 569–71. See also T. Brennan's fine study *Public Drinking and Popular Culture in Eighteenth-Century Paris* (Princeton, 1988), pp. 228–68.

19 E. Aerts, *Bier, brouwers en brouwerijen in Lier: institutionele, sociale en economische aspecten van een stedelijke industrie tijdens de late middeleeuwen en de nieuwe tijd, 1400–1800*, unpublished doctoral thesis, Louvain, 1988, pp. 384–5.

20 G. Elewaut, *Herbergen in Gent, 1656–1795*, unpublished Licentiate thesis, Ghent, 1985, pp. 288–300. The last figure is based on SAG, MA, series R, no. 362. From a count probably taken around 1780 it appears that Brussels had one public house for every 132 residents. P. Cnops, 'De Brusselse herbergen in de tweede helft van de 18e eeuw', *Eigen Schoon en de Brabander*, 52 (1979), pp. 121–2.

21 F. Theerens, 'Op herbergbezoek te Brugge (1750–1850)', *Volkskunde*, 84 (1983), pp. 28–36; E. Van Autenboer, 'De Brusselse speelkaartenindustrie in de 18e eeuw', *Kontaktblad van het Nationaal Museum van de Speelkaart*, 13 (1985), pp. 30–1; Elewaut, *Herbergen*, p. 151; F. Cremers, 'Speelkaarten anno 1789', *Taxandria*, new series, 61 (1989), pp. 329–42. See also G. Bigwood, 'La loterie aux Pays-Bas autrichiens', *Annales de la Société royale d'Archéologie de Bruxelles*, 26 (1912), pp. 53–134, and P. Bertholet, 'Les jeux de hasard à Spa au XVIIIe siècle: aspects économiques, sociaux, démographiques et politiques', *Bulletin de la Société verviétoise d'Archéologie et d'Histoire*, 66 (1988), pp. 92–6, 110–16.

22 J. Gilissen, 'Ouderlijke macht in het oud-Belgische recht', *Tijdschrift voor Rechtsgeschiedenis*, 29 (1961), pp. 484–506. See also Godding, *Droit privé*, pp. 121–2.

23 C. Lis, *Social Change and the Labouring Poor* (New Haven and London, 1986), pp. 8–14. The quotation comes from SAA, KK 2127.

24 J. Vermaut, *De textielnijverheid in Brugge en op het platteland in westelijk Vlaanderen voor 1800*, unpublished doctoral thesis, Ghent, 1974, *passim* (especially pp. 272–4).

25 Y. Vanden Berghe, 'De algemene armenkamer te Brugge (1776–1925)',

Standen en Landen, xliv (1968), p. 271; J. Denolf, *Brugge 1748*, unpublished Licentiate thesis, Ghent, 1981, p. 271.

26 M. Kin, 'Economische transformaties en verarming te Gent in de achttiende eeuw', *Tijdschrift voor Sociale Geschiedenis*, viii (1982), pp. 34–5; I. Pisters, *Eenvoud en luxe binnenshuis: studie van Gentse interieurs uit de 18e eeuw*, unpublished Licentiate thesis, Ghent, 1983, pp. 34–57.

Chapter 3 Rich Kids, Street Boys and Little Whores

1 SABs, file 442.
2 C. Vandenbroeke, *Sociale geschiedenis van het Vlaamse volk* (Beveren, 1981), p. 80.
3 K. Vander Plaetse and G. Verbeurgt, 'Voorhuwelijks seksueel gedrag te Gent, 1700–1850', *Driemaandelijks Tijdschrift van het Gemeentekrediet*, 44 (1990), pp. 111–17. See also M.-C. Gyssels, 'Het voorechtelijk seksueel gedrag in Vlaanderen (1700–1880)', *Tijdschrift voor Sociale Geschiedenis*, x (1984), pp. 71–104, and C. Lis, 'Gezinsvorming en vrouwenarbeid tijdens een versnellingsfase in de ontwikkeling van het kapitalisme, 1750–1850', ibid., pp. 380–405.
4 C. Vandenbroeke, 'De sociale leefwereld van het kind in Vlaanderen, 17e–19e eeuw', *Tijdschrift voor Geschiedenis*, 94 (1981), p. 418.
5 K. Degryse, *De Antwerpse fortuinen: kapitaalaccumulatie, -investering en-rendement te Antwerpen in de 18e eeuw*, unpublished doctoral thesis, Ghent, 1985, pp. 626–38, 641–4.
6 SAA, PK 888, f° 101, PK 889, f° 65–6; Degryse, *Antwerpse fortuinen*, pp. 649–50.
7 SAA, PK 891, f° 168.
8 Regarding Gerard van Wangen: SAA, PK 869, f° 141, PK 927, f° 229v°–231; Degryse, *Antwerpse fortuinen*, p. 647. Regarding Josephus De Heuvel: SAA, PK 877, f° 36.
9 Degryse, *Antwerpse fortuinen*, p. 644.
10 SAA, PK 455, f° 23–77; F. Prims, 'Het eerste theaterspel in vastentijd te Antwerpen, 1785', *Antwerpiensia*, xvii (1947), pp. 139–47.
11 SAA, PK 815, f° lv°, PK 819, f° 240, PK 832, f° 258, PK 835, f° 56, PK 839, f° 149v°, PK 847, f° 248v°.
12 M. Mortier, 'Het wereldbeeld van de Gentse almanakken, 17e en 18e eeuw', *Tijdschrift voor Sociale Geschiedenis*, x (1984), p. 282. See also H. Storme, *'Die trouwen wilt voorsichtelijck': predikanten en moralisten over de voorbereiding op het huwelijk in de Vlaamse bisdommen, 17e–18e eeuw* (Louvain, 1992), pp. 265–72.
13 SAA, PK 824, f° 104, PK 832, f° 241v°, PK 838, f° 32, PK 839, f° 83v°, PK 846, f° 103, PK 850, f° 101, PK 857, f° 217, PK 859, f° 16.
14 ROPBA, xi, pp. 187–9.
15 A. Farge and M. Foucault, *Le désordre des familles* (Paris, 1982), p. 188.
16 SAA, PK 880, f° 145v°.
17 SAA, PK 875, f° 24, and PK 878, f° 162.
18 SAA, PK 869, f° 130.
19 SAA, PK 878, f° 180.
20 SAA, V 107–8, V 111, V 113, V 118, V 163, V 246 and V 282.

21 L. Van Damme, *Misdadigheid, te Antwerpen, 1765–1794*, Ghent, 1973, pp. 38–9.

22 See H. Soly, 'Materiële cultuur te Gent in de 18e eeuw: een terreinverkenning', *Oostvlaamse Zanten*, 63 (1988), pp. 3–15, and D. Roche, *La culture des apparences: une histoire du vêtement, XVIIe-XVIIIe siècle* (Paris, 1989).

23 C. Lis, *Social Change and the Labouring Poor* (New Haven and London, 1986), pp. 9, 15, 176. The quotation can be found in SAA, PK 451, no. 55.

24 SAA, V 282.

25 B. Schotte, *Bestrijding van 'quaed gedragh' te Brugge in de 18e eeuw*, unpublished Licentiate thesis, Ghent, 1982, p. 381.

26 In this connection, see the important conclusions by R. W. Jongman, 'Over macht en onmacht van de sociale controle: ontwikkelingen in de Nederlandse criminaliteit', *Tijdschrift voor Criminologie*, 30 (1988), pp. 4–31.

27 SAA, PK 873, f° 34.

28 J. Ruwet, *Soldats des régiments nationaux au XVIIIe siècle. Notes et documents* (Brussels, 1962); B. Peeters, 'Ronseling van recruten voor de nationale regimenten in de Oostenrijkse Nederlanden', *Belgisch Tijdschrift voor Militaire Geschiedenis*, 25 (1983), pp. 49–60, 191–200 26 (1984), pp. 387–400. See also R. Boumans, 'Hebben de Belgische eenheden in het leger van de Oostenrijkse Habsburgers (1716–1794) het pressen gekend?', *Het Leger: De Natie*, ix, 2 (1954), pp. 8–9.

29 C. Huyghe, *Onlusten te Antwerpen en te Gent aan de vooravond van de Brabantse Omwenteling (1784–1788)*, unpublished Licentiate thesis, Ghent, 1970. See also Y. Vanden Berghe, 'De sociale en politieke reacties van de Brugse volksmassa op het einde van het ancien régime (1770–1794)', *Belgisch Tijdschrift voor Nieuwste Geschiedenis*, iii (1979), pp. 141–68.

30 Degryse, *Antwerpse fortuinen*, pp. 633–4.

31 SAA, PK 844, f° 184, PK 867, f° 58v°, PK 870, f° 39v°.

32 M. Bruggeman, *Brugge en kant* (Bruges, 1985), pp. 224–40; C. Deneweth, *Vrouwenarbeid te Bruggae in de achttiende eeuw*, unpublished Licentiate thesis, Ghent, 1987, pp. 51–8; Lis, *Social Change*, pp. 7–9, 12, 14–15; A. K. L. Thijs, *Van 'werkwinkel' tot 'fabriek': de textielnijverheid te Antwerpen (einde 15de – begin 19de eeuw)* (Brussels, 1987), pp. 112–13, 358–9.

33 S. Bocher, *Opsluiting op verzoek te Brugge in de 18de eeuw (1740–1789)*, unpublished Licentiate thesis, Ghent, 1988, pp. 247–8.

34 F. Vanhemelryck, *De criminaliteit in de ammanie van Brussel* (Brussels, 1981), pp. 140–1.

35 A.-M. Roets, *'Rudessen, dieften ende andere crimen'*, Ghent, 1987, p. 284.

36 SAA, PK 873, f° 47v°, and V 283.

Chapter 4 Marriages Made in Hell

1 H. Storme, 'Het 18de-eeuwse katholiek discours over huwelijk en sexualiteit in de Mechelse kerkprovincie', *Documentatieblad Werkgroep Achttiende Eeuw*, xvii (1985), p. 40. On the legal position of women, see J. Gilissen, 'Le statut de la femme dans l'ancien droit belge', *Recueil de la Société Jean Bodin*, xii, *La femme*, 2 (Brussels, 1962), pp. 255–321.

2 M. Mortier, 'Het wereldbeeld van de Gentse almanakken', *Tijdschrift voor Sociale Geschiedenis*, x (1984), p. 285.

3 A. Farge and M. Foucault, *Le désordre des familles* (Paris, 1982), p. 24.
4 L. Dresen-Coenders, 'De machtsbalans tussen man en vrouw in het vroeg-moderne gezin', in H. Peeters, L. Dresen-Coenders and T. Brandenbarg (eds), *Vijf eeuwen gezinsleven: liefde, huwelijk en opvoeding in Nederland* (Nijmegen, 1986), pp. 57–98.
5 SAA, PK 820, f° 20, PK 846, f°g 161v°.
6 SABs, file 445 (22 August 1772 and 12 November 1773).
7 S. Bocher, *Opsluiting op verzoek te Brugge in de 18de eeuw*, Ghent, 1988, p. 236.
8 SAA, PK 882, f° 94v°.
9 A.-M. Roets, '*Rudessen, dieften ende andere crimen*', Ghent, 1987, pp. 339–43 and appendices 129–30.
10 SAA, PK 876, f° 52v°.
11 SAA, PK 815, f° 222v°, PK 854, f° 5v°, PK 859, f° 167v°; SABs, file 431.
12 SAA, PK 825, f° 197v°.
13 SAA, PK 873, f° 13v° and f° 23.
14 SAA, PK 876, f° 3v°.
15 SAA, PK 827, f° 92v°, PK 829, f° 125v°.
16 SAA, PK 871, f° 249v°, PK 884, f° 191v°.
17 I. Pisters, 'Gentse woninginterieurs uit de 18de eeuw', *Oostvlaamse Zanten*, 63 (1988), pp. 74–8.
18 See note 9.
19 SAA, PK 869, f° 196v°, PK 870, f° 137v°, PK 873, f° 65.
20 See H. Soly, 'Social Aspects of Structural Changes in the Urban Industries of Eighteenth-Century Brabant and Flanders', in H. van der Wee (ed.), *Rise and Decline of Urban Industries in Italy and the Low Countries during the Middle Ages and Early Modern Times*, (Louvain, 1988), pp. 244–6; C. Deneweth, *Vrouwenarbeid te Brugge in de achttiende eeuw*, Ghent, 1987; K. Daems, *Vrouwenarbeid te Antwerpen in de 18de eeuw*, unpublished Licentiate thesis Ghent, 1988.
21 For Leiden, D. Haks, *Huwelijk en gezin in Holland in de 17de en 18de eeuw* (Assen, 1982), pp. 184–218, and H. A. Diederiks, D. J. Noordam and H. D. Tjalsma (eds), *Armoede en sociale spanning: sociaal-historische studies over Leiden in de achttiende eeuw* (Hilversum, 1985). For London, N. Tomes, 'A Torrent of Abuse: Crimes of Violence between Working-Class Men and Women in London, 1840–1875', *Journal of Social History*, 12 (1978), pp. 328–45.
22 O. Hufton, *The Poor of Eighteenth-Century France, 1750–1789* (Oxford, 1974).
23 For a European overview, see R. Phillips, *Putting Asunder: A History of Divorce in Western Society* (Cambridge, 1989). On the United Provinces, see L. J. Van Apeldoorn, *Geschiedenis van het Nederlandsche huwelijksrecht voor de invoering van de Fransche wetgeving* (Amsterdam, 1925); Haks, *Huwelijk*, pp. 177–84; J. Joor, 'Echtscheiding en scheiding van tafel en bed in Alkmaar in de periode 1700–1810', *Tijdschrift voor Sociale Geschiedenis*, xi (1985), pp. 201–2.
24 H. Hasquin, 'La tolérance et la question du marriage', in R. Crahay (ed.), *La tolérance civile* (Brussels, 1982), pp. 129–38.
25 W. Buntinx, 'De zaak Maria-Anna Buens – Judocus-Mattheus du Bois: een echtscheidingsprocess (1ste helft 18de eeuw) als bron voor sociale geschiedenis', in *Album Carlos Wyffels* (Brussels, 1987), pp. 57–68.

26 J. De Brouwer, *De kerkelijke rechtsoraak en haar evolutie in de bisdommen Antwerpen, Gent en Mechelen tussen 1570 en 1795*, 2 vols (Tielt, 1971–2), *passim*.

27 ROPBA, xii, pp. 380–5. See also P. Godding, *Le Droit Privé dans les Pays-Bas méridionaux* (Brussels, 1987), pp. 111–12, and Phillips, *Putting Asunder*, pp. 201–2.

28 J. R. Watt, 'Divorce in Early Modern Neuchâtel, 1574–1806', *Journal of Family History*, 14 (1989), pp. 137–55. On towns in Holland, see Haks, *Huwelijk*, pp. 184–7, 201–3; and especially Joor, 'Echtscheiding', pp. 204, 221–2. See also the remarks by V. Verhaar and F. van den Brink, 'De bemoeienis van stad en kerk met overspel in het achttiende-eeuwse Amsterdam', in S. Faber (ed.), *Nieuw licht op oude justitie: misdaad en straf ten tijde van de Republiek* (Muiderberg, 1989), pp. 80–3.

29 J. Mulliez, 'Droit et morale conjugale: essai sur l'histoire des relations personnelles entre époux', *Revue Historique*, 563 (1987), pp. 56–8.

30 De Brouwer, *Kerkelijke rechtspraak*, vol. I, pp. 145–52.

31 SAA, PK 868, f° 81v°, and PK 873, f° 37v°.

32 SAA, PK 873, f° 36v° and f° 47.

33 Haks, *Huwelijk*, pp. 181–4.

34 Roets, *Rudessen*, pp. 339–42.

35 Phillips, *Putting Asunder*, pp. 256–76, and all the literature cited therein.

36 See Susan M. Edwards, *Policing 'Domestic' Violence: Women, the Law and the State* (London, 1989). Outstanding as a case-study is L. Gordon, *Heroes of Their Own Lives. The Politics and History of Family Violence: Boston, 1880–1960* (New York, 1988).

Chapter 5 The Eyes of Others

1 A. Farge and M. Foucault, *Le désordre des familles* (Paris, 1982), p. 36.

2 See the fine study by D. Garrioch, *Neighbourhood and Community in Paris, 1740–1790* (Cambridge, 1986), as well as A. Farge, *La vie fragile: violence, pouvoirs et solidarité à Paris au XVIIIe siècle* (Paris, 1986), pp. 17–30; V. Mespoulet, 'Espaces et criminalité: les relations de voisinage à Toulouse au milieu du XVIIIe siècle', *Sources: travaux historiques*, 14 (1988), pp. 43–57; P. Peveri, 'Voisinage et contrôle social au XVIIIe siècle', *Mentalités*, no. 4 (1990), pp. 89–104.

3 See E. Varenbergh, 'Les voisinages de Gand', *Bulletin de l'Académie royale de Belgique*, 2nd series, xxv (1868), pp. 364–86; P. Claeys, *Pages d'histoire locale gantoise*, vol. II (Ghent, 1880), pp. 37–46; and especially G. Van Severen, *Het gebuurte en dekenijleven te Gent vroeger en nu* (Ghent, 1977).

4 General overviews can be found in J. Le Goff and J.-C. Schmitt (eds), *Le charivari: actes de la table ronde organisée à Paris (25–27 avril 1977) par l'Ecole des Hautes Etudes en Sciences Sociales et le Centre National de la Recherche Scientifique* (Paris, 1981), and M. Jacobs, 'Charivari en volksgerichten: sleutelfenomenen voor sociale geschiedenis', *Tijdschrift voor Sociale Geschiedenis*, xii (1986), pp. 365–92. The last-mentioned author is working on a comprehensive project about charivari in Europe, the results of which are to be published in 1996. On the Low Countries, see the special issue of the *Volkskundig Bulletin*, 15, 3, October 1989: 'Charivari in de

Nederlanden: rituele sancties op deviant gedrag' (especially the contributions by Anton Blok, Marc Jacobs and Gerard Rooijakkers).

5 Jacobs, 'Charivari', pp. 365–8, 385–6.

6 T. Romme, 'Charivari-rituelen in de Meijerij: de zaak Jan van Es te Oss', *Volkskundig Bulletin*, 15 (1989), pp. 335–50. See also B. C. M. Jacobs, 'Van gericht tot gerecht: justitieel optreden tegen charivari's in Oostelijk Brabant', ibid., pp. 355–7.

7 SAG, OA, series 108b, nos. 13 and 196, and series 110, no. 2.

8 H. Soly, 'Social Aspects of Structural Changes in the Urban Industries of Eighteenth-Century Brabant and Flanders', in H. van der Wee (ed.), *Rise and Decline of Urban Industries in Italy and the Low Countries during the Middle Ages and Early Modern Times* (Louvain, 1988), pp. 247–8, 250–1 (and the literature cited therein).

9 See the pertinent remarks by G. Mak, 'De Amsterdamse paradox', *NRC-Handelsblad*, 17 June 1989, Saturday supplement, pp. 1–2.

10 Haks, *Huwelijk en gezin in Holland in de 17de en 18de eeuw* (Assen, 1982), p. 64. See also C. A. Davids, 'De migratiebeweging in Leiden in de achttiende eeuw', in H. A. Diederiks, D. J. Noordam and H. D. Tjalsma (eds), *Armoede en sociale spanning* (Hilversum, 1985), pp. 151–2.

11 S. Bocher, *Opsluiting op verzoek te Brugge in de 18de eeuw*, Ghent, 1988, p. 219.

12 SAA, PK 873, f° 37.

13 SAA, V 282.

14 Bocher, *Opsluiting*, p. 237.

15 SAA, V 282.

16 SAA, PK 873, f° 34v°.

17 V. Verhaar and F. van den Brink, 'De bemoeienis van stad en kerk met overspel in het achttiende-eeuwse Amsterdam', in S. Faber (ed.), *Nieuw licht op oude justitie* (Muiderberg, 1989), p. 88.

18 See the surveys by R. Mols, 'De seculiere clerus', and M. Cloet, 'Het gelovige volk in de 18de eeuw', in *Algemene Geschiedenis der Nederlanden*, vol. IX (Haarlem, 1980), pp. 376–88 and 396–412.

19 SABg, OA, file 188, portfolio 1760–61.

20 Quoted by Cloet, 'Gelovige volk', p. 411.

21 Quoted by P. Bonenfant, *Le problème du paupérisme en Belgique à la fin de l'Ancien Régime* (Brussels, 1934), p. 65, note 3.

22 SABs, files 444–5.

Chapter 6 The Language of Authority

1 C. Lis, H. Soly and D. Van Damme, *Op vrije voeten? Sociale politiek in West-Europa, 1450–1914* (Louvain, 1985), pp. 12–14.

2 For Ghent, A. M. Roets, *Rudessen, dieften ende andere crimen*, Ghent, 1987, appendices, pp. 2–3, 14–15, 233, 236. For Antwerp, L. Van Damme, *Misdadigheid te Antwerpen, 1765–1794*, Ghent, 1973, pp. 75–90. For Bruges, E. Van Keirsbilck, *Heuristiek en methodologie van de studie der stedelijke criminaliteit*, unpublished Licentiate thesis, Ghent, 1982, pp. 63–73.

3 ROPBA, ix, pp. 332–3. See the pertinent remarks of C. Bruneel, 'Le droit

pénal dans les Pays-Bas autrichiens: les hésitations de la pratique (1750–1795)', *Etudes sur le XVIIIe siècle*, xiii (1986), pp. 51–3.

4 ARAB, GRO 578.

5 SAA, PK 927–8; SABg, OA, series 120; SABs, registers for 1720–2; SAG, OA, series 108b, no. 196, and series 110, no. 5.

6 For a general overview, see C. Lis and H. Soly, *Poverty and Capitalism in Pre-Industrial Europe* (Brighton, 1982), pp. 202–6. For Antwerp, C. Lis, 'Sociale politiek in Antwerpen (1779)', *Tijdschrift voor Sociale Geschiedenis*, ii (1976), pp. 146–66. For Ghent, M. Kin, *Evolutie van de sociale politiek te Gent in de achttiende eeuw*, unpublished Licentiate thesis, Ghent, 1979, pp. 99–104, 108–17, 194–204; and R. Felix, *Bedelarij in Gent in de achttiende eeuw*, unpublished Licentiate thesis, Ghent, 1986, pp. 25–30, 112–23. For Bruges: Y. Vanden Berghe, 'De algemene armenkamer te Brugge (1776–1925)', *Standen en Landen*, xliv (1968), pp. 267–88; and J. Bassens, *De openbare weldadigheid te Brugge, 1776–1830*, unpublished Licentiate thesis, Ghent, 1987.

7 SAG, OA, series 107, no. 29, and series 108b, nos. 13 and 196; G. Elewaut, 'Herberg en overheid: politionele en fiscale aspekten van het overheidsoptreden betreffende herbergen in de Zuidelijke Nederlanden en in het bijzonder te Gent, 17e–18e eeuw', *Handelingen van de Maatschappij voor Geschiedenis en Oudheidkunde te Gent*, new series, xl (1986), pp. 123–4.

8 Felix, *Bedelarij*, pp. 244–7.

9 SAA, PK 927, f° 277, and PK·928, f° 1–2.

10 SAA, PK 258, f° 51–52v°; H. Soly, 'Openbare feesten in Brabantse en Vlaamse steden, 16de–18de eeuw', in *Het openbaar initiatief van de gemeenten in België: historische grondslagen (Ancien Régime)* (Brussels, 1984), pp. 629–30; E. Put, *Onrust in de zielzorg: J. T. L. Wellens, 17de bisschop van Antwerpen, en zijn pastoraal beleid 1776–1784* (Brussels, 1983), pp. 111–14.

11 J. Art, 'Van heilige tijd naar vrije tijd', *Spiegel historiael*, 18 (1983), pp. 594–8. The quotation can be found in *Verzameling van alle de herderlijke brieven, vastenbullen, etc., uytgegeven door wijlen zijn doorlugtigste hoogweerdigheyd J. T. L. Wellens, bisschop van Antwerpen* (Antwerp, 1784).

12 SAA, PK 928, f° 30v°–31. See also G. Elewaut, *Herbergen in Gent, 1656–1795*, Ghent, 1985, pp. 123 and 151.

13 SAA, V 282–3 and V 1822.

14 F. Vanhemelryck, 'Bijdrage tot de studie van het politieapparaat in het Ancien Régime', *Belgisch Tijdschrift voor Filologie en Geschiedenis*, 50 (1972), pp. 356–94; A. Deroisy, 'Un aspect du maintien de l'ordre dans les Pays-Bas autrichiens après 1750: la lutte contre le vagabondage', *Etudes sur le XVIIIe siècle*, v (1978), pp. 133–45, and 'Juridictions particulières chargées des poursuites contre les vagabonds dans les Pays-Bas autrichiens au XVIIIe siècle', in *La Belgique rurale du Moyen Age à nos jours: mélanges offerts à Jean-Jacques Hoebanx* (Brussels, 1985), pp. 295–308; X. Rousseaux, 'L' incrimination du vagabondage en Brabant (14e–18e siècles): langages de droit et réalités de la pratique', in G. van Dievoet, P. Godding and D. van den Auweele (eds), *Langage et droit à travers l'histoire: réalités et fictions* (Louvain and Paris, 1989), pp. 167–83.

15 Quoted by Bruneel, 'Droit pénal', p. 35.

16 See P. Lenders' important article, 'De eerste poging van J. J. P. Vilain XIIII tot het bouwen van een correctiehuis (1749–1751)', *Handelingen der Zuid-*

nederlandse Maatschappij voor Taal- en Letterkunde en Geschiedenis, xii (1958), pp. 167–87. The same author has made a penetrating analysis of the personality of Vilain XIIII: 'De Gentse voorschepen J. J. P. Vilain XIIII (1755–1777): enkele trekken van zijn persoonlijkheid', *Handelingen van de Maatschappij voor Geschiedenis en Oudheidkunde te Gent*, new series, xl (1986), pp. 159–77.

17 Bonenfant, *Le problème du paupérisme en Belgique à la fin de l'Ancien Régime* (Brussels, 1934), pp. 103–9; M. S. Dupont-Bouchat, 'La réforme du droit pénal dans les Pays-Bas autrichiens à la fin de l'Ancien Régime (1765–1787)', in G. Macours (ed.), *Acta Falconis. Cornua Legum: actes des Journées internationales d'histoire du droit et des institutions* (Antwerp, 1987), pp. 74–7; and 'L'invention de la prison moderne', in D. Van Damme, F. Simon, J Dekker and B. Kruithof (eds), *Beyond the Pale, Behind Bars: Marginalization and Institutionalization from the 18th to the 20th Century* (Ghent, 1990), pp. 63–98 (*Paedagogica Historica*, xxvi, no. 2).

18 E. Hubert, *Un chapitre de l'histoire du droit criminel dans les Pays-Bas autrichiens au XVIIIe siècle: les mémoires de Goswin de Fierlant* (Brussels, 1895).

19 J. J. P. Vilain XIIII, *Mémoire sur les moyens de corriger les malfaiteurs et les fainéants à leur propre avantage et de les rendre utiles à l'Etat*, 2nd edn, pubd by C. H. Vilain XIIII (Brussels, 1841).

20 Bonenfant, *Problème*, pp. 264–7 (quote on p. 264).

21 J. W. Bosch, 'Belgische en Hollandse hervormingsplannen in de 18de eeuw', *Tijdschrift voor Strafrecht*, 70 (1961), pp. 167–86 (quote on p. 180).

22 L. Uytterhoeven, *Enkele aspecten van het provinciaal correctiehuis van Gent, 1773–1794*, unpublished Licentiate thesis, Ghent, 1989, p. 244.

23 SAA, PK 1798, f° 287v°.

24 SAA, PK 455, f° 330–6; SABs, file 447.

25 SAA, PK 455, f° 339–40.

26 SAA, V 282–3.

27 In this connection, see the pertinent remarks by E.-M. Benabou, *La prostitution et la police des moeurs au XVIIIe siècle* (Paris, 1987), pp. 33–5, 40, 65–6, 69–70.

28 SAA, PK 833, f°260.

Chapter 7 Sledge-Hammers and Treadmills

1 ROPBA, x, p. 504.

2 P. Spierenburg, 'Financiën en familie-eer: opsluiting en opgeslotenen op verzoek te Leiden, 1680–1805', in H. A. Diederiks, D. J. Noordam and H. D. Tjalsma (eds), *Armoede en sociale spanning* (Hilversum, 1985), p. 120, notes the same thing for Leiden.

3 SAA, PK 873, f° 25.

4 Ibid., f° 13v°.

5 Ibid., f° 10v° and f° 46v°.

6 Ibid., f° 36v°.

7 C. J. Kaufmann, *The History of the Alexian Brothers from 1300 to 1789*, 2 vols (New York, 1976–8); *Werken van Barmhartigheid: 650 jaar Alexianen in de Zuidelijke Nederlanden* (Louvain, 1985).

8 S. Bocher, *Opsluiting op verzoek te Brugge in de 18de eeuw*, Ghent, 1988. p. 175.

9 SAG, OA, series lxviii, no. 14.

10 SABg, OA, file 188, portfolio 1776–7 (10 October 1777).

11 F. H. Mertens and K. L. Torfs, *Geschiedenis van Antwerpen*, vol. VI (Antwerp, 1851), pp. 632–4.

12 Quoted by J. Geldhof, *Pelgrims, dulle lieden en vondelingen te Brugge, 1275–1975* (Bruges, 1975), p. 149.

13 SAG, OA, series lxviii, nos. 126 and 129.

14 Ibid., no. 13.

15 ARAB, GRO 835. See also Y. Vanden Berghe, *Jacobijnen en traditionalisten: de reacties van de Bruggelingen in de Revolutietijd (1780–1794)* (Brussels, 1972), pp. 94–5.

16 SAG, OA, series lxviii, no. 16.

17 R. Wellens, 'L'hospice de Saint Charles Borromée à Froidmont: notice historique et inventaire des archives', *Archives et Bibliothèques de Belgique*, 35 (1965), pp. 159–95.

18 Bocher, *Opsluiting*, p. 178.

19 See the contributions of A. Liégeois and B. Pattyn in P. Vandermeersch (ed.), *Psychiatrie, godsdienst en gezag: de ontstaansgeschiedenis van de psychiatrie in België als paradigma* (Louvain and Amersfoort, 1984); also F. De Potter and J. Broeckaert, *Geschiedenis der stad St.- Nicolaes*, vol. II (Ghent, 1882), pp. 107–24, and R. Weemaes, *Het Sieckhuys, 1710–1985: 175 jaar Zwartzusters van de Heilige Philippus Neri te Sint-Niklaas* (Tielt, 1985). For Geel there is a penetrating study by M. H. Koyen, 'Gezinsverleging van geesteszieken te Geel tot einde 18de eeuw' *Jaarboek van de vrijheid en het land van Geel*, xii (1973).

20 A. Henne and A. Wauters, *Histoire de la ville de Bruxelles*, vol. III (Brussels, 1845), pp. 510–13. See also SABs, files 421–3.

21 Geldhof, *Pelgrims*, pp. 147–50, 192–3.

22 OCMWA, OA, GH 170, f° 241–2.

23 Geldhof, *Pelgrims*, pp. 140–5.

24 P. Bonenfant, 'L'ancienne Maison des insensès', *Annales de la Société royale d'Archéologie de Bruxelles*, 45 (1941), pp. 133–7.

25 See the studies on urban houses of correction mentioned on pp. 220–1.

26 ARAB, RB, Fiscal Office, boxes 1308 and 1310, and *Vonnisboeken* (sentence-registers) nos. 1063–7; C. Bruneel, 'A rude école: le régime pénitentiaire de la maison de correction de Bruxelles', *Cahiers Bruxellois*, xi (1966), pp. 216–49. See also R. De Peuter, *Negocianten en entrepreneurs in een regionale hoofdstad: Brussel in de achttiend eeuw* (Utrecht, 1994), pp. 595–611.

27 M. Ignatieff, *A Just Measure of Pain: The Penitentiary in the Industrial Revolution, 1750–1850* (New York, 1978), pp. 44–79. See also M. Foucault, *Surveiller et punir: naissance de la prison* (Paris and Geneva, 1984); M. Perrot (ed.), *L'impossible prison: recherches sur le système pénitentiaire* (Paris, 1960); J. G. Petit (ed.), *La prison, le bagne et l'histoire* (Paris and Geneva, 1984), and *Ces peines obscures: la prison pénale en France, 1780–1875* (Paris, 1990).

28 J. J. P. Vilain XIIII, *Mémoire sur les moyens de corriger les malfaiteurs et les fainéants*, 2nd edn (Brussels, 1841), *passim*. The articles by P. Lenders cited in note 16 of ch. 6 should also be consulted.

29 J. Howard, *The State of the Prisons in England and Wales* (London, 1784), pp. 145–8. For further information on the motives of this reformer, see R. Morgan, 'Divine Philanthropy: John Howard Reconsidered', *History*, 62 (1977), pp. 388–410.
30 For the factual details regarding the provincial penitentiaries we relied on the studies mentioned on p. 221.

Epilogue: Power and Powerlessness

1 Calculations based on C. Quétel, '*De Par Le Roy*' (Toulouse, 1981) pp. 131–2, and the literature cited on p. 234. The Parisian *lettres de cachet* edited by A. Farge and M. Foucault, *Le désordre des familles* (Paris, 1982), do not permit the calculation of an annual average per 10,000 inhabitants because the archives are incomplete, as the authors acknowledge on p. 17.
2 Data taken from P. Spierenburg, *The Prison Experience: Disciplinary Institutions and Their Inmates in Early Modern Europe* (New Brunswick and London, 1991), p. 227. It should be noted that the number of admissions to the public asylums in Maastricht and 's-Hertogenbosch grew rapidly from the middle of the eighteenth century onwards. See J. C. G. M. Jansen, 'Waanzin en repressie', *Studies over de Sociaal-Economische Geschiedenis van Limburg*, 23 (1978), *passim*, and A. C. M. Kappelhof, 'De gestichtsbevolking van Reinier van Arkel in Den Bosch, 1650–1840', *Noordbrabants Historisch Jaarboek*, 5 (1988), pp. 95–120.
3 Farge and Foucault, *Désordre*, p. 364, note 2.
4 F.-X. Emmanuelli, 'Ordres du roi et lettres de cachet en Provence à la fin de l'Ancien Régime', *Revue historique*, 373 (1974), p. 376.
5 For more detail, see P. Spierenburg, 'Imprisonment and the Family: An Analysis of Petitions for Confinement in Holland, 1680–1805', *Social Science History*, 10 (1986), pp. 127–30.
6 J. Geesink, 'Opsluiting op verzoek in Dordrecht', *Kwartaal en Teken*, 15 (1989), pp. 3–7.
7 Jansen, 'Waanzin', *passim*, and Kappelhof, 'Gestichtsbevolking', pp. 107–9.
8 C. Quétel, 'En maison de force au siècle des Lumières', in *Marginalité, déviance, pauvreté en France, 14e–19e siècles* (Cahiers des Annales de Normandie, no. 13; Caen, 1981), pp. 76–9, and his '*De Par le Roy*', pp. 156–8; Spierenburg, *Prison Experience*, pp. 250–1.
9 From that viewpoint the developments in the Austrian Netherlands were no different from those in France. See R. Muchembled, *L' invention de l'homme moderne: sensibilités, moeurs et comportements collectifs sous l'Ancien Régime* (Paris, 1988), p. 358. See also M. Vovelle, 'Le tournant des mentalités en France, 1750–1789: la sensibilité pré-révolutionaire', *Social History*, 2 (1977), pp. 605–9.
10 The theoretical speculations of Norbert Elias often underpin such interpretations. See, for example, Spierenburg, *Prison Experience*, pp. 17–18, 248–9.
11 J. Bossy (ed.), *Disputes and Settlements: Law and Human Relations in the West* (Cambridge, 1983). See also D. Black, 'Social Control as a Dependent Variable', in D. Black (ed.), *Toward a General Theory of Social Control* (New York, 1984), pp. 1–29.
12 For an overview of what is currently known about changes in urban

neighbourhood life at the end of the *ancien régime*, see C. Lis and H. Soly, 'Neighbourhood Social Change in West European Cities: Sixteenth to Nineteenth Centuries', *International Review of Social History*, 38 (1993), pp. 1–30.

13 N. Castan, 'The Arbitration of Disputes under the Ancien Régime', in Bossy (ed.), *Disputes*, pp. 219–60.

14 See R. Chartier (ed.), *Histoire de la vie privée*, vol. III: *De la Renaissance aux Lumières* (Paris, 1986), pp. 80–3.

15 This was also the case in the United Provinces. See V. Verhaar and F. van den Brink, 'De bemoeienis van stad en kerk met overspel in het achttiende-eeuwse Amsterdam', in S. Faber (ed.), *Nieuw licht op oude justitie* (Muider-berg, 1989), pp. 80–3.

16 See the pertinent remarks by C. Quétel, 'Lettres de cachet et correctionaires dans la généralité de Caen au XVIIIe siècle', *Annales de Normandie*, 28 (1978), p. 154.

17 A. Scull, *The Most Solitary of Afflictions* (New Haven and London, 1993), pp. 353 and 363.

18 Ibid., p. 362.

19 J. K. Walton, 'Lunacy in the Industrial Revolution', *Journal of Social History*, 13 (1979), *passim*.

20 Cf. C. Lis and H. Soly, 'Total Institutions and the Survival Strategies of the Laboring Poor in Antwerp, 1770–1860', in P. Mandler (ed.), *The Uses of Charity: The Poor on Relief in the Nineteenth-Century Metropolis* (Philadelphia, 1990), p. 60.

21 T. Szasz, *The Myth of Mental Illness* (New York, 1961), and *The Manufacture of Madness* (New York, 1970).

Sources and Literature

This study is based mainly on archive sources. The most important of these are of course the requests for confinement presented to the aldermen by housemates or relatives of the unwanted person. We have taken into consideration only those files relating to the residents of the cities under scrutiny – namely, Antwerp, Brussels, Bruges and Ghent.

In Antwerp, requests for confinement for the first time and for extensions, transfers and releases were written up in special registers, the so-called *Requestboeken*, found in the *Privilegekamer* of the City Archive; numbers 787–896, covering the period 1700–94, were gone through systematically. Two checks ensured that the source showed no gaps, with the exception of the years 1700–9 and 1790–4. On the one hand we did not come across any requests for extensions that were related to cases of which the initial confinement could not be found in the *Requestboeken*. On the other we made random checks in the archives on a number of institutions in which residents of Antwerp had been confined by other members of their family – namely, the mental hospital at Antwerp, the house of correction at Brussels and the provincial penitentiary at Vilvoorde. For these three institutions there are series of registers or files in which the detainees are mentioned by name, with a specification from the courts that permission had been granted and the procedure that had led to that person's admission there. We were able to find all the residents of Antwerp who ended up in one of the aforementioned institutions around 1780 in the *Requestboeken*.

In the Brussels City Archive we came across no comparable source. While the decisions of the magistrate were registered in the *Resolutie-boecken der Tresorie*, we can deduce from these only who was put under lock and key and when, at whose expense and (sometimes) for how long. For this reason we have based ourselves on the files concerning people who, through the intervention of their families, ended up in the mental institution (files 426–33) or the house of correction (files 441–6). Comparisons with the *Resolutieboecken* on the one hand and some lists of detainees (registers 1384–6 and 2896–7) on the other show that all the initial requests for confinement during the decades 1740–9 and 1770–9 have been preserved. We did not make use of the (otherwise interesting) article by Claude Bruneel entitled 'Les prisonniers de la maison de correction de Bruxelles: étude statistique', *Cahiers Bruxellois*, xii (1967), pp. 40–68, in which the demographic characteristics of the inmates are discussed. Given that the author had completely different purposes, he paid no attention to certain aspects which are of central importance in our study, the consequence of which was, among other things, that his arrangement of the information makes it impossible to answer all sorts of questions in which we are interested.

In both Bruges and Ghent the requests for confinement for the first time and those for extensions, transfers and releases are spread over several ranges of sources which largely supplement each other. As regards Bruges, principal mention should be made of the *Criminele Informatieboeken* and the *Criminele Vervolgen* or *Tichten* ['Criminal Prosecutions'] (State Archive, Bruges records, numbers 639–58 and 704–24), the *Criminele Informatiën* and the lists of detainees in the *Rasphuis* (City Archive, Old Archive, series 188 and 197) and the requests for the confinement of insane persons (Public Centre for Social Welfare, Sint-Juliaans records, numbers 20–4). Abstracts were systematically made of all these sources and statistically processed by Sabine Bocher in *Opsluiting op verzoek te Brugge in de 18de eeuw (1740–1789)*, unpublished Licentiate thesis, Ghent, 1988. Since we sometimes use other arrangement and incorporation criteria, our figures do not always tally with those of the author; obviously, we bear full responsibility for the interpretations. The Ghent files are to be found in the City Archive, Old Archive, series 328 and 339–40. For the periods 1755–64 and 1775–84 they were analysed by Anne-Marie Roets, '*Rudessen, dieften ende andere crimen'. Misdadigheid te Gent in de zeventiende en achttiende eeuw: een kwantitatieve en kwalitatieve analyse*, unpublished doctoral thesis, Ghent, 1987. Here too, we take full responsibility for all interpretations.

It should be mentioned that a comparison of the Bruges and Ghent material with archives from the penal and mental institutions has brought to light the fact that some requests are missing. Sadly enough, it is not always mentioned in the lists of detainees who was confined on request and even less whether the request had been made by other members of the family or third parties, so that it is not always possible with this material to track down all the lacunae. It could nonetheless be assumed that the numbers were small, because a systematic check showed that an initial request for confinement was always available when we came across a petition for a prolongation of confinement. Whatever the case may be, account should be taken of the fact that the final picture could be slightly distorted.

Private confinement during the *ancien régime* has until now received little attention from Belgian historians. For France, on the other hand, several interesting monographs are to hand: F.-X. Emmanuelli, 'Ordres du roi et lettres de cachet en Provence à la fin de l'Ancien Régime', *Revue Historique*, 373 (1974), pp. 357–92; C. Quétel, *'De Par Le Roy': essai sur les lettres de cachet* (Toulouse, 1981) and the articles by the same author 'Lettres de cachet et correctionnaires dans la généralité de Caen au XVIIIe siècle', in *Annales de Normandie*, 28, 1978, pp. 127–59, and 'Entre la faute et le délit: la correction par lettre de cachet', in *Justice et répression de 1610 à nos jours* (Paris, 1984), pp. 43–57; A. Farge and M. Foucault, *Le désordre des familles: lettres de cachet des Archives de la Bastille* (Paris, 1982); G. Minois, 'Morale et société: les internements féminins en Bretagne au XVIIIe siècle', in *Justice et répression*, pp. 117–34. On the legal and administrative framework, see B. E. Strayer, *'Lettres de cachet' and Social Control in the Ancien Régime, 1659–1789* (New York, 1992). Research on this subject has also been carried out in the Netherlands. For an overview, see P. Spierenburg, *The Prison Experience: Disciplinary Institutions and Their Inmates in Early Modern Europe* (New Brunswick and London, 1991), pp. 223–5; also H. Diederiks and P. Spierenburg, 'L'enfermement non criminel en Hollande, XVIIIe-XIXe siècles', in J. G. Petit (ed.), *La prison, le bagne et l'histoire* (Paris and Geneva, 1984), pp. 43–55. Information from Leiden is discussed in more detail by P. Spierenburg, 'Financiën en familie-eer. opsluiting en opgeslotenen op verzoek te Leiden, 1680–1805', in H. A. Diederiks, D. J. Noordam and H. D. Tjalsma (eds), *Armoede en sociale spanning: sociaal-historische studies over Leiden in de achttiende eeuw* (Hilversum, 1985), pp. 117–35, of which a revised version has been published under the title 'Imprisonment and the Family: An Analysis of Petitions for Confinement in Holland, 1680–1805, *Social Science History*, x (1986), pp. 115–46. The compulsory admission of 'insane' persons has been studied by J. C. G. M. Jansen, 'Waanzin en repressie. de zinnelozen en hun behandeling in Maastricht in de 18e eeuw', *Studies over de sociaal-economische geschiedenis van Limburg*, 23 (1978), pp. 63–97, and A. C. M. Kappelhof, 'De gestichtsbevolking van Reinier van Arkel in Den Bosch, 1650–1840', *Noordbrabants Historisch Jaarboek*, 5 (1988), pp. 95–120.

Little is known about perceptions of madness and attitudes towards people with psychological disturbances in the Austrian Netherlands. Only Jozef Geldhof, *Pelgrims, dulle lieden en vondelingen te Brugge, 1275–1975* (Bruges, 1975), has looked into patterns of behaviour that were considered to be insane. Information on the treatment of patients is to be found in P. Bonenfant, 'L'ancienne Maison des Insensés (*Simpelhuys*) de Bruxelles', *Annales de la Société royale d'Archéologie de Bruxelles*, 45 (1941), pp. 129–40; M. H. Koyen, 'Gezinsverpleging van geesteszieken te Geel tot einde 18de eeuw', *Jaarboek van de vrijheid en het land van Geel*, xii (1973); P. Vandermeersch (ed.), *Psychiatrie, godsdienst en gezag: de onstaansgeschiedenis van de psychiatrie in België als paradigma* (Louvain and Amersfoort, 1984). For the situations in other parts of Western Europe, see P. Spierenburg, *De verbroken betovering: mentalititeitsgeschiedenis van pre-industrieel Europa* (Hilversum, 1988), pp. 189–219. There is no detailed study available on the *Cellebroeders* in the Southern Netherlands. This is all the more regrettable because they were very active in the care of mental patients. We must content ourselves with C. J. Kaufmann, *The History of the Alexian Brothers from 1300 to 1789*, 2 vols. (New York, 1976–78), and *Werken van Barmhartigheid: 650 jaar Alexianen in de Zuidelijke Nederlanden* (Louvain, 1985).

It is impractical here to list all the books and articles which provide information on deviant behaviour that was not associated with madness. In the first place we must consult studies on urban crime. For Antwerp: L. Van Damme, *Misdadigheid te Antwerpen, 1765–1794*, unpublished Licentiate thesis, Ghent, 1973. For Bruges: B. Schotte, *Bestrijding van 'quaed gedragh' te Brugge in de 18e eeuw*, unpublished Licentiate thesis, Ghent, 1982, and E. Van Keirsblick, *Heuristiek en methodologie van de studie der stedelijke criminaliteit*, unpublished Licentiate thesis, Ghent, 1982. For Brussels: F. Vanhemelryck, *De criminaliteit in de ammanie van Brussel van de late middeleeuwen tot het einde van het Ancien Régime, 1404–1789* (Brussels, 1981). For Ghent: the aforementioned doctoral thesis by A.-M. Roets. Attitudes towards the addiction to drink are discussed by A. Cosemans, 'Alcoholisme en drankbestrijding in vroeger eeuwen', *Handelingen der Zuidnederlandse Maatschappij voor Taal- en Letterkunde en Geschiedenis*, x (1956), pp. 81–127. For the changes in the prosecution of 'sexual crimes', see F. Vanhemelryck, *Misdadigers tussen rechter en beul, 1400–1800* (Antwerp and Amsterdam, 1984), pp. 155–88. The repression of beggary is discussed by P. Bonenfant, *Le problème du paupérisme en Belgique à la fin de l'Ancien Régime* (Brussels, 1934), supplemented by R. Felix, *Bedelarij in Gent in de achttiende eeuw*, unpublished Licentiate thesis, Ghent, 1986.

Several studies throw some light on daily life in penal institutions. For the urban houses of correction, see L. Stroobant, 'Le Rasphuys de Gand',

Annales de la Société d'Histoire et d'Archéologie de Gand, iii (1898), pp. 240–71; A. Hallema, 'Het Antwerpsche tuchthuis, een Hollandsche navolging', *Antwerpsch archievenblad*, second series, vi (1931), pp. 3–26; C. Bruneel, 'Un épisode de la lutte contre la mendicité et le vagabondage: la maison de correction de Bruxelles', *Cahiers Bruxellois*, xi (1966), pp. 29–72; F. Mahy, *De Brugse tuchthuizen in de 17e en 18e eeuw: een onderzoek naar hun maatschappelijke functie*, 2 vols, unpublished Licentiate thesis, Ghent, 1982. There is much information on disciplinary methods in the Dutch houses of correction to be found in H. C. M. Michielse, *Welzijn en discipline. Van tuchthuis tot psychotherapie: strategieën en technologieën in het sociaal beheer* (Amsterdam, 1989), pp. 33–54. For the provincial penitentiaries, see the unpublished Licentiate theses by M. Van Opdenbosch, *Het provinciaal correctiehuis te Gent (1770–1792) en de gevangenen uit het Land van Aalst*, Louvain, 1968; R. Vanderwielen, *Het provinciaal correctiehuis te Vilvoorde, 1773–1794*, Louvain, 1971; C. De Pauw, *Het tuchthuis te Vilvoorde, 1772–1794*, 2 vols, Ghent, 1981 and L. Uytterhoeven, *Enkele aspecten van het provinciaal correctiehuis van Gent, 1773–1794*, Ghent, 1989.

All aspects of private law are thoroughly discussed by P. Godding, *Le droit privé dans les Pays-Bas méridionaux du 12e au 18e siècle* (Brussels, 1987). See also J. Gilissen, 'Ouderlijke macht in het oud-Belgische recht', *Tijdschrift voor Rechtsgeschiedenis*, 29 (1961), pp. 484–506, and 'Le statut de la femme dans l'ancien droit belge', in *Recueil de la Société Jean Bodin*, xii, *La femme*, 2 (Brussels, 1962), pp. 255–321. We have no detailed study on criminal law in the eighteenth century, but information can be found in C. Bruneel, 'Le droit pénal dans les Pays-Bas autrichiens: les hésitations de la pratique (1750–1795)', *Etudes sur le XVIIIe siècle*, xiii (1986), pp. 35–66, and M.-S. Dupont-Bouchat, 'La réforme du droit pénal dans les Pays-Bas autrichiens à la fin de l'Ancien Régime (1765–1787)', in G. Macours (ed.), *Acta Falconis. Cornua Legum: actes des Journées internationales d'histoire du droit et des institutions* (Antwerp, 1987), pp. 71–97. For ecclesiastical administration of justice, see J. De Brouwer, *De kerkelijke rechtspraak en haar evolutie in de bisdommen Antwerpen, Gent en Mechelen tussen 1570 en 1795*, 2 vols (Tielt, 1971–72).

In comparison with neighbouring countries the history of the family is still at a very elementary stage in Belgium. It is true there are numerous monographic studies available on the subject, but these do not enable a judgement to be made on the relationships between spouses and between parents and children, their experiences and feelings, their values and attitudes. C. Vandenbroeke, *Vrijen en trouwen van de middeleeuwen tot heden: seks, liefde en huwelijk in historisch perspectief* (Brussels and Amsterdam, 1986), largely supports foreign examples which are not necessarily representative of the Southern Netherlands. More useful (from our perspective) is the short survey by the same author 'De sociale leefwereld van het kind in Vlaanderen, 17e–19e eeuw', *Tijdschrift voor geschiedenis*, 94 (1981), pp. 412–26. The attitudes of the clergy towards marriage and sexuality are analysed by H. Storme, 'Het 18e-eeuwse katholiek discours over huwelijk en sexualiteit in de Mechelse kerkprovincie', *Documentatieblad Werkgroep Achttiende Eeuw*, xvii (1985), pp. 29–48.

The social developments that took place in the cities of this study have been sketched out by H. Soly, 'Social Aspects of Structural Changes in the Urban Industries of Eighteenth-Century Brabant and Flanders', in H. van der Wee (ed.), *Rise and Decline of Urban Industries in Italy and the Low Countries during the Middle Ages and Early Modern Times* (Louvain, 1988), pp. 255–77. The most important monographs for Antwerp are: K. Degryse, *De Antwerpse fortuinen: kapitaalaccumulatie, -investering en -rendement te Antwerpen in de 18de eeuw*, unpublished doctoral thesis, Ghent, 1985; C. Lis, *Social Change and the Labouring Poor: Antwerp, 1770–1860* (New Haven and London, 1986), and A. K. L. Thijs, *Van 'werkwinkel' tot 'fabriek': de textielnijverheid te Antwerpen (einde 15de – begin 19de eeuw)* (Brussels, 1987). For Bruges: Y. Vanden Berghe, *Jacobijnen en traditionalisten: de reacties van de Bruggelingen in de Revolutietijd (1780–1794)*, 2 vols (Brussels, 1972), and J. Vermaut, *De textielnijverheid in Brugge en op het platteland in westelijk Vlaanderen vóór 1800*, unpublished doctoral thesis, Ghent, 1974. For Brussels: R. De Peuter, *Negocianten en entrepreneurs in een regionale hoofdstad: Brussel in de achtiende eeuw* (Utrecht, 1994). For Ghent: M. Kin, 'Economische transformaties en verarming te Gent in de achttiende eeuw', *Tijdschrift voor Sociale Geschiedenis*, viii (1982), pp. 34–53, and H. Soly, C. Terryn, J. Van Ryckeghem, I. Bourgeois and I. Pisters, 'Materiële cultuur te Gent in de 18de eeuw', *Oostvlaamse Zanten*, 63 (1988), pp. 3–80.

Index

Aalst, 142, 171
absolutism, 2, 5
'acting mad', 25
adolescents, frustrations of, 48–9, 196; *see also* generation conflict; youths
Adrians, Joannes Servaes, 167
adultery, 96, 99, 116, 127, 139, 199; and charivari, 118, 120; as a ground for divorce/separation, 100–1; husbands charge wives with, 89, 90, 155
adulthood, 43, 101
alcohol abuse, 37–41, 139, 168, 199; as a cause for confinement, 33, 38, 125–6, 128–9; and insanity, 38, 93, 201; as major charge of wives against husbands, 34, 41, 128–9; and violence, 93, 95, 201
alcohol consumption *see* beer; drinking houses; gin
Alexian Brothers, 17, 53, 54, 56, 93, 162, 163, 164–9
Alkmaar, 103, 104
almoners, 72, 79, 112, 150; confinement requests of, 140–1, 151–2
Amelot, minister, 2
Amsterdam, 90, 91, 127, 175
animality, 23, 30, 93, 95, 125, 127, 130, 181
Antwerp, 6, 16, 27, 108, 122, 170, 181; Alexian Brothers in, 53, 54, 93, 162–3, 165; categories of objectionable behaviour in, 33–4; crime in, 35–6, 61–70, 73, 133–4; drinking houses in, 40; generation conflict in, 54–5; house of correction, 141, 175–6, 179; irreligion in, 130–1; mad and madhouse in, 24, 76, 88–9, 91–2, 172–4; neighbourhood life in, 116–17; neighbours

and private confinement in, 113, 125–6; petitions for confinement in, 9–15, 19–21, 74; parent–child conflicts in, 53–4, 56–7, 59–60, 75, 79, 126; population of, 123; poverty in, 45, 70, 140–1; private prisoners sent to Vilvoorde, 149–50; prostitution in, 35, 79, 89–90; segregation in, 123; social policy in, 137, 138–41, 150–1; spouses, conflicts between, 82–8, 90, 91–5, 96; textile industry, 44–5, 70–1, 76–7, 97–8, 137; 'uncontrollable' children and adolescents in, 47–51, 56, 58, 75–6, 79
army, 73–4
assault and battery, 33; husbands charge wives with, 25–6, 87–8; parents charge children with, 71; wives charge husbands with, 33, 36, 69, 92–5, 119, 120, 125, 127, 129, 161
asylums *see* madhouses
Ath, 136
authority: familial, 5, 195; language of, 152–4, 199–200; patriarchal, 81–2, 85, 102, 104; *see also* father

Bacheli, Jean-Joseph, 87
Baecke, Catharina, 118
Baelen, Anna, 29
Baesten, Jean, 182
Bal, Engelbert, 94
Batkin, Philippus Carolus, 56
Baut, Jacob, 29
Beccaria, Cesare, 143
bed and bedding, importance of, 95–6
Bedlam, 175
Beeckmans, canon, 141

behaviour, 128; and indissolubility of
  marriage, 83, 100
Rome, 185, 187
Rooms, Frans, 62–3
Rooms, Gerard, 62–3
Rottiers, Maria Isabella, 11
Rousseau, Anthoon, 183–4
Rousseau, Jean-Jacques, 104
Rousseau, Peter, 65

St Joris' Hospital, 121
St Julian's Hospital, 11, 17, 173
Sas, Cornelius Franciscus, 32
Sas, Hendrina Josina, alias Moeder Cato,
  66–7
Sas, Jacob, 67
Scull, Andrew, 201
Sechele, Joannes, 64
segregation, 123–4
senile dementia, 29
separation from bed and board: abandonment
  without formal, 102–3; causes of, 103–4;
  choice between private confinement and,
  105–7; grounds for, 101–2; and the
  questions of guilt, 108; and social class,
  105–6; *see also* divorce
servants, theft by, 68, 133
Seven Years' War, 74
sexual offences, 93, 96; *see also* adultery,
  immorality; incest; prostitution
's-Hertogenbosch, 61, 120, 194, 215
shoplifting, 62–5, 133
Shrove Tuesday Uproar, 122, 138–9, 160
Simpelhuys (Brussels), 14, 17, 29, 31, 172,
  174, 205
Sint-Jan-ten-Dullen, 173
Sint-Niklaas, 88, 170, 171
Sira, Jacob, 57, 163
Slim Tist *see* Claessens, Jan-Baptist
Smulders, Louis, 56
social problem, definitions of, 132, 142–7,
  196–7; *see also* social policy
social policy, 133–40, 150–1, 196; *see also*
  social problem
solitary confinement, 169, 185–6, 187–8
sons: ages of 'uncontrollable', 48; confined,
  51, 56, 58; rebellious, 43, 56, 130, 131;
  unruly lives of, 22, 48, 54, 56, 57, 61–7,
  161; work-shy, 34, 44, 60, 72, 126; *see also*
  father; mother; parents
Spain, 76
Speltincx, Laurent, 25
Spierenburg, Pieter, 194
spouses: changing relationships between,
  87–8, 97–9, 198; conflicts between, 82,
  84–5, 87, 89–90, 91–6, 127
Stadskind (ward of the city), 52, 54

stepchildren, 51
stepfather, 49, 50–1
Stevens, 168
Stienon, Liliane Rosalie, 203
suicide: change in attitude to, 26–7; impulse
  to, cause for confinement, 27–8, 92
Swaen, Joannes, 57
Swaens, Jan, 32
Swyn, Jean, 31
Szasz, Thomas, 201–2

Taintenier, Jean-François, 136–7
Teegers, Johanna, 127
Temse, 63
textile industry, restructuring of, 44–6, 70–1,
  97–8; *see also* cotton spinners; lace industry
Theatre Question, 54–5
theft, 133; of clothes, 63, 64, 65, 67, 68; of
  foodstuffs, 63, 65; at home, 59–60, 140;
  see also fencing; pickpocketing; shoplifting
Thijs, Jan Franciscus, 66
Tielemans, Christiane, 30
't Kint, Barthélemy, 180
tolerance threshholds, 2, 117, 124, 155,
  196–7, 201
Tournai, 170
Turnhout, 171

unemployment, 45, 49, 64, 66
United Provinces: charivari in, 120–2; divorce
  and separation in, 100, 103, 104–5, 107,
  127; ideas about the exercise of marital
  power in 109; madhouses in, 175; numbers
  of petitions for confinement in, 193–4;
  tuchthuizen in, 2, 175, 178; *see also*
  Reformed Church
unruly living, categories of, 32–46
urban house of correction, 17, 131, 141–2,
  147, 175–84, 200

vagrants, 136, 137, 142, 149–50;
  imprisonment of, 143–4, 175–6
Valck, Albert, 59–60
Van Bortel, Jacoba, 89
Van Campen, Franciscus, 141
Van Coekelberghe, Petronella, 76
vandalism, 134–5, 160
Van de Houten, Martine, 28
Vandekerckhove, Jan, 128
Van Den Eynden, Gommarius, 95
Van Den Eynden, Maria, 95
Van den Hoeck, Jan, 66
Van den Huyse, Elisabeth, 31
Van der Achteren, Joannes, 26
Vander Haeghen, Jacob, 168
Van der Meiren, Barbara, 87
Van der Meiren, Philippus, 87